1970

W9-AFR-863

3 0301 00004666 0

AMERICAN ART MUSEUMS

AMERICAN ART MUSEUMS

An Introduction to Looking

Eloise Spaeth

Revised Edition

LIBRARY
College of St. Francis
JOLIET, ILL.

McGraw-Hill Book Company
New York   Toronto   London   Sydney

Copyright © 1960, 1969 by Eloise Spaeth.

All Rights Reserved. Printed in the United States of America. No part of this publication may be reproduced, stored in a retrieval system, or transmitted, in any form or by any means, electronic, mechanical, photocopying, recording, or otherwise, without the prior written permission of the publisher.

Library of Congress Catalog Card Number: 68–55274
First Revised Edition
59850

FOREWORD

708.13
8733

This book is not meant to be a definitive guide, but rather an introduction to looking. Although the space is limited I have tried to cover all the major museums and as many as possible minor-major art museums and galleries. In selecting, I have frequently had to be somewhat arbitrary in my choices. The emphasis, but for a few exceptions, is on the *general* art museum; the few have been included because geographically near a particular museum under discussion.

In choosing university and college museums, I have given preference to those which have their own museum buildings and which act as community museums as well. The winnowing has been difficult, since practically every self-respecting university has or is building a museum or an art center on campus. The large metropolitan museums, under the title "The Big Seven," are given a description too brief in relation to their importance, on the assumption that everyone knows where they are. Moreover, their sales desks have catalogues and literature on their collections in abundance. Tours and docents (museum jargon for lecturer-guides) are plentiful.

In a few lines, I have tried to capture the quality, character and mood of each museum listed. Each has its own. In some museums I have singled out specific works of art, sometimes the works chosen are the museum showpieces, sometimes the choice has been my own. The works discussed belong to the permanent collections; however, it is advisable to request a floor plan when visiting a particular institution, for frequently museum directors rearrange the collections and what is here today is elsewhere tomorrow.

The title of works of art, the spelling of artists' names (whether to h or not to h Brueghel), and all attributions follow museum labels. 5-3891

CONTENTS

[*Note: Museums and galleries within regional subdivisions are
entered alphabetically by states, cities, and museum names.*]

MIDDLE ATLANTIC ART MUSEUMS

NEW YORK CITY MUSEUMS

SOUTHEASTERN ART MUSEUMS

EASTERN CENTRAL ART MUSEUMS

WESTERN CENTRAL ART MUSEUMS

SOUTHWESTERN ART MUSEUMS

WEST COAST ART MUSEUMS

AMERICAN ART MUSEUMS

HOW MUSEUMS CAME TO BE

The American art museum as a public and formal institution is of fairly recent vintage. Fortunately, to assemble and put on view historical treasures is an old human impulse. In colonial times the Dutch in New York and the British in both New England and the South felt a desire to establish traditions in their adopted land.

The Charleston South Carolina Library Society, formed in 1773, was the first group to establish a museum. Though the stress was on history, china, bits of jewelry, miniatures and portraits were also on display.

After the Revolution, a number of historical societies were formed from the Carolinas to Maine, to preserve and keep up to date the story of the new country. Maps, land grants, and firearms hung beside grim portraits of civic and political leaders, on the whole of more historical than artistic interest. Although colonial America was too busy making history to think much about art, painting began to improve and painters to be patronized. Master craftsmen who decorated colonial carriages and furniture were soon testing their skill on canvas.

In Philadelphia, about 1783, Charles Willson Peale, the saddler's apprentice who became a painter, held exhibitions at home. His artist son Rembrandt Peale erected in Baltimore the first building designed specifically as an art museum. Although the Pennsylvania Academy of the Fine Arts had been established in Philadelphia, Peale's museum holds the honor of being the first building in America to house only works of art.

At the same time, other institutions over the country were struggling to establish and maintain themselves. The National Academy of Design opened in New York in 1826, with Samuel F. B. Morse (the inventor of the telegraph who was also a painter) as its first president. The Boston Atheneum, a library since 1807, began to show paintings. Actually, Harvard College had been the pioneer. In 1760, Harvard established a "Museum Room" which was the basis for its university collection. James Bowdoin, of Bowdoin College, returned from Europe in 1811 with a collection of paintings which he gave the college, thus making Bowdoin's the oldest college art collection, while Yale, through the purchase of John Trumbull's paintings of the American Revolution, was the first university to emphasize the housing of the arts by opening its Trumbull Gallery in 1832. In 1844, the Wadsworth Atheneum opened its new picture gallery with some eighty paintings.

These beginnings were followed by a real expansion when in the year 1870 the Boston Museum of Fine Arts, New York's Metropolitan and the Corcoran Gallery in Washington, D.C., were incorporated as museums.

But it was the avid private collectors of the mid-century who hastened the emergence of the museum as a separate entity. In those days making the Grand Tour of Europe was a requisite for young men of wealth before they settled down. Often, during these travels, men of education and discernment bought and brought home paintings in quantity. James Jackson Jarves, the most astute of them all, brought back a magnificent group of thirteenth- to seventeenth-century Italian paintings, 119 in all. Most of them are now at the Yale University Art Gallery. Men like William Walters of Baltimore, the first of our great collectors of Oriental art, and William Corcoran, the Washington banker, set the pattern for the Morgans, Fricks, and Mellons of later years.

The tradition of the millionaire patron of the arts carried into the twentieth century. Though the bounty is not always of top quality, often the museums are bequeathed many a happy choice of minor masters. But men like Widener, Morgan, Johnson, Frick, Bache, Freer, Lehman, Havemeyer, Huntington, and later Mellon, Kress, Hanna, Dale, Rockefeller, Guggenheim, Pulitzer, Hirschhorn have and are giving America priceless examples from almost every known civilization. Whatever their motives—pride, generosity, love of the beautiful, vanity—every citizen in the United States now has the privilege of seeing these collections in public museums. Many a small place has its surprises: The selection of Spanish colonial paintings in Davenport, Iowa, is second only to the collection in the Philadelphia Museum. Indianapolis boasts two marvelous twelfth-century Spanish frescoes from San Baudelio de Berlanga, Omaha displays a fine Titian portrait, San Diego a splendid Goya, and so on. It used to be a cliché among Easterners that the rest of the country was a cultural desert with occasional watering holes in Chicago, St. Louis and Kansas City; those who still think so provincially had better take to the road.

While the chief purpose of museums is to collect, preserve and exhibit works of art, the modern concept goes far beyond such a definition. Now the museum has, in many instances, become the cultural heart of the community it serves. Its broad educational programs, films, libraries, concerts, theatrical performances, are aimed both at children and adults. Many museums are establishing rental galleries where, for a small fee or as a membership privilege, a subscriber can take home for a period of time a work of art of his choice. Baltimore, Dayton, Columbus, Buffalo and Milwaukee are five cities of many with galleries reporting lively traffic.

Building programs, attendance figures and activities can be cited, but above all there is the immeasurable importance of the impact of a single painting or piece of sculpture on the most casual visitor. The communication established between the two may open doors of the mind or the spirit never touched before.

AN INTRODUCTION TO LOOKING

The collector Philip Lehman's son Robert was born with a golden Renaissance spoon in his mouth and took his first steps among the glories of Persian faïence and Italian majolica because his father had a penchant for them. But most of us encounter our first great works of art in a museum and, with increasing familiarity, gain the feeling of being at home with them, not passively accepting, but recognizing such beauty as a force in our daily lives. Unfortunately, many of us never learn to make the most of our treasure houses. On a first visit, the temptation is to take in everything at once. The result is a confused mind, cultural indigestion, and museum feet.

Going from gallery to gallery, continents and centuries are jumped. Standing before the elegant statue of an *Athenian Youth* in New York's Metropolitan Museum, you are in the Acropolis, with the smell of olive blossoms and thyme in the air, a witness of immortality. The Athenian boy of the fifth century B.C. is not far from a goddess of the third century A.D. Nearby the life of the Nile is present. Pharaohs build the pyramids and artists hammer out golden necklaces as dynasties succeed one another. In another museum we step into our own historical past. Tea is dumped in Boston Harbor and a wilderness is cleared. *Paul Revere, Silversmith,* painted by John Singleton Copley, in the Boston Museum of Fine Arts is the same Paul Revere who spread the word through every Middlesex village and farm.

Or perhaps we are taken with the extravagances of the French courts; with porcelains, bric-a-brac and painters like Boucher and Fragonard giving evidence of refined abandon in the reigns of the worldly kings named Louis. Or maybe we fear the tyranny of tradition and gravitate to the contemporary galleries, where we are challenged by current audacities. From a confusion of remembered shapes and colors, somehow a small Vermeer painting or a giant Lehmbruck sculpture will force their way to the conscious surface of our minds, refusing to be obscured.

Whatever our interest or curiosity, we go back to what has touched us most. Works of art seldom yield their mysteries to a first glance.

E. S.

Georges Seurat: *A Sunday Afternoon on the Island of La Grande Jatte* (1884) (The Art Institute of Chicago; Helen Birch Bartlett Memorial Collection)

Gustave Caillebotte: *The Place de l'Europe on a Rainy Day* (1879) (The Art Institute of Chicago; Charles H. and Mary F. S. Worcester Collection)

THE BIG SEVEN

ART INSTITUTE OF CHICAGO

Michigan Avenue at Adams, Chicago, Illinois
Hours: Mon.–Sat., 10–5; Sun., holidays, 12–5; Thurs., 10–8:30
P.M.; closed Christmas.
Library.
Restaurant. Free.

The zest and foresight with which Chicagoans built their city
(was it an accident that H. H. Richardson, Louis Sullivan, and
Frank Lloyd Wright erected some of their earliest monuments
here?) was matched in the building of their collections. Mrs.
Potter Palmer was purchasing Renoirs in Paris as early as 1892.
Only Mrs. Horace Havemeyer in New York, aided by Mary
Cassatt, was buying the controversial Impressionists for America
at that time. In purchasing, Mrs. Palmer usually went it alone.

The Chicago Academy of Design, established in 1866, was the
wellspring of the present institute. Its name change occurred in
1882 and its move to the present Italianate structure was made
at the closing of the 1893 World's Columbian Exposition. The
building erected to house the fair's Congress of Religions has been
home to the Art Institute ever since. Many additions have been
made; the latest is the Morton Gallery, which holds the splendid
collection of twentieth-century European art: Modigliani, Marc,
Miró, Léger, Delaunay, Giacometti, Balthus, Etienne-Martin, and
Picassos from 1901 to his great *Nude under a Pine Tree* (1959).
Special exhibitions are also held here.

The painting section proper starts with fifteenth-century Europeans. Facing each other across a grandiose stair well are two of
the museum's stars: El Greco's *Assumption of the Virgin,* discovered by Mary Cassatt in Spain in 1901 and purchased by the
institute in 1906; and the *Ayala Altar.* Dated 1396, this altar,

consisting of sixteen scenes from the lives of Christ and the Virgin, is one of the most important Iberian works to be found outside Spain. Other distinguished paintings: *The Life of John the Baptist* by Giovanni di Paolo and four large canvases by Giovanni Battista Tiepolo depicting episodes from the story of Rinaldo and Armida. The latter have been brought to a luminous grandeur through cleaning and reinstallation. The museum's truly great group of French nineteenth-century paintings is based on the Mrs. Potter Palmer, Fredrick C. Bartlett, and L. L. Coburn collections, while the Ryerson and Worcester gifts range from Italian primitives to the nineteenth century. The American painters march straight through from Robert Feke, one of our first native artists, to the latest ventures into kinetic art with Len Lye's *Loop*, a tintinnabulation of sounds. With the renovation of the painting galleries, small mood alcoves sparingly furnished with period pieces of furniture, sculpture, and canvases have been installed.

The print and drawing department is superlative and is constantly being strengthened, not only with grand pieces but also with sketch books and intimate-study sheets. The Japanese group is second only to Boston's. The Gauguin holdings are the most complete extant. Numerically, the decorative arts section is the strongest in the museum as well as being distinguished for the quality of its holdings. One is introduced to the Oriental and East Indian wing by Kuan-Yin (Chinese, late Ming), sleeping above the trickling waters of her fountain bed. The Thorne collection of miniature period rooms installed in shadow boxes show significant European and American interiors. Fun for the amateur they are also invaluable source material on furniture for the professional and student.

For decades the Art Institute has been the cultural halfway house of the nation. Between stopovers of trains or planes, travelers have rushed through its hospitable doors to bathe their eyes and charge their spirits with Seurat's masterpiece, *Sunday Afternoon on the Grande Jatte* (this perfectly pitched painting represents the apex of the Pointillist movement), Monet's *The River*, Van Gogh's *Bedroom at Arles*, Toulouse-Lautrec's *At the Moulin Rouge*, Degas' *The Millinery Shop*, to say nothing of nineteen Renoirs.

Building on strength, the museum has recently added a distinguished Jacques-Louis David of 1792, *Portrait of the Marquise de Pastoret*, and what may well become a runner-up to the *Grande Jatte* in popularity, Gustave Caillebotte's 7- by 9-foot canvas

El Greco: *The Assumption of the Virgin* (1577) (The Art Institute of Chicago; gift of Nancy Atwood Sprague in memory of Albert Arnold Sprague)

Place de l'Europe on a Rainy Day (see page 6). Painted seven years before the Seurat, the figures in the canvas have the same static monumentality.

As the gifts pour in, tomorrow's grandchildren may well say—as did Chauncey McCormick, a former president, when asked how the institute could afford such valuable French paintings—"We do not buy them; we inherit them from our grandmothers."

MUSEUM OF FINE ARTS, BOSTON

465 Huntington Avenue, Boston, Massachusetts
Hours: Tues.–Sat., 10–5; Wed. (Oct.–May), 10–10;
Sun., 1:30–5:30.
Library,
Restaurant. Adults 50¢; children under 18, 25¢.

On February 4, 1970, the Museum of Fine Arts will celebrate its centennial. Like many United States museums, its collections were begun in a library, the Atheneum. Emerson wrote in 1822 that the paintings "attract the eye . . . from the tedious joys of reading and writing." Those paintings formed the nucleus of the museum's collection when it was founded in 1870 on Copley Square. The present building dates from 1909.

Today, having outgrown every department, the museum pushes outward with new additions for the decorative arts, sculpture, and textiles. A large wing is being added on Museum Road which will be the new entrance and will hold the painting galleries, libraries, laboratories, and restaurant. Meantime, renovation of old galleries goes on. The museum's great monuments of antiquity—given added space and light—breathe again.

The intellectual leaders of Boston, traveling far and wide, made the museum their project. Probably the first Egyptian art to reach America were New Kingdom pieces brought from Luxor in 1835 by John Lowell. Harvard University and the museum engaged in a prolonged dig that resulted in great Old Kingdom pieces for the department. The "grand tours" of Edward Perry Warren brought collections of classical antiquities, including some of Boston's glorious Greek vases, to the museum.

Under the guidance of Ernest Fenollosa, one of the first American scholars seriously to study Japanese art, the Asiatic department—which includes work from China, Korea, Japan, and Cambodia—had its beginnings. Slightly later another scholar-teacher, Denman Ross, brought Dr. Ananda Coomaraswamy and his renowned Indian collection to the museum. Dr. Ross was also instrumental in forming the historical textile collection which, together with tapestries, rugs, and costumes, contains more than fifty thousand pieces.

The painting collection goes back to the twelfth century with a rare and beautiful fresco taken from the apse of a Catalan church, Santa Maria de Mur, now installed in its own small chapel. It proceeds through Italian and Spanish masters such as Duccio, Tintoretto, El Greco, and Velásquez. The Spanish gallery is pure joy. The Northern schools hold fine examples of Rogier van der Weyden, Lucas van Leyden, Rubens, Rembrandt, and

Martyrdom of St. Hippolytus (Flemish, late fifteenth century) (Museum of Fine Arts, Boston)

Pablo Picasso: *Rape of the Sabines* (Museum of Fine Arts, Boston)

Ruisdael. A recent addition is *The Martyrdom of St. Hippolytus,* a stunning triptych (Flemish, late fifteenth century). French painting culminates in Monet's figure *La Japonaise,* Renoir's *Le Bal à Bougival,* and what Gauguin considered his masterpiece, *Where Do We Come From? What Are We? Where Are We Going?* Eminent Americans are here, too: Stuart's portraits of *George* and *Martha Washington,* which we all grew up with; Copley, Trumbull, and a host of artists who recorded our leaders, our ancestors, our historical past. A room is devoted to Boston's native son Paul Revere. Here Copley's portrait of the patriot silversmith hangs, and here priceless pieces of his silver are displayed. The Karolik group is rich in seventeenth- and eighteenth-century American furniture, nineteenth-century American paintings, and drawings by both obscure and well-known artists. The contemporary group continues to grow in importance, especially with examples of the quality of Giacometti's *Femme Qui Marche* and Picasso's powerful *Rape of the Sabines.* The print section is vast, with holdings of distinction in every category but especially in fifteenth-century Italian and German.

Boston's latest triumph is the acquisition of Starboard House, home of Forsyth Wickes in Newport, Rhode Island. The predominantly eighteenth-century French collection will be installed in the new decorative arts wing in such a way as to recreate the original atmosphere, in paintings, furniture, *objets d'art,* sculpture. Mr. Wickes, with the commitment of the true connoisseur, assem-

Virgin and Child (ca. 1200) (Museum of Fine Arts, Boston)

bled only works of the highest quality; to quote the museum's director, Perry Rathbone, "The collection is a stunning ensemble, a many-sided testimony to the creative genius of France during the age of the Enlightenment." The hundredth anniversary will doubtless see the unveiling of many treasures which the museum is understandably keeping quiet about now.

BROOKLYN MUSEUM

Eastern Parkway and Washington Avenue, Brooklyn, New York
Hours: Mon.–Sat., 10–5; Sun. and holidays, 1–5.
Library,
restaurant.
Free.

The approved plans of this McKim, Mead and White building called for a quadrangle of which the present museum is only one side. Opened in 1897, Brooklyn was one of the first in the field to emphasize primitive arts. The Hall of the Americas on the first floor exhibits fifty centuries of colorful and exotic art of the Indian people from the Arctic to Argentina: the giant totem poles, house posts, and masks of the Northwest Coast tribes; the textiles and pottery of the Pueblo culture; war bonnets and shields of the Plains Indians; stone and jade sculptures of the

Maya, Aztec, and Olmec; gold pieces from Costa Rica; Peruvian, Chilean, and Argentinian work from the Chavin period, 1000 B.C., to the conquest of the Inca in the sixteenth century. The outstanding collection of African art, begun a half-century ago, has been augmented by ancient bronze and wood sculpture from Nigeria, Mali, and the Congo.

The Egyptian department, while not as large as Boston's or that of the Metropolitan, ranks with them in quality. Brooklyn's interest in Nile civilizations is less historical or archeological than aesthetic. Selecting what to praise is impossible. The extensive library of Egyptology is open both to scholars and an interested public. The arts of Islam and the Indian East are set in handsome new quarters.

In the small European painting section are Hals, Ribera, and some French Impressionist canvases including Monet's *Ducal Palace*. A recent acquisition is the collection of Brooklyn-born Mrs. Albert C. Barnes, wife of one of America's distinctive collectors (see Barnes Foundation, Merion, Pa.). The paintings, many by the nineteenth-century French artists her husband collected, are intimate in scale. The museum's American group, a significant historical collection, begins with *The Van Cortland Boys* by an unknown artist, ranges through the colonial, Federal, and Hudson River schools to excellent examples of individualists, such as George Caleb Bingham's *Shooting for Beef*, the romantic Quidor's *Money Diggers*, and Eakins' portrait of *William Rush*

LEFT: *Stone Statue* (Huaxteca, Mexico); (The Brooklyn Museum) RIGHT: Pedy-Ma-Hes, *Priest and Scribe* (ca. 665 B.C.); (The Brooklyn Museum)

Carving His Allegories of the Schuylkill. The knitting duenna attending the female nude model was included in the canvas. Rush's carving *Winter* is also at the museum. William Rush, one of our first native sculptors, did these carvings for the Philadelphia waterworks. They can now be seen at the Philadelphia Museum. There are galleries for the American Impressionists, The Eight, the American Scene painters. "Listening to Pictures" is an invaluable innovation in the contemporary section, with taped commentaries on their works by such artists as Edward Hopper, Jack Levine, Louise Nevelson, Charles Sheeler, Ben Shahn, Larry Rivers, and many more. Another innovation is the Paintings Study Gallery. One thousand paintings have been brought from storage into a well-lighted, humidity-controlled gallery. A long wall contains sliding panels of well-categorized and documented canvases. More important ones are displayed on forty-four, three-sided, rotating pylons. Open 1 to 4 Wednesday and Saturday for guided tours; by appointment other days.

The decorative arts section counts among its displays entire houses. The Jan Martense Schenck House (1675) is the earliest intact New York building. Colonial and Victorian rooms abound. The "Turkish Room," that delightful innovation of the pipe-smoking, turn-of-the-century male, is bedizened with bead portieres, divans, and braziers. It was removed intact from John D. Rockefeller's house on 53rd street. Brooklyn's watercolor gallery alone displays more than two hundred works, including eighteen Winslow Homers. The drawings of the nineteenth and twentieth centuries rate highly, while the prints reach their apex with twentieth-century American and French artists, the German Expressionists, and Secessionist works (the Secessionists, led by Max Lieberman, revolted against the romanticism of the Academy).

To the great store of treasures in the museum, only a short subway ride from Times Square, another first has been added: a sculpture garden for the preservation of America's vanishing architectural past—corbels, lintels, capitals, friezes, caryatids, every form of ornament saved from distinguished buildings, the Park Lane Hotel and Pennsylvania Station being the latest. Other examples include a cast-iron railing from the *Police Gazette* building in San Francisco and a fierce lion of formed zinc from Steeplechase Park; a giant bull's head from a tannery in lower Manhattan will be mounted dramatically on a white brick shaft; classical stone or terra cotta medallions rest on beds of ivy;

nostalgic gas street lamps cluster about. Generations of Americans raised on the austerities of glass-box construction will be grateful for this "Remembrance of Things Past."

METROPOLITAN MUSEUM OF ART

Fifth Avenue at 82nd Street, New York, New York
Hours: Daily, 10–5; Tues., 10–10; Sun. and holidays, 1–5.
Library,
restaurants.
Free.

No single American institution presents a more complete expression of man's artistic endeavor under one roof than the "great gray lady of upper Fifth Avenue." Now that the lady contemplates major surgery, including face-lifting, she should be by her one hundredth birthday in 1970 in real ferment. John Jay, lawyer, diplomat, abolitionist, and one of the founders of the Republican Party, is credited with instigating the founding of the museum. A Union League clubman, he roused fellow members to action— including artists John Kensett and Worthington Whittredge (the same Whittredge who posed as Washington in Emanuel Leutze's famous *Washington Crossing the Delaware*). In 1870, the Metropolitan Museum of Art was incorporated. It moved from its first home, the Allen Dodworth Dancing Academy, to the Douglas Manor (later the Salvation Army training school on West 14th Street) before it came to rest in Central Park a decade later. As early as 1893, William Morris Hunt designed a new front for the building. The latest expansion produced, in 1964, the handsome Thomas J. Watson Library, largest art reference library in the United States, together with print galleries where for the first time the general public can see continuous changing exhibitions from the important print collection.

The Egyptian section spans every aspect of the ancient Nile Valley through forty centuries, from the reconstructed tomb of Per-Neb, a Memphite dignitary of the fifth dynasty, to the skillfully wrought pendants of queens. Extending from the Egyptian sculpture court and encased in what must be the biggest glass box extant will be that refugee from the onrush of waters of the new Aswan Dam, the Temple of Dendur. It was given in gratitude by the Egyptian government for America's part in saving the great monuments of Abu Simbel from the same deluge. This colossal moving venture is already under way and 1972 should see Dendur established as a sunny appendage to the museum.

The Greek holdings are strong in Cypriot art, partially because General Luigi Palma de Cesnola, an Italian who won his stripes in our Civil War, made important excavations in Cyprus. In 1879 he became the Metropolitan's first director. The Near Eastern department contains great Assyrian sculpture, while the Far Eastern galleries are dominated by a huge wall painting, a *Buddha Assembly*, Chinese, Yuan Dynasty XIV century and a great sandstone *bodhisattva,* both from Shensi. With the exception of Istanbul's Topkapi Museum, the Islamic section is unmatched in the world. Wonders of the Middle Ages are shared between the museum and The Cloisters it administers. The arms and armor collection ranks third in the world, while one of the prides of the fabulous Renaissance trove is the *Rospigliosi Cup,* attributed to Cellini. Building plans include space for 4,000 musical instruments, playing back into prehistory, and seldom seen pre-Columbian material.

A stroll through the Elysian fields of painting takes one from Italian primitives through practically every school and country, with such magnificence as two Raphaels, over thirty Rembrandts, four Vermeers, including the oft-reproduced *Woman with a Water*

View of one of The Metropolitan Museum of Art's galleries of Far Eastern art, showing figure of a Bodhisattva from the Northern Ch'i Dynasty (550–577) (The Metropolitan Museum of Art; photograph by Gary Winogrand)

LEFT: *Bury St. Edmond's Cross* (The Metropolitan Museum of Art; The Cloisters Collection, 1963) **RIGHT:** El Greco: *View of Toledo* (The Metropolitan Museum of Art; H. O. Havemeyer Collection)

Jug. El Greco's only complete landscape, *View of Toledo,* hangs in a gallery opulent with Spanish treasures. In the French galleries one sees Poussin's women being abducted, Boucher's and Fragonard's ladies swinging, flirting, posturing, and a galaxy of breathtaking Impressionist and Post-Impressionist canvases.

The new American wing will house paintings the scope and importance of which few Americans have realized. Out of the stacks will come the primitive portraits, the Wests, the Copleys, the Peales, the Hudson River boys, the Sargents, Hassams, The Eight, right up to Jackson Pollock's enormous *Autumn Rhythm,* Adolph Gottlieb's *Sun-Moon Thrust,* De Kooning's *Easter Monday,* Ellsworth Kelly's *Blue, Red, Green,* and sculptor Lippold's blazing *Sun.*

Whole civilizations are recreated in period rooms that contrast the frescoed bedroom of a first-century Roman villa and the simplicities of colonial America, the fulsome baroque of a Venetian boudoir and the elegance of an Adam dining room. You can walk up the only known staircase done by famed British carver Grinling Gibbons. The beautiful Spanish patio from the castle of Velez Blanco, Almería (1512–1515), was bequeathed by George Blumenthal, former Metropolitan president.

The Costume Institute, with its own entrance at 83rd Street and Fifth Avenue, reviews dress historically, aesthetically, and engagingly. The Junior Museum has its entrance at 81st Street and Fifth Avenue. With peepholes, slides, filmstrips, acoustical guides, vivid and scholarly exhibitions from which adults can also profit are assembled for the young. A library, auditorium, and snack bar complete the junior picture.

At a visitors' booth by the main entrance such questions as "The shortest way to Aristotle?" are answered, and tours are plotted to conform with an individual's time and interest.

It seems a foregone conclusion that former New York City Commissioner of Parks Thomas P. F. Hoving, now the museum's director, will do everything possible to integrate the museum and the park more closely. Certainly Rodin's great *Thinker*, claustrophobically set in a forest of sculpture on the Metropolitan's balcony, could concentrate better on the park's green hillside.

THE CLOISTERS

*Fort Tryon Park, off Riverside Drive, just south of Dyckman
Street, New York, New York
Hours: Tues.–Sat., 10–5; Sun. & holidays, 1–5; May to Sept., 1–6.
Free.*

High above the Hudson is a monastic medieval world abounding with everything but chanting monks. Architectural elements including five cloisters have been welded into a harmonious whole. A Spanish Romanesque apse from the Church of St. Martin, Fuentidueña, Spain, was reassembled stone by stone. It took persistence and horse-trading on the part of James Rorimer, long-time curator of The Cloisters, to pry the apse from a reluctant Spanish government. The assemblage that is The Cloisters was made possible through the generosity of John D. Rockefeller, Jr., but the growth and direction of the medieval enclave is a testament to James Rorimer, the late director of the Metropolitan and The Cloisters. Other greats include the St. Guilhem Cloister, the medieval sculpture group; the Hunt of the Unicorn tapestries; the Spanish gallery, which holds *Annunciation with St. Joseph and Donors* by the Master of Flémalle (accepted by most scholars as Robert Campin); the Treasury, three rooms set aside for smaller works of exceptional quality, such as the *Chalice of Antioch*, reliquaries, illuminated manuscripts, enamels, and bronzes. From the sculpture harvest that the sculptor George Grey Barnard gathered from abandoned French farms and ruined churches and which the Metropolitan bought in 1925 to the latest important purchase, the *Bury St. Edmond's Cross,* acquisitions have always been of the highest quality. The cross, though only 2 feet high, is brilliantly carved on both sides with 108 figures and many inscriptions in Latin and Greek. So akin to the spirit of the Europe of the Middle Ages are its cloisters, walks, and medieval gardens that moments of peace can be found here even in twentieth-century Manhattan.

CLEVELAND MUSEUM OF ART

11150 East Boulevard, Cleveland, Ohio
Hours: Tues., Thurs., 10–6; Wed., Fri., 10–10; Sat., 9–5; Sun.,
    Jan. 1, May 30, 1–6.
Closed Mon., July 4, Thanksgiving, Dec. 25.
Library, restaurant.
Free.

Since its founding in 1916, this museum has been blessed with enlightened trustees, donors, and directors. William Milliken, curator from 1919 and director 1930–1958, brought international fame to the institution with the purchase of the cream of the treasures of the Guelphs—a princely German family. This was the greatest medieval cache to come on the market in a century. Hitler bought what was left for the Third Reich. Recent medieval acquisitions, a group of early Christian sculptures, include four tours de force in marble of *Jonah and the Whale.*

Money, rapacity, and "eye for excellence" have fashioned Cleveland's superb collections. What is now acknowledged one of the most important ancient Chinese objects in America, *Cranes and Serpents* (late Chou, 600–22 B.C.), was turned down years ago by Boston and the Freer before being picked up by Cleveland. *The Death of Adonis,* by José de Ribera, was found dirty and unattributed in a Geneva library by Sherman Lee, the present director. The same discernment was demonstrated when a striking early Velásquez, *Portrait of the Jester Calabazas,* came into the Cleveland fold. In 1967 alone 132 works of art were purchased. *The Descent from the Cross* has been described by Sherman Lee as one of the most important baroque ivories known. Commissioned by Prince Eusebius von Liechtenstein from sculptor Adam Lenckhardt in 1646, the 17½-inch piece includes eight figures carved from a single piece of ivory.

Velázquez: *Portrait of the Jes-
ter Calabazas* (The Cleveland
Museum of Art; Leonard C.
Hanna, Jr., Bequest)

Western painting starts with an Italian primitive an early donor
had the wit to purchase from James Jackson Jarves (see Yale)
and with Giovanni di Paolo's *St. Catherine Invested with the
Dominican Habit*. Filippino Lippi's tondo of the *Holy Family with
St. Margaret and St. John* is one of the great Lippis. Rembrandt's
moving *Old Man Praying* has lately joined three other Rembrandts
here. *Diana and Her Nymphs Departing for the Hunt* is an early
work of Rubens' mature period, a style little known in America. Cleveland's smallest painting is one of its most famous:
a 7 by 5 inch section of a larger polyptych of *St. John the Baptist,*
attributed to the Master of Flémalle (see The Cloisters). The
galleries ring with Titian, Tintoretto, El Greco. Goya's portrait
of the *Infante Don Luis de Borbon* is one of the great Goyas in
America. Monet's shimmering *Water Lilies* with the sweet sleepy
smell of the garden about them and Picasso's *La Vie* from his
Blue Period, indicate the strength of the Impressionist and Post-
Impressionist section. Since the addition of its 1958 wing, the
museum has broadened its historical American art survey by more
than five hundred works. The contemporary section could con-
stitute a small museum of modern art; Mark Rothko, Ellsworth
Kelly, Frank Gallo, Richard Lindner, and William De Kooning
are among those represented.

In the smaller departments one finds rich and rare examples, whether of Egyptians, Medes, Persians, Greeks, or Etruscans: the little *Negro Beggar,* an Alexandrian bronze of the second century; the noble Olmec *Stone Figure* and terra cotta and turquoise mask of the Mixtec culture from Mexico; a tenth-century stone sculpture of the Khmer civilization from Cambodia. The Oriental section holds the delectable Chinese Album of paintings, three great early landscape scrolls, Shang-Yin and Chou bronzes, and the Imperial Collection of Sung Dynasty porcelains, choice Cambodian pieces, a generous sampling of Indian sculpture and paintings, and the only group in the Western world of Japanese Buddhist wood sculpture of the seventh and eighth centuries.

Cleveland's Hispano-Islamic and Spanish textiles, eighteenth-century French furniture, tapestries, porcelains, American silver, and fifteenth-century Venetian glass (the world's largest collection) are dazzling. Prints range from fifteenth-century Italians and Germans to the present. A late acquisition from Prince Liechtenstein's collection is Antonio Pollaiuolo's *Battle of Naked Men,* which has been identified as a previously unrecognized first state of the work.

To speak of the Cleveland Museum and not pay tribute to Leonard Hanna would be like ignoring Andrew Mellon in speaking of the National Gallery. Through long years the Hanna fund aided the museum in its purchases. Hanna's fine collection of some forty nineteenth-century French paintings was left, together with his munificent estate, to the museum. Like Mellon a modest man, he would not allow the wing his money built to bear his name. Another wing was added in 1966, but the building program cannot seem to keep pace with the buying. A new wing designed by Marcel Breuer, architect of New York's Whitney Museum, will house an auditorium, classrooms, galleries and a visual aid center.

PHILADELPHIA MUSEUM OF ART

Benjamin Franklin Parkway at 26th St., Philadelphia,
  Pennsylvania
Hours: Daily, 9–5; closed national holidays.
Admission 50¢; children 6–12, 25¢. Free Monday.

Gone are the days when the museum's founding fathers worried about what to put in the vast Greek temple they were building at the apex of the Benjamin Franklin Parkway. Erected after World War I, the museum today houses some of the richest collections in America. Among these, in the fine and diverse painting division, are the John G. Johnson, Arensberg, and Gallatin groups. The Johnson is a truly encyclopedic amalgam of Western European painting from the tenth century to the dawn of Impressionism, with its most important holdings in the Flemish primitives of the fifteenth and sixteenth centuries, early Spanish and French, and unrivaled masterpieces of Italian Renaissance and seventeenth-century Dutch art. Rogier van der Weyden's *Christ on the Cross with Virgin and St. John* is probably one of the most poignant and sublime religious paintings in America. As Aline Saarinen relates in *The Proud Possessors,* a flip of a coin brought the two altar wings together in Philadelphia. Johnson and his collector friend P. A. B. Widener were shown them by a Paris dealer, who would sell them only as a pair. Johnson persuaded Widener to buy one. They flipped a coin and the panel *Virgin and St. John* went to Johnson. Later Widener, who could not find a spot in his home for the *Crucifixion,* offered it to his friend for the purchase price. Jan van Eyck's tiny, masterful *St. Francis* was sold as a Dürer in the 1820s in Portugal for $40. In 1941 it was valued at $500,000.

The Arensberg collection is a stupendous and beautifully integrated assemblage of 500 works of art, from the twentieth century (twenty magnificent Brancusis) back to the primitives. Extraordinary, monumental, pre-Columbian sculptures are harmoniously installed with eminent Cubist works by Braque, Picasso, Gleizes, and Juan Gris. Thirty Marcel Duchamp paintings include the show-stopper of the Armory exhibition, *Nude Descending the Staircase.* The A. E. Gallatin group, with such outstanding canvases as Léger's *The City* and Picasso's *Three Musicians,* complements the Arensberg. The Louis Stern collection of nineteenth- and twentieth-century French and American painting is intimate in scale and hangs together as it did in Mr. Stern's home, interspersed with examples of antiquities, primitive and modern sculpture. The Carroll Tyson and Wilsbach bequests have strengthened the already fine nineteenth-century French group.

Important works of Philadelphia painter Thomas Eakins, such as *The Concert Singer,* are shown against red-velvet walls sympathetic to the ambiance of the period in which Eakins painted. The museum owns fifty-five works, major paintings and drawings.

The print and drawing department has an inviting gallery for changing exhibitions as well as a permanent display of the tech-

TOP: Marcel Duchamp: *Nude Descending a Staircase, No. II* (1912) (Philadelphia Museum of Art, Louise and Walter Arensberg Collection) BOTTOM: Renoir: *The Bathers* (1884–1887); (Philadelphia Museum of Art; W. P. Wilstach Collection)

niques of print-making. A pleasant print-study room is open to the public. The range is wide, the quality distinguished.

Perhaps because the museum's first and long-time director, Fiske Kimball, was an architectural historian of note, some of the best period rooms in the country are in Philadelphia, their interiors a composite of the fine and decorative arts. In the great hall of a Chinese palace of the late Ming Dynasty is the rock crystal collection of the eighteenth-century Emperor Ch'ien Lung. The Japanese ceremonial teahouse and Buddhist temple with its green garden of fir and bamboo is unique in America. A new gallery of Thai and Cambodian treasures is dominated by a carved sandstone Cambodian figure of the pre-Khmer period (seventh to ninth century). Romanesque cloisters and portals are the setting for art of the Middle Ages. The architecture and sculpture of sixteenth-century India blend in a pillared hall from

Interior detail of Mandapam (South India, sixteenth century) (Philadelphia Museum of Art)

Madura to form an ensemble unmatched outside India. There are Flemish, Dutch, Italian Renaissance, Jacobean, and French interiors, and impressive English manor-house drawing rooms.

With charming chauvinism, most of the American wing is oriented to Philadelphia and her renowned cabinetmakers, silversmiths, and architects; the surrounding countryside contributes Pennsylvania Dutch interiors and artifacts.

In the extensive decorative arts section are fashion galleries that trace American dress from demure eighteenth-century Quaker garb to Grace Kelly's wedding gown. A wing is being opened that will house a children's museum with its own entrance.

Though contemporary art, with the exception of sculpture, has not been collected to any degree, hopeful signs appear with the inclusion of such artists as Lee Krasner, Leon Kelly, Franz Kline, Morris Louis, and Robert Rauschenberg. The museum also administers the nearby Rodin Museum (Benjamin Franklin Parkway and 22nd St.), which houses an extensive collection of the artist's work, and three colonial houses in the park—Mount Pleasant, Cedar Grove, and Letita Street House.

Many of the great collections that Fiske Kimball, with gargantuan verve and sometimes equally gargantuan nerve, gathered for the museum are being given brilliant new installations.

NATIONAL GALLERY OF ART

Constitution Avenue at 6th Street, N.W., Washington, D.C.
Hours: Mon.–Sat., 10–5; Sun., 2–10; April 1–Labor Day, 10 A.M.–
10 P.M. weekdays, 12 noon–10 P.M. Sun.;
closed Jan. 1, Dec. 25.
Restaurant.
Free.

In 1937 Andrew Mellon, Secretary of the Treasury under three presidents, gave to the people of America the Andrew Mellon collection of works of art and provided for a building worthy of them. No less important than the gift was the structure Mr. Mellon devised for the gifts' protection. The National Gallery, though technically a bureau of the governmental Smithsonian Institution, is autonomous and governed by its own board of trustees. The chairman is the Chief Justice of the United States; other trustees are the Secretaries of State and the Treasury, the secretary of the Smithsonian, and five citizens who may not be government employees. Thus the highest offices in the nation guard the Gallery.

Mellon's aim was ambitious: to establish the nucleus of a great national collection. He succeeded. There are examples of almost every artist whose influence was felt through seven centuries. His great *coup* was the purchase in 1930 of twenty-one masterpieces from the Hermitage collection in Leningrad. These include Botticelli's *Adoration of the Magi*, Raphael's *Alba Madonna*, Perugino's *Crucifixion*, Van Eyck's *Annunciation*, Titian's *Venus with a Mirror*, and works by Van Dyck, Hals, and Rembrandt.

Other important collectors took up Mr. Mellon's challenge. When the gallery opened in 1941, the Smauel H. Kress collection had been added and the Kress Foundation continues to make munificent gifts. Joseph A. Widener's group came next. The superb Lessing Rosenwald print collection followed, an anthology of 20,000 prints ranking in quality with the world's greatest. The impressive French nineteenth- and twentieth-century collection of Chester Dale came together at last in the National Gallery. Cézannes, Monets, and Renoirs that many of us grew up with in Chicago or Philadelphia are now in continuous flow through newly arranged galleries. Eighty-eight treasures such as Degas' *Mme. Malo* came directly from the Dale home and had never been on public view before.

The American section contains some fine early works. *The*

LIBRARY
College of St. Francis
JOLIET, ILL.
5 3891

Skater is a masterpiece of Gilbert Stuart's English period. Copley's *Watson and the Shark* was recently acquired from Christ Hospital, London. It had been bequeathed to the hospital by Sir Brook Watson, who commissioned the painting either to commemorate the losing of his leg or the saving of his life (see Detroit). From Whistler, Homer, and Eakins we move to the American Impressionists and the school of The Eight.

Jewels of rare value plucked from castle walls or auction blocks continue to enhance the National's holdings. One is *St. George and the Dragon*, a minuscule painting once attributed to Hubert van Eyck but now given to Rogier van der Weyden. To show the "thumb-sized hero slaying a three-inch dragon," the Gallery displays it in a glass case in which is mounted a magnifier, which brings out every detail of the artist's minute, lovely world. Matthias Grünewald's small crucifixion was found in the attic of a house in Essen, Germany, in 1922. Surely *Young Girl Reading* is one of Fragonard's most pleasing canvases. The diadem seems to have been placed in the National Gallery's crown with the purchase of

LEFT: Jean-Honoré Fragonard: *A Young Girl Reading* (The National Gallery of Art, Washington, D.C.) RIGHT: Leonardo da Vinci: *Ginevra de' Benci* (ca. 1480). (The National Gallery of Art, Washington, D.C.)

da Vinci's portrait of the pensive but arrogant *Ginevra de' Benci,* the only painting by Leonardo in the Western Hemisphere.

Invaluable for a first visit is the free booklet of general information available at the sales desk on the ground floor. A separate floor plan, color-keyed by periods, makes it easy to find what is where. Most galleries have free fact sheets of paintings on exhibit. But do not try to see everything on one visit. Three to four tours, one general, the others on specific facets of the collection, are given each day. If you prefer to be on your own, Acousti-guides with an introductory talk by the director, John Walker, are available in four languages. The extension services continue to expand. The department lends films, slides, filmstrips, reproductions, all available by writing the Curator of Extension Services. On Sunday evenings (except in summer) free concerts are given in the Garden Court.

Paul Mellon and his sister Ailsa Mellon Bruce, following their father's generous examples, have given the National Gallery $20 million to construct an adjacent building that will add exhibition space and house a center for advanced studies in visual arts.

NEW ENGLAND ART MUSEUMS

WADSWORTH ATHENEUM

25 Atheneum Square North, Hartford, Connecticut
Hours: Tues.–Fri., 10–5; Sat., 9–5; Sun., 1:30–5:30;
closed major holidays, Sat.–Sun. preceding Labor Day, Good
Friday. Restaurant. Free.

There is a staid sort of madness about this oldest of U.S. museums. (Others, for instance the Peale Museum in Philadelphia, can cite earlier founding; but for continuous operation as a public institution, the Atheneum takes the trophy.) The Tudor Gothic building opened in 1844. Later a brick addition that can only be called American Gothic was tacked on the back. Next came the Junius S. Morgan wing, in the best 1910 public library style. In 1934 the Avery wing made a simple architectural statement and harmonized the whole. Now, with the new James Lippincott Goodwin wing, the museum comes full circle. The original Tudor Gothic structure again provides the main entrance. Ingenious cantilevering reformed the gallery space and connected Goodwin to Avery. Gothic windows bricked up in 1890 were unbricked, regained their places in the façade. The whole flows uninterruptedly around an open center court, with a raised platform at one end for sculpture or summer theater, and, for the audience, aluminum bleachers which appear and disappear effortlessly. Off the garden cafeteria, a special room beckons children and their box lunches. The public street along the Morgan wing has reverted back to the museum, will become a sculpture mall.

Paintings hung for public viewing in the older 1807 Atheneum. But the original collection was greatly expanded by eighty-six paintings purchased by the donor of the 1844 building, Daniel Wadsworth, and a group of Hartford citizens. John Trumbull, president of the American Academy of Fine Arts when it became defined in 1836, was Wadsworth's brother-in-law. Although Sir Thomas Lawrence did two other portraits of the expatriate painter Benjamin West, Hartford's version is the original. In the robes of the Royal Academy's president, West lectures on "The Immutability of Colours." Among other splendid seventeenth- to nineteenth-century American paintings, Ralph Earl's *Portrait of Chief Justice Oliver Ellsworth and His Wife, Abigail Wolcott,* has Ellsworth holding the Bill of Rights, which he helped to write. Through the window is a view of his house, which still stands in Windsor, Connecticut. *Portrait of a Woman Knitting,* once titled *Mrs. Seymour Fort,* is one of the finest Copleys in America. Copley probably painted it after he left permanently for England, but the vigor and forthrightness of his American period gleams. Fifteen Thomas Coles illumine the wonderful Hudson River school canvases.

The Morgan wing still gives shelter to acquisitions of that insatiable but selective collector J. P. Morgan, Sr., son of Junius S. Morgan, merchant of Hartford, later of London, in whose memory the wing was built. Greek, Roman, early Christian, and Italian Renaissance bronzes enliven this wing, which also holds the most comprehensive German Meissen collection in this country. An immensely voluptuous seventeenth-century fountain figure, *Venus Attended by Nymph and Satyr* by the Flemish sculptor Pietro Francavilla, rises in mannered elegance into the stark three-story court of the Avery wing. The Prince of Wales brought *Venus* from Florence to England in 1750. It was then lost (quite a feat; *Venus* is 8 feet tall) and was dug up in a rose garden near Croyden in 1919.

Ralph Earl: *Portrait of Chief Justice and Mrs. Oliver Ellsworth* (Wadsworth Atheneum, Hartford, Connecticut)

The vagrant *Venus* is a fitting clue to the Atheneum's treasures, since its brilliant director from 1927 to 1944, A. Everett Austin, was strongly biased in favor of baroque and rococo art. The rapturous marvels of the baroque collection owe their presence here to Mr. Austin's use of a bequest from Frank C. Sumner, president of the Hartford Trust. Mr. Sumner, himself a flamboyant figure who rode in a purple Rolls-Royce, was never known to buy a painting or visit a museum, yet his fund is still the major source of the museum's purchase-income today.

Random winners from various galleries: designs for the sets of the Lifar Ballet Company, drawings by Derain, Matisse, Picasso, Max Ernst, which Lifar, last of Diaghilev's great male dancers, inherited from the maestro. In Strozzi's *St. Catherine of Alexandria*, the figure sits in theatrical dignity against the almost psychedelic brilliance of the draperies. See Caravaggio's *Ecstasy of St. Francis*; a dark, glowing *Crucifixion* by Poussin; and the magnificent Zurbarán, *St. Serapion*, crucified with ropes for preaching the gospel to the Mohammedans. Rather new to the Spanish gallery is the *Portrait of Don Pedro Arascot* by Francisco Bayen, brother-in-law of Goya. An early Goya and an El Greco hang in the same room. Hartford has the pen-and-ink sketch for *View of the Piazzetta, Venice* by Guardi, as well as the charming painting he made from it. *The Tiger Hunt* by Rubens, smaller version of the one in the museum of Rennes, France, has the advantage of being entirely by the master. Rembrandt's *The Boy*, *Turkish Women Bathing* by Delacroix, and *Jane Avril Leaving the Moulin Rouge* by Toulouse-Lautrec also command interest.

Bernardo Strozzi: *St. Catherine of Alexandria* (Wadsworth Atheneum, Hartford, Connecticut)

Giovanni Pannini's *Interior of a Roman Picture Gallery* provokes an entertaining guessing game. Most of the canvases-within-a-canvas, hung and stacked against the walls, are copies of well-known masterpieces.

In the Dutch gallery the small canvases are strung around the wall like pearls in a necklace. *The Feast of the Gods* by Cornelis van Poelenburg sings as loud as the huge Tiepolo in the next gallery. In the French room there is a whole wall of small masterpieces: Pissarro's *Portrait of Minette,* Monet's *Beach at Trouville,* Courbet's *A Bay with Cliffs,* Picasso's minute *Nude,* which couldn't be more monumental if it were 8 feet square. (The Atheneum held the first museum retrospective of Picassos in the United States in 1934.) The seductive, mad, dreamy, and sometimes mischievous world of Surrealism is evoked in the contemporary section by De Chirico, Dali, Max Ernst, and others. In the Wallace Nutting collection, the museum has a comprehensive display of Connecticut furniture and artifacts. The whole Pilgrim century is involved, a thorough review of our founding fathers' cabinetmakers and artisans.

Then there are the drawings. Daumier's *The Mountebanks Changing Place* will halt the most restless of gallery gobblers in mid-flight. If *Mountebanks* has changed its place, it is because it is sought for loan exhibitions more often than anything else in the museum. Exhibitions change in the new Austin galleries. The Susan M. Hilles gallery of twentieth-century art keeps the Atheneum *avant.*

NEW BRITAIN MUSEUM OF AMERICAN ART

56 Lexington Street, New Britain, Connecticut
Hours: Tues.–Sun., 1–5.
Closed major holidays.
Free.

On a shady side street in New Britain, this pleasant house offers a brief, nicely edited course in American art. It commences with striking primitive portraits, then goes on to John Trumbull, Benjamin West, Ralph Earl, John Smibert, Gilbert Stuart, Thomas Sully, and S. F. B. Morse. A beautiful Frederick Church, *Haying Near New Haven,* demonstrates the Hudson River school. *View of St. Peter's* is an early major work of landscapist George Inness,

George Bellows: *The Big Dory* (The New Britain Museum of American Art, New Britain, Connecticut; photograph by E. Irving Blomstrann)

and one of six Innesses here. Numerous Henris, Glackenses, Sloans, Lukses, Prendergasts, Doves, Lawsons, Shinns, and a fine small Bellows, *The Big Dory*, speak up for the school of "The Eight." Some of The Eight come off better than others in New Britain, but it is good to have them hanging about together as they did in the days when they stirred the New York art world with their exhibition of 1908. The genre work of Eastman Johnson, William Sidney Mount, and E. L. Henry and the realism of William Harnett, John Haberle, and John Peto are shown in first-rate examples. Of five Andrew Wyeths, *McVey's Barn*, a large tempera canvas, is perhaps the most important. And Thomas Hart Benton's *The Arts in America* sounds a nostalgic note with its permanent installation in the last gallery. For years these four large murals hung in the old Whitney on Eighth Street, in New York, the first museum wholly given over to this country's art.

YALE UNIVERSITY ART GALLERY

1111 Chapel Street, New Haven, Connecticut
Hours: Tues.–Sat., 10–5; Sun., 2–5;
closed Thanksgiving, Christmas, New Year's, July 4.
Free.

Shortly after the fledgling university in New Haven had been given his name, Elihu Yale presented it with its first work of art, a portrait of the reigning monarch, George I, from the workshop of Sir Godfrey Kneller, England's official court painter. To Kneller is ascribed the dubious practice of "factory painting," in which the master does the face of the sitter then passes the canvas, assembly-line fashion, to his specialists in hat, hands, or ruffles. (This system is not to be confused with the earlier European custom of apprentice of workshop painting, such as Rubens employed.)

In 1832 Yale purchased John Trumbull's series of paintings of Revolutionary battles, miniatures, and portraits, and the John Trumbull Art Gallery became the first college art museum in the country. Trumbull, former aide to George Washington, was a diplomat and architect as well as a painter. Its course set, the university has continued through gift and purchase to build one of the top collections in America, metropolitan museums excepted. In 1864 Samuel F. B. Morse gave his alma mater a painting by his former teacher, Benjamin West. In 1871 Yale purchased the James Jackson Jarves collection of 119 early Italian paintings, priceless today. Jarves, scholar and connoisseur, peddled his finds to many museums before they came to rest at Yale.

The present building is composed of two units, the first a 1928 "Ruskin Gothic" museum, the second a buff brick and glass extension of the parent edifice, adroitly created by architect Louis Kahn, its interior admirably adapted to the collection and the varied exhibitions that make up a museum calendar. From the first- and second-floor galleries one looks out to the giant women of sculptors Moore and Maillol set against a wooded campus. On warm days art majors in rumpled slacks lounge about the sculpture bases.

The ground-floor gallery is usually reserved for the Société Anonyme collection. The Société was founded by Katherine Dreier, with the help of artists Marcel Duchamp and Man Ray. A determined spinster from Brooklyn Heights who became an astute and militant patron of the arts, Miss Dreier wished her

Neroccio and Francesco di Giorgio: *Annunciation* (Yale University Art Gallery, James Jackson Jarves Collection)

Société to promote art, not personalities (hence the name). This exposition of various progressive movements in American and European art from 1909 to 1949 includes 169 artists from twenty-three countries. Emphasis is on the early Russian constructivists, Dadaists, Surrealists, and the German Expressionists. Klee, Miró, Malevich made their bow to America under its auspices; some others in the group are Schwitters, Gorky, Kandinsky, Gabo, Arp, Archipenko, Campendonk, Dove, and Mondrian.

Current exhibitions and the contemporaries are on the entrance floor. A few important contemporary canvases are: Motherwell's *La Resistance*, Tworkov's *B.S. 7*, Rico Lebrun's *Women of the Crucifixion*. One second-floor gallery holds a staggering compendium of nineteenth- and twentieth-century American classics; among them seven Eakinses, including *Girl with Cat–Katherine* and *John Biglen in a Single Scull*, Homer's *Game of Croquet*, Sargent, Bellows, and Hopper.

In the main galleries the Aztecs surround Picasso, while Soutine and Francis Bacon hold their own amidst the Bambara, Gura, and Boga tribes of Africa. Van Gogh's famous *The Night Café* is here, along with *Reclining Young Woman in Spanish Costume* by Manet. The third-floor holdings are unbelievably rich in European art: the Jarves and Maitland F. Griggs collections of Italian art and the Rabinowitz group which contains, besides the Italian, Northern Renaissance paintings such as Hieronymus Bosch's *Allegory of Intemperance* and Lucas Cranach the Elder's *Crucifixion with the Converted Centurion*. One could spend days in these galleries, for the old building opens from the European section into our American past. A pivotal canvas, *Bishop Berkeley and Family*, is by John Smibert, one of the first professional artists to reach our shores. He was brought over by the Bishop. Canvases by Benjamin West, Wollaston, Blackburn, Earl, and a great covey of Copleys hang about the walls. In the room of Trumbulls, cornerstone of the Yale Gallery, is Gilbert Stuart's portrait of *Trumbull* and Trumbull's own *George Washington at the Battle of Trenton*, all 6 feet 2 inches of him; also his minute oil-on-wood portrait of Ben Franklin in fur cap with spectacles sliding rakishly down his nose. The Garvin collection of American silver and furniture is superb.

The Oriental galleries, the Dura–Europos section (in 1928 Yale cooperated with the French Academy on a dig at this ancient site between Antioch and Damascus), medieval sculpture, and classical antiquities round out this impressive horde.

Projected in the future is the new Paul Mellon gallery. Though

John Smibert: *The Bermuda Group* (Yale University Art Gallery; gift of Isaac Lothrop)

no official name has been chosen, the building will contain Mr. Mellon's British paintings and will be a study center for the arts of Great Britain. It will occupy the block directly opposite the present gallery, from High to York Streets.

ALDRICH MUSEUM OF CONTEMPORARY ART

45 Main Street, Ridgefield, Connecticut
Hours: Fri., Sat., Sun., 2–6. Also by special appointment.
Library.
Admission 50¢.
Children free.

Again revolution takes place in Ridgefield, where General Benedict Arnold once barricaded Main Street to halt the British. Today the vanguard of modern art takes its stand on that same street—behind the barricades of a white clapboard church façade. "Old Hundred" was its name to the original tenants, the "Old Hundred" grocery and hardware store. Built in 1783, it became a home in 1883, a church sometime later. Naturally, to create functional and airy galleries required interior changes, but New England still prevails. The original polished oak floors, the corner fireplaces, the economy of color and severity of line serenely harmonize with the art inside that prim façade. Baumeister and Bolomey, Paolozzi, Penalba, even Picasso, bloom well in this alien soil.

Main Street view of The Larry Aldrich Museum; The Aldrich Museum of Contemporary Art, Ridgefield, Connecticut; photograph by Malcolm Smith

Aldrich Museum, entrance and center galleries showing, left to right, Hartung, Youngerman, Bengston, Tam Suden; sculpture by Metcalf. The Aldrich Museum of Contemporary Art, Ridgefield, Connecticut; photograph by Malcolm Smith

Larry Aldrich, long known in both the worlds of collecting and couture, is the man responsible for the idea and the accomplishment of this vital little museum. The permanent and expanding collection sounds its guns in the first two floors' flexible galleries. Once or twice a season, a traveling exhibition or invited works of other collectors are shown. Landscape and figure paintings include Cicero, Dubuffet, Freilicher, Giacometti, Golub, Oliveira, and Rivers. For the neo-Dada symbolic image, there are works by Baruchello, Al Bengston, Holden, Indiana, Ostlihn, Trova, and Willenbecher. The "optical magicians" Anuszkiewicz, Avedisian, Fukui, Jensen, Kelly, Riley, Sander, Stanczak, and Vasarely stir up visual excitement.

A library and reading room on a lower floor leads out to the lawn, a generous carpet for what Mr. Aldrich claims is the only purely nonobjective sculpture garden in the country.

BOWDOIN COLLEGE MUSEUM OF ART

Walker Art Building, Brunswick, Maine
Hours: Sept.–June: Mon.–Sat., 10–12, 2–4; Sun., school holidays,
2–4. July–Labor Day: Mon.–Sat., 10–5, 7–9; Sun., 2–5;
closed national holidays.
Free.

Charles F. McKim of McKim, Mead and White built this museum in 1894, on one of the most beautiful small campuses in America. Its grandiose little entrance hall is muraled by semicircles of Cox, LaFarge, Thayer, Vedder. Given in 1811 by founder James Bowdoin III, this oldest collection of any college group contained seventy paintings, including portraits of Jefferson and Madison by Gilbert Stuart that Bowdoin commissioned. Among 142 drawings, appraised at the time for $7.50 the lot, are fine specimens of Luca Cambiaso, Nicholas Poussin, and Pieter Brueghel the Elder.

But the fame of the collection rests primarily on portraits of the Bowdoins themselves, terrific testimonials to a family who played a strong role in shaping colonial history. There is no likeness of Pierre Baudouin, who, fleeing from the Huguenot persecution in France, established the clan in New England; but his son *James Bowdoin I,* who anglicized the name, was painted in both youth and maturity by skillful "unknowns" and also by Joseph

Badger, the house and sign painter who acquired a facility far beyond likenesses. There are handsome portraits of *James Bowdoin II*, one done as a youth by John Smibert, another later by Robert Feke. Christian Gullager, who did the Salisbury family in Worcester (see Worcester Museum), also painted James II. Robert Feke, portraying James's wife, tried to live up to her husband's poem to her particular charms, "Her tempting breast the eyes of all command,/ And gently rising court the am'rous hand," by painting her in what must have been spicy décolletage for the old New England Puritans. There are many portraits of collateral Bowdoins, but we will cling to the trunk of the tree, departing only to mention two: *Brigadier Samuel Waldo*, whose second wife was a Bowdoin—his full-length portrait is considered Feke's masterpiece; and Copley's arresting portrait of *Thomas Flucker*, Tory conspirator married to a Bowdoin. One of the most delectable portraits of children to be found anywhere is Joseph Blackburn's of *James Bowdoin III and His Sister Elizabeth*. Gilbert Stuart did *James Bowdoin III and His Wife*. Mrs. Bowdoin—young, coiffed, and ruffed, and set against a classical background—is especially appealing. Several years after his death, James III's widow presented the family portraits to the college. A scholarly and lively catalogue of their history has been done by Marvin Sadik, former director of the museum.

Five huge Assyrian reliefs (see Amherst) came to the college in 1857. Much of its fine classical antiquity section is the gift of Edward Perry Warren, who aided both the Metropolitan and the Boston Museum in establishing departments of antiquities. The Salton Renaissance and baroque medals and plaquettes have joined the museum. Maine-stater Winslow Homer is well represented. *Fountains at Night* is an atypical Homer canvas in myriad tones of gray. Some contemporaries here: Philip Guston, John Grillo, Jack Tworkov, Franz Kline, Peter Agostini, Reuben Nakian.

Joseph Blackburn: *James Bowdoin and His Sister Elizabeth* (Bowdoin College Museum of Art, Brunswick, Maine)

MUSEUM OF ART OF OGUNQUIT

Shore Road, Ogunquit, Maine
Hours: June 28–Sept. 10: Mon.–Sat., 10:30–5; Sun., 1:30–5.
Free.

The Ogunquit museum is unusual in that it is strictly a summer museum. However, during that blithe period the place pulsates with all the activity of a city museum. Changing exhibitions are put on, and the permanent collection continues to grow in stature every year. The building was erected in 1952 in memory of Charles and Adeline Strater of Louisville, Kentucky. Built on a rocky promontory of Narrow Cove, the place has a salty fragrance. Though probably not by design, much of the collection seems indigenous to Maine and the sea: Marsden Hartley's *Lobster Pots and Buoy* and *Mt. Katahdin,* Marin's *Cape Split, Maine,* John Flannagan's *Pelican.* The site on which the museum was built was an artists' preserve for years. Here Walt Kuhn, Kuniyoshi, and a host of others used to set up their easels to try to catch that grandeur of cliff and sea peculiar to Maine.

From the center court of the clean-lined little building a glass façade frames the ocean. Sculpture resting out of doors is silhouetted against its blue. Restricted to American art, some of the museum's holdings are in Tobey, Graves, Kuniyoshi, Demuth, Tom Hardy, Maldarelli, and Walt Kuhn. Kuhn, a long-time summer resident, was almost as much a part of the tall pines and green firs of Maine as of the sawdust arenas of the "Big Top."

Ogunquit is surpassed in the state only by Bowdoin College's distinguished museum (the oldest college collection in the United States), Colby College, and the University of Maine's growing collections.

COLBY COLLEGE ART MUSEUM

Mayflower Hill, Colby College, Waterville, Maine
Hours: Mon.–Sat., 10–12; 1–5; Sun., 2–5;
closed Christmas, New Year's, July 4, Labor Day.
Guides provided in summer; apply information center.
Free.

On the edge of the Colby campus, the Bixler Art and Music Center houses a small museum and a brisk program—for example,

Alexander Calder: *Black Dot in the Air*
(Colby College Art Museum, Waterville,
Maine)

Rosati, Marca-Relli, and Guston exhibitions, with each artist
coming for one week as artist-in-residence, and the museum purchasing a work of each. Such exhibitions rotate during the school
year with the permanent collection. In the summer, classrooms
adjacent to the museum cleverly transform into galleries so that
more of the collection can be seen.

The American Heritage collection of seventy-eight canvases, a
1956 gift to the college, consists primarily of New England primitives, 1800–1869. In the museum's estimable cache of colonial
portraits, John Smibert, Joseph Badger, and Joseph Blackburn
turn up. John Singleton Copley was twenty-two when he did the
Portrait of Mrs. Metcalf Bowler. The panels of Mrs. Bowler's
living room are now built into the American wing at the Metropolitan. The earliest portrait is of *William Burnett,* godson of
William of Orange, who migrated to the Colonies and became
governor of Massachusetts and New Hampshire, which then included Maine. A Maine artist painted him. Nineteenth-century
America is represented by Birch, Doughty, Cole, Kensett, Inness
and Eastman Johnson. Of the Winslow Homer watercolor holdings, fourteen in all, *The Trapper, Adirondacks 1870* and *The
Berry Pickers* are the most frequently reproduced. With such
artists as Noguchi, Townley, Chadwick, Rosati, Guston, Zao
Wou-Ki, and Marca-Relli, the collection is leaping ahead.

AMHERST COLLEGE: MUSEUM OF FINE ARTS, MEAD ART BUILDING

Amherst College, Routes 9 and 116, Amherst, Massachusetts
Hours: 9–5 Mon.–Sat.; Sun., 11:30 A.M.–5 P.M. during
academic year.
Summer: 9–12, 2–4; closed August.
Free.

Lord Jeffrey Amherst, who saved New England from the French
in the Battle of Louisburg (1758) and became Governor General
of North America, hangs in Gainsboroughian splendor and honor
at the Mead Art Museum (a copy hangs in the National Portrait
Gallery in London). The building, erected in 1949 by McKim,
Mead and White, was a gift of William R. Mead, a member of the
firm. Studios and lecture rooms branch off from the changing
exhibitions and the permanent collection in the central portion.
As with many another campus art museum, only a small portion
of the permanent holdings can appear at one time. The collection
is strong in American art: Copley in two portraits, *Mr. and Mrs.
Benjamin Blackstone,* Benjamin West, John Wollaston, Ralph Earl,
John Trumbull, Charles Willson Peale and Rembrandt Peale, and
Thomas Sully. The Gilbert Stuart holdings number seven, the
rarest a portrait of his Irish period, *Robert Shaw Terenure,* ancestor of George Bernard Shaw. The Rotherwas Room (1611)
is an outstanding piece of Elizabethan decoration. The house
itself existed from 1086 and was mentioned in the Domesday
Book of William the Conqueror. When it was dismantled in 1930,

Gilbert Stuart: *Portrait of Robert Shaw
Terenure* (Amherst College, Amherst,
Massachusetts)

Herbert L. Pratt purchased the room and moved it to Glen Cove, Long Island. He gave it to Amherst in 1945. The elaborately carved and richly polychromed mantelpiece is held up by figures of Fortitude, Justice, Prudence, and Temperance.

The Ninevah Room contains large reliefs from the palace at Nimrud, capital of the Assyrian empire (ninth century B.C.), as well as other antiquities. When Sir Austin Henry Layard, an English archeologist, dug up pieces, the Reverend Henry Lobdell (Amherst, 1844), a missionary in nearby Mosul, was on hand. Sawed from the face of the huge alabaster blocks they rested on, the reliefs were packed on the back of camels, who marched 500 miles to the nearest port with their burden. The dig should have been titled "Operation Missionary," because Dartmouth, Middlebury, Bowdoin, Williams, Yale, and the University of Vermont all have similar reliefs sent home in the 1850s by alumni missionaries to the Middle East (see S. Lane Faison's *Art Museums of New England*). There is a Kress study collection and a decorative arts section quite rich in textiles and American and European furniture. While little of the latter can be on view, it is accessible to anyone interested.

ADDISON GALLERY OF AMERICAN ART

Phillips Academy, Andover, Massachusetts
Hours: Mon.–Sat., 9–5; Sun., 2:30–5.
Closed holidays.
Free.

If rules were made to be broken, this is the place to break the rule. Our concern is with the community and college art museum, but Phillips Academy is unique among secondary schools in that it established an art museum for its students before such an aid to education was a gleam in many a college president's eye.

A gift of Thomas Cochran, class of 1890, the museum opened in 1931, a tidy package replete with objects of art, maintenance and endowment funds. The permanent collection is exclusively American, but loan exhibitions may and do go far afield. A new building, the Arts and Communications Center, joins the museum via the long gallery facing an outdoor sculpture court. Auditorium, studios, and workshops are here.

There is a small but fine hoard of silver, glass, and furniture in the Addison. Old ship models, figureheads, and skillfully

Elie Nadelman: *Seated Woman* (1917) (Addison Gallery of American Art, Phillips Academy, Andover, Massachusetts)

wrought trade signs fill one gallery with pure American delight. The painting section starts with John Smibert, a Scot who came to New England in 1729; John Singleton Copley is here; so are Benjamin West and many of his pupils—Washington Allston, Gilbert Stuart, John Trumbull, and Samuel F. B. Morse, who graduated from Phillips Academy in 1805 at the age of fourteen. There are splendid Hudson River paintings, but it is the holdings of that turn-of-the-century triumvirate Eakins, Homer, and Ryder that are most enviable. Homer's *Eight Bells, West Wind,* and the early *New England Country School* come to mind. The latter is a factual happy painting of children playing at recess. It is done in the direct manner of earlier genre scene painters but elevated beyond that level by Homer's particular genius. *West Wind,* much more loosely done, is one of the artist's acknowledged masterpieces. It shows a solitary little woman pushing against the wind in a broodingly lonely landscape.

Professor Henry A. Rowland, a physicist of Johns Hopkins University, was painted by Thomas Eakins, conjurer of mood. This is an instance of the frame being almost as telling as the portrait, for it is etched with mathematical formulas selected by the professor.

Others here in fine examples: James McNeill Whistler, Childe Hassam, Maurice Prendergast, George Luks, William Glackens, George Bellows, and Edward Hopper. The Addison's spirit of quest and adventure led them to acquire such people as Jackson Pollock, Andrew Wyeth, and Charles Sheeler before they attained broad demand and prices beyond most museum budgets.

INSTITUTE OF CONTEMPORARY ART

Soldiers Field Road, Boston, Massachusetts

Since its 1936 nativity, the scope here has been international and inclusive. The institute chalked up first comprehensive exhibitions, generously circulated, of Kokoschka, Munch, Ensor, and Fritz Wotruba. Its special and basic goal is to perform as a study center for current creativity. Changing exhibitions and the involment of Boston's urban artists is the present goal.

Because its quarters on Newbury Street have been sold, the institute is moving back to its old home on the banks of the Charles River. During this period of transition it would be best to telephone as to hours and activities.

ISABELLA STEWART GARDNER MUSEUM

280 The Fenway, Boston, Massachusetts
Hours: Tues., Thurs., Sat., 10–4; first Thurs., 10–10;
closed Mon., Wed., Fri., holidays, and August.
Free.

Fenway Court, as Bostonians call it, is as much a triumphal monument to Isabella Stewart Gardner as it is a museum. This remarkable woman, a New Yorker who at twenty married into an old Boston family, alternately shocked and dazzled her adopted city.

Mrs. Gardner started out collecting rare editions, but one day Henry James took her to John Singer Sargent's London studio, where she saw his famous *Portrait of Madame X* (now at the Metropolitan). The ebullient Mrs. Gardner put aside the pursuit of first editions for the warmer climes of the visual art world. Trips to European *palazzi* and museums developed the love affair. She made a few intoxicating purchases on her own, one a glorious Vermeer, $6000 at auction. A couple of bangs of the gavel would bring it down to a million today. Though she did not realize it at the time, she was bidding against the directors of the Louvre and the National Gallery, London. In 1894, under the tutelage of Bernard Berenson, she turned from erratic buying to serious collecting. Berenson, only a few years out of Harvard, was already a brilliant art historian, and by the time he died at ninety-four, in 1959, would be acknowledged a world authority on early Italian and Renaissance art. Although she occasionally took fliers on her own and advice from others, his was the genius behind her acquisitions.

Mrs. Gardner called Rembrandt's *Self-Portrait as a Young Man* her cornerstone, because its purchase forced on her the realization that her Beacon Street house would burst if she added one more painting. (Today some scholars attribute the work to Jan Lievens, a contemporary of Rembrandt.) She also realized that she had a nucleus of works of art so important that they belonged some day in the public domain. She designed a house, based on Venetian palaces of the fifteenth and sixteenth centuries, large enough to become a museum. Mrs. Gardner was on the job every day, bringing her lunch as the workmen did. She acted, in fact, as master foreman, changing plans (the architect was largely ignored), countermanding, rolling up her sleeves to show a laborer how to get an unorthodox effect she wanted.

For years she had been picking up architectural fragments from all over Europe: capitals, doors, an odd assortment of columns, furniture, and fountains. Because of her innate taste and sense of scale, they all fell into place as though plans had been drawn for them.

When Fenway Court was opened to the public after Mrs. Gardner's death, it was still her house—even the varieties of flowers under certain paintings remain essentially the same. Under Zurbarán's *A Doctor of Law* stands a Chinese beaker (Chou, 1122–249 B.C.) that reiterates the reds and browns of the doctor's robes: a bowl beside is filled with flaming nasturtiums, the color of his great orange collar. This masterful arrangement was originally conceived by Mrs. Gardner.

The front door opens directly into a Spanish gallery designed to set off *El Jaleo, the Spanish Dancer* by Mrs. Gardner's friend John Singer Sargent. To create for this huge brilliant canvas an atmosphere approximating the cafés in Spain where such dancing was seen, Mrs. Gardner lighted it dramatically from below so that the dancing figure in the painting really seems on stage. The corridor turns into the court, which rises in three tiers of Venetian arches to a skylighted glass roof. Balconied windows look down on a jungle of tropical plants that border a first-century Roman tile floor from the villa of Emperor Augustus' wife, Livia. High banks of flowers are a year-long extravaganza of color—chrysanthemums in autumn; a hanging waterfall, stories high, of nasturtiums in spring. An Egyptian hawk rests pertly in the foliage, and

Gardner Museum, court as seen from second floor north (Isabella Stewart Gardner Museum, Boston; photograph by Barney Burstein)

a Roman seat has a footstool, daringly compounded by Mrs. Gardner from two Ionic capitals back to back.

In the first gallery of the Italian rooms on the second floor is Piero della Francesca's *Hercules,* his only fresco outside Italy and his only painting of a pagan subject. Masaccio's *Young Man in a Scarlet Turban* is one of the earliest of secular paintings. While it seems strangely flat-planed, it is a strong and penetrating introduction to the portraiture of succeeding generations. With Simone Martini's melancholy *Madonna and Child with Four Saints,* the humanistic tradition instituted by Giotto (there is a Giotto in the Gothic room) moves a step forward. This is the only large and complete altarpiece by Simone Martini outside Italy. In a case with Persian plates and a melange of objects are two Chinese bronze bears of the Han period. Scholars travel far to see this playful pair.

The Raphael gallery has two paintings by the master, a *Pietà* and his *Portrait of Tommaso Inghirami,* painted between 1509 and 1513. A copy, probably of the same century, of the Inghirami portrait is in the Pitti in Florence. In the Inghirami Palace at Volterra is another copy made at the time of the sale (as has often been done by families forced to sell their ancestral paintings) to fill the place left empty by the original.

As I walked into the great tapestry hall one of the guards was playing a Chopin nocturne on the piano. Music was always a part of the life of the house, and musicales are given frequently in this gallery as they were when Mrs. Gardner entertained. In the Dutch room are two Holbein portraits, four Rembrandts, and a beauty of a Rubens, *Portrait of Thomas Howard, Earl of Arundel*—Earl Marshal under Charles I and one of the first great private collectors. Here is the baroque grandeur of court life, the full armor in smoky grays and blacks dramatizing the noble, intelligent face. Vermeer's *The Concert*, Mrs. Gardner's auction prize, is genre painting at its height, distilled, refined to perfection.

Upstairs, in the Titian room, is the picture some scholars rate as the finest canvas in America: Titian's *Rape of Europa*. Beside the painting is a small sketch of it by Van Dyck. The Titian hung in Madrid's Royal Palace for a century and a half, and it was there that Rubens did a copy of it. Since Van Dyck never went to Spain, it is presumed that his sketch was done after the Rubens copy. Cellini's bust of a banker and art patron, Bindo Altoviti, for which he was praised by Michelangelo, is in this room, one of the few authentic Cellini bronzes in America. The long gallery is full of memorabilia and treasures, such as Botticelli's *Madonna of the Eucharist*, a painting touched with sadness and mysticism. Above the altar, in the chapel at the end of the gallery, is a fine thirteenth-century French window. High Mass is celebrated here by an Anglican priest on Mrs. Gardner's birthday, as provided for in her will.

By the window in the Gothic room is Giotto's *Presentation of the Child Jesus in the Temple*, humane beyond anything his Byzantine predecessors had dreamed of. With splendid disregard for the logic of time and place, Mrs. Gardner, who delighted in

Titian: *The Rape of Europa* (Isabella Stewart Gardner Museum, Boston)

each object she owned for its own sake and mixed at will, hung Sargent's portrait of her so that it dominates the room. *Portrait of Mrs. Gardner* was considered so outrageous when it was painted (she chose to wear her famous pearls to delineate her tiny waist, instead of around her neck where they belonged) that Mr. Gardner had it put away, and only after his death was it brought out and placed where it now is.

Fenway Court celebrates the passion, the daring, and the taste of Isabella Stewart Gardner and the brilliantly selective eye of Bernard Berenson. In the worthy catalogue prepared by him, Sir Philip Hendy states: "It is probably the finest collection of its compact size in the world."

In her last years Isabella Gardner, obsessed with the importance of perpetuating Fenway Court, is said to have turned miser and put her servants on rations when she wanted to buy a painting. Aline Saarinen recounts in *The Proud Possessors* how Mrs. Gardner used to send her secretary and curator to a corner store each day for an orange. One day, to save himself time, he bought two. "What's the matter," asked the storekeeper. "The old lady having a party?"

FOGG ART MUSEUM (HARVARD UNIVERSITY)

Quincy Street, Cambridge, Massachusetts
Hours (during academic year): Mon.–Sat., 9–5; Sun., 2–5;
closed Sat., Sun., July 1–Sept. 15, and holidays.
Library.
Free.

The pleasantly dimensioned Renaissance lobby at the Fogg is the center around which revolve collections encompassing the whole evolution of art. Arriving late on the university museum scene, the first museum opened in Hunt Hall in 1895 and moved to the present site in 1927. Through such distinguished men as art historian Charles Eliot Norton and Paul Sachs, teacher, curator, director, and father figure to a host of museum directors, the museum soon took a prominent place in both training programs and collections. Its range covers Eastern and Western, prehistoric to modern. The strongest holdings are in Chinese bronzes and archaic jades and in the print and drawing section, the latter being rivaled only by the Metropolitan Museum and the Morgan

RIGHT: Horse tomb figurine (Chinese, T'ang Dynasty, 718–907 A.D.) (Fogg Art Museum, Harvard University; bequest of Mrs. John Nicholas Brown) BELOW: Nicholas Poussin: *Holy Family* (Fogg Art Museum, Harvard University)

Library. Singling out examples from the more than fifty thousand prints and drawings is difficult, but the Paul and Meta Sachs group of nineteenth-century French drawing is nothing short of superb, and the Ingres group is considered the finest outside France.

For a small museum, its variety is wide, from the compelling little figure on an English hammer beam (*circa* 1430) to the marble sophistication of Guillaume Coustou the Elder's bust of *Louis XV;* from Simone Martini and Lorenzetti to contemporary painters Kenneth Noland and Morris Louis.

In the field of classical art, Greek and Roman sculptures include the marble *Meleager* after Skopas, a leading artist of the Alexandrine period, and a portrait of the Emperor Trajan. The medieval section contains several Romanesque capitals from Moutier–St. Jean, and an eleventh-century Virgin from Santa Maria de Tahull. In cleverly lighted cases are twelve unique terra cotta Bernini sketches, some for his famous monuments, such as the angel for the altar of the Sacrament in the Vatican. Fra

Angelico, Filippo Lippi, and Lorenzo Lotto represent the Renaissance; Rubens and Delacroix the baroque period. Some eighteenth-century painters are Guardi, Tiepolo, Gainsborough, and our own John Singleton Copley with a great portrait, *Mrs. Thomas Boylston, Sr.* Early nineteenth-century French painters, besides Delacroix, are David, Gericault, and Ingres with *Odalisque and Slave.* If the casual visitor is sometimes bemused to see copies, frankly fakes, and masterpieces hanging side by side, it is because the Fogg really takes itself seriously as a teaching museum—and why not? Many of America's leading directors and curators call it alma mater. If a gallery is less than perfectly installed, it is likely that a student has been given the assignment of hanging a show or arranging objects to be discussed. Usefulness and liveliness win over display here.

A bastion of scholarship, the Fogg manages an engaging air of informality. Storage racks easily accessible from main galleries allow the visitor to see old favorites not on display. On two floors below ground is one of the most efficient and comprehensive libraries in existence. A passageway links the library with the new art school, housed in a splendid building designed by Le Corbusier, his only work in America.

HARVARD UNIVERSITY: BUSCH-REISINGER MUSEUM OF GERMAN CULTURE

Kirkland Street at Divinity Avenue, Cambridge, Massachusetts
Hours: Mon.–Sat., 9–5;
closed Sat. in summer.
Free.

Another specialized museum not to be missed, the Busch-Reisinger holds the largest collection of German culture outside that country. It is administered in cooperation with the Fogg.

Though showing Gothic and medieval works, the strength of the collection lies in its twentieth-century work, much from the Bridge and Blue Rider groups (see Pasadena). The Bridge was formed by Erick Heckel, Ernst Kirchner, and Karl Schmidt-Rottluff to bring together artists of different schools, as the name suggests. Emil Nolde, whose group of religious paintings is outstanding, was a part of the movement for a short time. Sculptors Gerhard Marks and Ernst Barlach make strong statements.

HARVARD UNIVERSITY: PEABODY MUSEUM OF ARCHAEOLOGY AND ETHNOLOGY

Divinity Avenue, Cambridge, Massachusetts
Hours: Mon.–Sat., holidays, 9–4:30; Sun., 1–4:30.
Free.

These world-famous collections have been gathered primarily from expeditions sponsored by the university. The major sections include prehistoric, Oceanic, African, and pre-Columbian. Though not displayed with elan, both quantitatively and qualitatively the Peabody collection is difficult to surpass.

DE CORDOVA AND DANA MUSEUM

Sandy Pond Road, Lincoln, Massachusetts
Hours: Tues.–Sat., 10–5;
50 cents admission 21 or over;
free Sun., 1:30–5.

New England artists are well nurtured in this lovely spot on a wooded hilltop. Long a community center for the arts with changing exhibitions, lectures, and concerts, the museum is now establishing a permanent collection. Already New Englanders Townley, Wolfe, Boyce, Chaet, Alcalay, Aronson, Kepes, Knaths, and Hyman Bloom are represented, along with such internationally known artists as Ortman, Von Wicht, Sutherland, Salemme, Hartung, Resnick, and Vasarely. Some eight major exhibitions are presented a year; while they tend to be contemporary, the arts of other times and cultures occasionally crop up.

SMITH COLLEGE MUSEUM OF ART: TRYON ART GALLERY

Elm Street, Northampton, Massachusetts
Hours: Mon.–Sat., 9–5; Sun., 2–4:30.
Summer: Mon.–Fri., 2:30–4:30
and by appointment;
closed holidays.
Free.

Through the bequest of Sophia Smith, Smith College came into being in 1871. Shortly after its founding the first purchases of art were made, mainly American and contemporary. Thomas Eakins' *In Grandmother's Time* was bought by the college in 1879 directly from the artist. But the important thrust took place in the early 1920s, when antiquarian Joseph Brummer gave five canvases by Spanish-born Juan Gris. The collection of eighteenth- through twentieth-century French masters illustrates the development of modern painting. *Pyramids* by Hubert Robert leads into David and Ingres. Of several Corots, *Italian Hill-town* and *View of the Romanesque of Jumieges* command special admiration. And Courbet's power-packed 8 feet of *Preparation of the Village Bride* is possibly the museum's proudest possession. The Impressionists are there in force: Degas' *Portrait of René de Gas,* Renoir's portrait of *Mme. Edouard Maitre,* Claude Monet's *The Seine at Bougival;* also Cézanne, Vuillard, Bonnard, and three Seurat studies for his *Un Dimanche à la Grande Jatte.* Picasso's *La Table* (*circa* 1920) complements the Juan Gris 1914–1916 quintet. German Expressionism is represented by a splendid Ernst Kirchner—*Dodo and Her Brother.*

From other lands, in other styles: some sixty archaic Chinese

Gustave Courbet: *Preparation of the Village Bride* (*ca.* 1864) (Smith College Museum of Art, Northampton, Massachusetts)

jades, Shang and Chou Dynasties: Dutch Hendrick Terbrugghen's *Old Man Writing by Candlelight;* contemporaries Bontecou, Kline, Marini, Moore, Baskin, Nickford, and a splendid Arp. In the Tryon Gallery (the museum's formal name), expect to see only a fraction of the pleasures on hand. This is especially true when some of the changing exhibitions the museum mounts are on stage.

MUSEUM OF FINE ARTS

49 Chestnut Street, Springfield, Massachusetts
Hours: Tues.–Sat., 1–5; Sun., 2–5;
closed Sun. in July, month of August and holidays.
Library.
Free.

A deft hand worked on this arrangement. Except for the print cabinet, a gallery of contemporary art, and two attractive galleries of fine Chinese bronzes and ceramics on the first floor, the collection flows in orderly succession around a two-story "tapestry court." In the Gothic room at the head of the stairs the focal piece, a carved wood Spanish altar, depicts scenes from the life of the Virgin. The Medieval gallery features *The Crucifixion Triptych* by Goswyn van der Weyden, grandson of the great Rogier van der Weyden, whose masterpiece *The Descent from the Cross* hangs in the Prado in Madrid. In the Dutch galleries nestle small succinct landscapes by Jacob van Ruisdael and Jan van Goyen and Gerrit Berckheyde's *The Great Church at Haarlem,* a scrubbed-looking street scene in brilliant lights and shadows, the oft-painted church in the background. Seventeenth- and eighteenth-century French galleries culminate in a handsome Chardin still life, *Refreshment.* Two nineteenth-century French portraits to note: Courbet's *Portrait of M. Nodler, the Younger,* a strong, straight rendering of a dour and troubled youth, and a Eugène Delacroix study for the portrait of *Ludwig August, the Baron von Schwiter.* Don't attempt to walk through the *trompe l'oeil* door next to the Harnett *trompe l'oeil Emblems of Peace* and don't miss Homer's *Promenade on the Beach* in the American section.

One of the oddities of American painting is set in the gallery devoted to the work of Erastus Salisbury Field: his 9- by 13-foot *Historical Monument of the American Republic.* Until the advent of the daguerreotype, Field was a successful New England folk

Erastus Salisbury Field (1805–1900): *Historical Monument of the American Republic* (1876) (Museum of Fine Arts, Springfield, Massachusetts; The Morgan Wesson Memorial Collection)

artist. Dr. Theodore B. Robinson, the museum's director, suggests in a brochure on Field that he did the work for a design competition for the Central building at the Philadelphia Centennial. Tower after tower rises like a tiered wedding cake, quotes from the Bible and historical scenes imposed on their surfaces. Field's involvement with the slavery issue prompted him to give Lincoln the place of honor. Each tower represents an important sequence in American history. Angels atop the tallest spires wave the stars and stripes.

Important holdings in the early print field concentrate on English, French, and American nineteenth-century works and over three thousand Japanese prints.

The museum's library entrance is on a pleasant quadrangle around which are a science museum, the city library, the William Pynchon Museum of Connecticut Valley History, and the George Walter Vincent Smith Art Museum, the latter a period piece of late nineteenth-century collecting propensities in jade, porcelain, armor, embroidery, and such.

BRANDEIS UNIVERSITY: ROSE ART MUSEUM

Waltham, Massachusetts
Hours: Daily, 1–5;
closed holidays.
Free.

The growth of the holdings of the Rose Art Museum since its opening is nothing short of a director's dream. Though the basic collection came into being in 1950, the 1961 erection of the handsome little glass and stone building added impetus. The interior forms one spacious high-walled room with additional space on the lower floor. Stairs float downward over a rectangular pool where sculptor Reg Butler's *Figure in Space* is anchored in a small round green island.

The scope ranges from the Egyptians to the present day, with more than twenty-five hundred works illustrating the historic winds of art. The rest of the campus shares some of this material. Oceanic art is on permanent exhibition in Schwarz Hall, prints and drawings in the Goldfarb Library. The new Spingold Arts Center next to the museum provides added exhibition space. While the Renaissance and baroque periods are covered, and the late nineteenth- and early twentieth centuries upheld by the likes of Boudin, Monet, Degas, Renoir, Bonnard, and Pascin, it is to the art of today, its experimentation and its exploration, that this young university museum is dedicated. An exhibition or two a year is done outside the twentieth century, but the main emphasis is on challenging exhibits that stress our time. Some artists in the permanent collection: Robert Indiana, James Brooks, Ellsworth Kelly, Grace Hartigan, Morris Lewis, Roy Lichtenstein, Matta, Marisol, Ludwig Sander, Claes Oldenburg, Robert Rauschenberg, De Kooning, Dubuffet, and Motherwell. The list is long.

Robert Motherwell: *Elegy to the Spanish Republic, No. 58* (1957–1961) (Brandeis University Art Collection, Waltham, Massachusetts, gift of Julian J. and Joachim Jean Aberbach)

WELLESLEY COLLEGE: JEWETT ARTS CENTER

Wellesley, Massachusetts
Hours (academic year): Mon.–Sat., 8:30–4:30; Sun., 2:30–5:30;
closed summer, college holidays.
Free.

Established in 1883, the Wellesley College Museum has found an excellent home in the Jewett Arts Center. Designed by Paul Rudolph, the pink brick building is in harmony with the campus complex. The museum forms a bridge between the two wings sheltering drama, music, and art activities. Changing print and drawing shows line the broad corridors. The impressive sculpture listing includes one of the most notable Roman copies of Greek sculpture in America, *Athlete, of Polykleitos.* Other distinguished pieces: a German carving, *Standing Saint or Apostle,* thought to be the only piece in the United States by the North German sculptor Henning von der Heide; Duchamp-Villon's stern and intellectualized bust of *Baudelaire* is one of the fine twentieth-century pieces in the group. The painting section harbors early Italian panel painting and works of Bernardo Strozzi, Marco Ricci, Pietro da Cortona, Salvator Rosa, and Alessandro Magnasco. Among the Dutch is an arresting little Gerard Terborch, *Soldiers at Night.* Terborch brings this mundane scene to life through his clever use of light and shade.

An early, atypical Corot, *The Inn at Montigny,* would be the "stump the experts" picture of any collection. Alfred H. Barr, Jr., long-time head of the Museum of Modern Art collections, but before that professor of art at Wellesley, says of it: "he made a composition which compels one to believe Picasso and Braque might have found in Corot sanction for the earliest phases of

Corot: *The Inn at Montigny*
(Jewett Art Center, Wellesley College, Wellesley, Massachusetts)

cubism." Among contemporary European paintings is a large 1913 Kokoschka, *Two Nudes*, Fernand Léger's forceful *Mother and Child*, canvases by Picasso and Paul Klee. Loren MacIvor, Walt Kuhn, Gyorgy Kepes, I. Rice Pereira are but a few in the twentieth-century American collection that represents either through draw-ings, graphics or oils almost every painter of importance. The Jewett Arts Center serves not only the students who, enviably cannot reach their classes in the Center without being exposed to works of art, but also the community of Wellesley, the town.

STERLING AND FRANCINE CLARK ART INSTITUTE

South Street, Williamstown, Massachusetts
Hours: Tues.–Sun., 10–5;
closed February.
Free.

When the Clark museum opened in 1955 it was the neatest surprise package ever delivered to an art world usually well aware of what the left and right hands are up to. Clark, retiring by nature, had his paintings, his prints, and silver scattered through four houses, two of them abroad. He had no art advisors, since he bought only to please himself, and used a variety of dealers. Any paintings he loaned were shown anonymously. Perhaps this reticence stemmed from the fact that his brother, Stephen Clark, from whom he was estranged, was a well-known collector (the Clark brothers were grandsons of Edward Clark, an early stockholder of the Singer Sewing Machine Company). But the paradox of the shy Mr. Clark was that when he realized his time was running out, he could not bear the idea of having his collection dispersed. There was noth-ing for him but to follow other major collectors and give to or build a museum.

The tomblike, white, Vermont marble edifice he erected in the idyllic college town of clapboard and brick houses in the Berk-shires is equally out of character with Williamstown and with Robert Sterling Clark. Some have referred to the building as "the tomb of the unknown collector." But the interior, all on one floor except for the print department, is inviting. Galleries, bays, and alcoves have been scaled to their contents, intimate or grandiose. A large addition for library, auditorium, and more gallery space is scheduled. With the exception of a few really distinguished pieces which have been and will continue to be purchased since Mr. Clark's death, the collection is the pure expression of his catholic taste. While buying his thirty-three Renoirs and Degas in depth, he was also indulging in the then-unfashionable French Salon painters—Gérôme and Carolus-Duran—and acquiring a bar-sized Bouguereau.

Chronologically, paintings extend from the later Middle Ages and Renaissance in Italy, France, and the Low Countries to the end of the nineteenth century. A slight indication of the riches to be found in Williamstown: a seven-part panel altarpiece by Ugolino da Siena; Piero della Francesca's *Madonna and Child with Four Angels* purchased by Mr. Clark in 1914 and never publicly seen until 1957; a predella panel from the Bichi altar by Luca Signorelli; Renaissance works by Mantegna, Crivelli, Memling, Mabuse, Solario. One gallery contains Rembrandt's *A Man Reading,* and an eighteenth-century etching of the same subject by Debucourt. Most of Clark's Renoirs, including *At the Concert* and *Onions,* date between 1875 and 1890—only *The Letter* giving a foretaste of his later "hot" period. Of the eleven Corots, *Mlle. du Puyparlier Dressed for a Sunday Country Walk* is a favorite. No wonder Corot hated to part with his pictures. He painted twenty-five years before he sold one, and then was desolate because his "collection of Corots was broken up."

When the Whitney decided to restrict itself to the twentieth century, Clark bought many of their eighteenth- and nineteenth-century holdings, among them the handsome Winslow Homer *The Bridle Path.* A clue to the present Clark purchasing policy is the quality of a late acquisition, Fragonard's *Portrait of a Man* (*The Warrior*) which Charles Sterling, curator of the Louvre, called one of the most beautiful and significant of Fragonard's *portraits de fantaisie* in existence.

The drawing section extends from Dürer to Monet, the prints from the fifteenth-century Italian Mantegna to the Swedish Anders Zorn, with the heaviest concentration in both media on the eighteenth and nineteenth centuries. The Degas and Lautrec prints alone deserve a special visit. Clark's silver collection is among the most distinguished in the country with its rare French pieces, Dutch, English, and American examples including five pieces by Paul Revere. A recent acquisition is a rare set of English Apostles spoons—one of seven known (the Metropolitan just became heir to another set which had been lying in the James B. Mabon family silver chest on Park Avenue for forty years).

Each Apostle's symbol or tool of martyrdom is sculpted on the spoon's handle. An impressive 1726 tea tray made in London by Paul De Lamerie is one of his thirty-five works in the group. Another beauty is a George III milk jug presented to Benjamin Franklin when he went to London to plead the Colonies' cause. An etched chain, symbolizing the unity of the mother country and America, joins the body of the jug to the lid—a lid America was soon to blow off.

Jean-Honoré Fragonard: *Portrait of a Man* (*The Warrior*) (Sterling and Francine Clark Art Institute, Williamstown, Massachusetts)

WILLIAMS COLLEGE MUSEUM OF ART

Lawrence Hall, Williamstown, Massachusetts
Hours: Mon.–Sat., 10–12, 2–4; Sun., 2–5;
closed holidays.
Free.

Founded in 1926, the Williams, like other such college institutions, developed as a general museum to aid in the teaching and in the appreciation of art. Its collection starts with antiquities, including Greek and Etruscan pottery, and comes down to the present. It wisely avoids concentration in areas where the nearby Clark Institute is strong. Through changing exhibitions and acquisitions, the college brings to students and to the community contemporary art, a field not exploited by the Clark.

The museum's home is an 1846 Greek Revival building with a large first-floor gallery, a formidable Ionic rotunda and smaller galleries upstairs. Set in the downstairs gallery, accompanied by proper furniture and *objets d'art,* are a series of Spanish paintings. Highlights are *The Annunciation* by Juan de Valdés-Leal of Seville, *The Executioner* by Ribera, *A Knight of Santiago* by Francisco Pacheco—a surprising bit of Iberian civilization in a high corner of Massachusetts. A second-floor gallery evokes the Middle Ages—panel paintings, sculptures, ivories, manuscripts. One medieval stained-glass panel, originally from France, turned up in a Williamstown barn. No one has been able to explain its curious migration. A recent acquisition is an almost-life-sized *Mater Domini.* Carved in wood and richly polychromed, the figure is shown in adoration. Two portrait heads, one an ancient Roman mosaic, the other a Byzantine fresco, are interestingly juxtaposed here.

Francesco Pacheco (1564–1654): *A Knight of Santiago* (Williams College Museum of Art, Lawrence Hall, Williamstown, Massachusetts)

The growing print and drawing collection holds old masters and contemporaries, and the rotunda shows ancient and modern pieces. The first work of art presented to the college, in 1850, is here in this formidable, many-pillared space; large ninth-century B.C. Assyrian reliefs, part of the Operation Missionary which sent to various New England colleges reliefs from the dig at Nimrud, capital of the Assyrian Empire (see Amherst).

WORCESTER ART MUSEUM

55 Salisbury Street, Worcester, Massachusetts
Hours: Mon.–Sat., 10–5; Sun., and holidays, 2–5;
Nov.–Apr., open to 10 P.M.;
closed July 4, Thanksgiving, Dec. 25.
Free.

Salisburys have been prominent in Worcester since Stephen Salisbury I came from Boston around 1767 and set up shop to dispense flour, nails, and rum, staples of the time. In the Salisbury room in the early American section are portraits of several Salisburys by Stuart, Gulliger and Harding; Samuel F. B. Morse's *Chapel of the Virgin at Subiaco* which Stephen II commissioned when he met Morse while doing the Grand Tour of Italy, and family heirlooms, including some splendid Paul Revere silver. Stephen Salisbury III, dying a bachelor in 1905, left almost his entire fortune to endow the museum.

Set in the foyer floor of the museum are two superb mosaics from second- to sixth-century A.D. Antioch. (Other examples from the same dig are the pride of Baltimore and Providence.) To the left is a complete twelfth-century Romanesque chapter house taken from a Benedictine monastery near Poitiers, France. The secular business of the monastery took place in the chapter house, and so evocative is the setting that it is easy to visualize the abbot sitting by the fire wondering what to do about Brother Hyacinth, who was late for matins again. Of the frescoes in the next gallery, *The Last Supper* (from near Spoleto, late thirteenth century) is the most powerful and has retained a great deal of clarity. Green predominates in the fading color because it was used as underpainting. A favorite among antiquities is a minute, wild-eyed figure (Sumerian, 3000–2500 B.C.) discovered in 1937 below the floor of a temple near Baghdad; it impressively demonstrates that a small piece can be monumental. A ravishing *Female*

Torso of the Fourth Dynasty, Egypt (2680–2560 B.C.), is one of the museum's important pieces.

The galleries of Asiatic and Oriental cultures flow into each other. In most museums the delicate subtleties of Persian art are absorbed into related periods, but Worcester, like New York's Hotel Plaza, has its own Persian Room; manuscripts, miniatures, fabrics, and trappings of that rich civilization are displayed together. One of the best and most comprehensive Japanese print collections in the country emphasizes seventeenth and early eighteenth centuries. Another Japanese treasure is a ninth-century, eleven-headed Kannon, life sized and carved in wood. Kannon is most often known as the deity of mercy. Resting on a headband are eleven small heads surrounding a figure of Amida Buddha. Upstairs the painting galleries begin with strong Italian primitives: *The Madonna and Child in a Rose Garden* by Stefano da Verona; the Florentine Pesellino depicting the triumph of prayer over magic in *The Miracle of St. Sylvester.*

San Donato of Arezzo and the Tax Collector by Lorenzo di Credi was done at a time when Italians took their taxes seriously and when both Di Credi and Da Vinci worked in Verrocchio's workshop. Some experts believe that Da Vinci painted this scene of the saint praying for a tax collector falsely accused of taking public funds or that he at least has a hand in it.

The Dutch and Spanish galleries need plenty of time for the Rembrandt, the Heda, the Saenredam, the Goya, the El Greco, the Ribera. Exciting new acquisitions are *Le Geste Napolitain* —a marvelously early Jean Baptiste Greuze—and a bronze Roman portrait, *Bust of a Lady of the Antonine Period* (165–185 A.D.). A skylight heightens the cheeriness of eighteenth-century England in Gallery 205. Gainsborough's *The Artist's Daughters*, tender and evocative, recalls the story of his younger daughter's insanity. With what gentleness the painter profiles the vacant little face. Here too is Sir Thomas Lawrence's outsize portrait of *Mr. and Mrs. Jacob Dunlop.* William Hogarth's subtly satirical portraits of Mr. and Mrs. William James are as fine a brace of paintings as Hogarth has done.

There are delights for the lovers of early American art. Ralph Earl, like many young colonial painters, went off to England to study; unlike most, he did not ape the fashionable London portrait school. His *Portrait of William Carpenter* has American directness and native charm, though it was done in England. Earl's *A View of Worcester* is, as it should be, in Worcester. A pre-Revolutionary painting of major importance is the *Self-*

Portrait by Thomas Smith, who arrived in America about 1650 from Bermuda as a sea captain, it is said. Instead of the usual landscape arbitrarily used as backgrounds for portraits, Smith painted himself against a brig sailing into battle.

The masterpieces of the American collection are the recently acquired portraits of *Mr. John Freake of Boston* and *Mrs. Freake and Baby Mary*. Though by an unknown painter, seldom have portraits come better documented. Mrs. Freake's birthday in Dorchester, Massachusetts, is recorded, as is young John Freake's arrival in Boston from England in 1658. He became a successful merchant, constable, and shipowner. Ever on the alert, the museum is conducting a serious study regarding attributions while a major cataloguing work is in process. Some surprises are in store.

The pre-Columbian gallery arrests one with its beautiful installation. Perhaps the fact that Stephen Salisbury III was truly interested in archeology accounts for the museum's unusual primitive material, bought long before the modern vogue for it. Contemporary art, long a stepchild, is being brought into balance with the requirements of a general museum. Fine drawings represent such diverse talents as Cuevas and Jack Wolfe. Kelly, Wesselmann, Kline, and Youngerman are but a few artists with important works here.

The Dial (1840–1929) was a little magazine synonymous with

LEFT: *Mrs. Elizabeth Freake and Baby Mary* (unknown Boston artist, *ca.* 1674) (Worcester Art Museum, Worcester, Massachusetts) **RIGHT:** Jack Youngerman: *Black-Orange-Red-Orange* (1965) (Worcester Art Museum, Worcester, Massachusetts)

the best in arts and letters. Its monuments endure at the Worcester Museum. *The Dial* collection consists of works assembled for reproduction in the magazine and its subsidiary, *Living Arts*. The drawing and watercolor section is naturally strong, especially in the line drawings used in the magazine's text. Egon Schiele's *Seated Nude Girl* and *Self-Portrait* and Charles Demuth's *After Sir Christopher Wren* stand out. A catalogue at the sales desk which portrays the spirit of the venture, as well as its history, includes an article called "Dial M for Modern." It is by the museum's distinguished director and scholar Daniel Catton Rich.

DARTMOUTH COLLEGE: HOPKINS ART CENTER

Hanover, New Hampshire
Hours: Mon.–Sat., 1–5; Sun., 7–10; Holidays 2–5;
Carpenter Hall: Daily 2–5. Closed Christmas, New Year's.
Free.

The Center named after one of Dartmouth's former presidents, Ernest Hopkins, and built in 1962 by Harrison and Abramovitz is a stunning complex which houses two theaters, a concert hall, workshops and, regretfully, only two small art galleries. As if to make up for this slight to the visual arts, the enormous second-floor lounge is probably the best place on any campus in America for showing large paintings. There Rothko, Kelly, Noland, Vicente, Anuszkiewicz, and Mathieu are displayed to best advantage. Called "The Top of the Hop" by the students, it faces one of the most beautiful village greens in New England.

The print section starts with the late fifteenth century but, as with painting and sculpture, it is strongest in twentieth-century holdings. Specific areas include: Greek icons from Crete; Oriental objets d'art; and many fine examples of Paul Revere silver. In 1773, Governor John Wentworth, a trustee, gave the college a silver bowl made by two of Revere's competitors, Daniel Henchman and Nathaniel Hurd, thus starting Dartmouth's art collection.

The galleries at Hopkins are used for changing exhibitions while Carpenter Hall, across the Green, contains part of the permanent collection in three galleries on the third floor. A small Oriental room has some fine Chou and Sung Dynasty bronzes. The group of Assyrian reliefs that came to the college in the

1850s (see Amherst) are impressive and less fragmented than many other similar pieces in university collections. Painters Fredrick Church, Albert Bierstadt, Thomas Eakins and John Sloan are shown in top examples. The influence of Dartmouth's famous alumnus, Daniel Webster, is everywhere. There is a room of Webster memorabilia in Baker Library. He successfully defended the college when the state tried to absorb it into the University of New Hampshire. The trustees maintained that Dartmouth received its charter from the King and should remain the independent college it is today. The school was founded in 1769 by Eleazar Wheelock, a missionary, as a college and seminary for Indians.

Baker Library, connected by a corridor with Carpenter Hall, contains the famous fresco murals by José Clemente Orozco, which caused much controversy when painted in 1932. With bold stroke and strident color the Mexican artist, then a teacher at Dartmouth, depicts in 3000 square feet the epic of civilization on the American continent. Telephone listening posts explain both the technique and the subject matter. "Two years went into the making of this mural which, quantitatively, is the largest fresco project yet executed in the United States."

CURRIER GALLERY OF ART

192 Orange Street, Manchester, New Hampshire
Hours: Mon.–Sat., 10–5; Sun., 2–5;
closed holidays.
Free.

Moody Currier, one-time governor of New Hampshire, was a self-made man most of whose wealth came from the stretch of cotton mills lining Manchester's Amoskeag Canal. Though showing no interest in art in his lifetime, he left his fortune, on his death in 1915, to build an art museum.

Italian Renaissance in style, it resembles a modest *palazzo*. The collection is small but unusually impressive. The result: the enjoyment of paintings of top quality in an uncluttered atmosphere.

Upper New England crafts predictably dominate the decorative arts section. The paintings range from Perugino and Joos van Cleve to a beauty by Picasso, at his lively, impudent best in

LEFT: Pablo Picasso: *Woman Seated in a Chair* (Currier Gallery of Art, Manchester, New Hampshire; photograph by Frank Kelly) **RIGHT:** Charles Sheeler: *Amoskeag Canal* (Currier Gallery of Art, Manchester, New Hampshire)

Woman Seated in a Chair. The chair resembles a bass viol on four legs and the woman's eyes are askew; the orange and green and gold sing out like a Handel "Hallelujah"; the composition is as intricate as a Bach fugue.

Monet's *The Seine at Bougival* is full of the splendor of his first experiments with light, expressed through a line of dusty trees. Other small landscapes by Ruisdael and Constable have all the qualities of their better-known works. Strong contemporary realists like Hopper, Wyeth, and Kuhn are here, and avant-garde exhibitions are held.

Few towns of 85,000 can boast so rounded a collection or one that includes a painting of such local interest as *Amoskeag Canal* by Charles Sheeler. It depicts the canal and mills that made up Manchester's history.

RHODE ISLAND SCHOOL OF DESIGN MUSEUM OF ART

224 Benefit Street, Providence, Rhode Island
Hours (Sept.–July): Tues.–Sat., 11–5; Sun., 2–5.
Columbus Day and Armistice Day, August by appointment only;
closed major holidays.
Free.

Three ladies from Providence came home from the Philadelphia Exposition of 1875 dissatisfied with the crafts in the Rhode Island section. Somehow $1,675 had been left over from the state's contribution to the Exposition and with this they launched the Rhode Island School of Design. Gradually rooms were added for use as a museum. In 1904 Pendleton House, an engaging Georgian dwelling full of such outstanding early Americana as Newport furniture, China-trade porcelains, and New England silver, was donated. Drawings by Copley, Feke, and Rhode Islander Gilbert Stuart adorn the walls. The main building of the museum joined Pendleton House in 1926.

Stepping through the Georgian doorway of the museum, you will see only a few classical marbles on view. No surfeit of material, no compulsion to show everything the museum owns at once will overcome you. Even extravagant Etruscan and Greek jewelry is sparingly displayed. In the first gallery, small ancient bronzes are set in shadow boxes, each little creature or vessel isolated so that you and it can hold private communion. Among ancient Greek and Roman sculptures is *Torso of a Woman* (520–10 B.C.). The blocklike strength recalls the Egyptians, but the slightly molded breasts and the fall of the drapery are Greek humanism. The classical collection—Roman fresco paintings and splendid portrait busts—is generally rated third in America, bowing to Boston and the Metropolitan only. An early thirteenth-century Spanish crucifix dominates the Medieval galleries, but treasures like the stone *St. Peter* from the abbey church in Cluny, France, quietly assert themselves. Tilman Riemenschneider, a German sculptor of the transition period, Gothic to Renaissance, used the linden wood *Pietà* here as a model for many of his larger pieces.

After the Medieval, small galleries flow along, offering in fine sequence the major periods of Western art. Gallery VII has a High Renaissance bronze by the sixteenth-century German Georg

Cluny St. Peter (French, *ca.* twelfth century) (Museum of Art, Rhode Island School of Design, Providence)

Vischer, and a small oil on panel, *Resurrection,* by the Italian Previtali. Turbulent *Jerusalem Delivered* and a darkly moving oil sketch, *The Combat Between Tancred and Clorinda,* are by Tintoretto, that long-lived artist who formed the bridge between High Renaissance and baroque. Baroque slips into effulgent rococo, with Tiepolo casting his talents on church, palace, and boudoir with gay and witty impartiality. His ceiling painting is from a Venetian *palazzo.* In another gallery neoclassicism revolts against rococo. Late romanticism and Delacroix move abruptly to the realism of Courbet. Much of Courbet is relentless, almost brutal. But in *The White Mill,* darkly accented white-on-white, Courbet achieved a serenity that comes close to poetry. Edouard Manet, contemporary of Courbet, did *Le Repos,* a portrait of the painter Berthe Morisot. Three small Monet beauties and Degas are in the same gallery.

With the exception of Renoir's glowing *The Shepherd Boy,* Cézanne, Van Gogh, and Lautrec drawings overshadow the paintings in the next gallery. Gallery XVII takes in Braque, Matisse, Kokoschka, and the contemporary sculpture of Manzú's *The Cardinal.* This 15-inch model for his large *Cardinal Enthroned* in Bologna predicts the latter's strength and dignity. Among superb Picassos: a 1911 Cubist still life.

When the Rhode Island School of Design moved to new quarters on campus, the museum gained gallery space for changing exhibitions, nineteenth- and twentieth-century Americans, and another interest—contemporary Latin American art, which introduces south-of-the-border artists to New England. A few are the Colombian Fernando Bolero, the Nicaraguan Armando Morales, the Argentinian Luis Filipe Noe.

Edouard Manet: *Le Repos* (*Portrait of Berthe Morisot*) (Museum of Art, Rhode Island School of Design, Providence)

The print and drawing section is bringing a new emphasis to the eighteenth century. Rodin's *Balzac,* the sturdy nude that caused an uproar in 1898 Paris, rests quietly in the museum's garden court. Richard Merkin's *Funeral of John Dillinger* and Leo Manso's *Samurai II* spice the contemporaries.

Upstairs, the primitives, the Orient, and the Near East hold sway. In the Abby Aldrich Rockefeller collection, 640 Japanese prints frequently change places.

SHELBURNE MUSEUM

Shelburne, Vermont
Hours (May 25–Oct. 20): daily, 9–5.
Admission: adults, $3; students, $1.

The museum enclave, the Shelburne, was founded by Mr. and Mrs. J. Watson Webb in 1947 to preserve America's heritage, and New England's in particular. Some thirty-three buildings filled with examples of early craftsmanship have been reassembled in Vermont's green hills. The Stagecoach Inn shows early American folk art: ship figureheads, weather vanes, signs, carrousel figures, the American eagles so popular with early carvers. The Lighthouse Gallery displays marine oils and historic prints of clipper ships. A bit large for inclusion, the 896-ton sidewheeler *Ticonderoga* rests in the open. On each side of this staunch old ship stands a new building, the Webb Gallery and the Electra Havemeyer Memorial Building.

The Webb Gallery of American art, starting with Pieter Vanderlyn and an anonymous portrait of George Washington, *sans* teeth, shows a collection of over two hundred paintings. It ranges through the eighteenth and nineteenth centuries with John Wollaston, John S. Copley, S. F. B. Morse, John Quidor, and Winslow Homer. A 10-foot statue of *Justice,* which formerly decorated the courthouse at Barnstable, Massachusetts, scales in hand and alarmingly alive, stands in the entrance foyer.

The Webb Memorial Museum, done in the Greek Revival style so popular in nineteenth-century New England, houses the collection of European paintings inherited from Mrs. Webb's parents, the Henry O. Havemeyers. The interiors, six paneled rooms, are furnished as they were in the J. Watson Webbs' New York apartment. Artists represented by important works include: Rembrandt, Goya, Courbet, Corot, Degas, Manet, Monet, and Cassatt.

"Goddess of Liberty" weathervane (Shelburne Museum, Inc., Shelburne, Vermont; photograph by Einars J. Mengis)

The main body of the Henry O. Havemeyer collection is a cornerstone of the Metropolitan Museum painting section and it would be difficult to say who were the more indefatigable collectors— Mrs. Webb or her parents.

There the likeness ceased. Electra Havemeyer's first purchase at the age of eighteen was a "cigar store Indian," and from that moment she left her parents with their El Grecos and Japanese tea jars and marched firmly back into the world of Americana. The Shelburne Museum is a unique testimonial to the heritage and accomplishment of this talented, charming, and spirited woman.

BUNDY ART GALLERY

Waitsfield, Vermont
Hours: Weekdays, 10–5; Sun., 1–5;
closed Tues., holidays, and Nov.
Library.
Free.

While meandering through Vermont's verdant countryside, it would be a pity to miss this arresting little gallery. A glass, copper, and brick building (1962), the Bundy rises beside a lagoon set in 80 wooded acres planned as a sculpture park. A classroom was incorporated into the plan to give free instruction to school children, as there is no art program in the local school. The orientation of the gallery is strictly international contemporary. A few in the permanent collection are: Afro, Nevelson, Marca-Relli, Mathieu, and Soulages. Changing exhibitions and summertime Sunday afternoon concerts are features.

THE WILMINGTON SOCIETY OF THE FINE ARTS, DELAWARE ART CENTER

2301 Kentmere Parkway, Wilmington, Delaware
Hours: Mon.–Sat., 10–5; Sun., 2–6;
closed major holidays.
Free.

The Delaware Art Center is talking of expansion. I know of no museum more in need of space, for only from April to October can its permanent collection, quite rich for a small institution, be shown. During winter months the spacious center gallery is reserved for changing exhibits.

At the entrance to the Pre-Raphaelite gallery, handsomely and permanently installed, is a chart showing the original group and their contemporaries in art, music, and literature. In addition to works by the major painters of the movement, there is an exten-

Andrew Wyeth: *Arthur Cleveland* (The Wilmington Society of the Fine Arts; Delaware Art Center Collection)

sive library on the subject. Works by the illustrator and native son Howard Pyle are always on view, along with his pupils, including various members of the Wyeth family. A general collection of American paintings, stored below stairs, is available to seriously interested visitors. Important holdings: American and English examples of Benjamin West, Rembrandt Peale, Church, Inness, Eakins, Luks, seven Burchfields, Hopper's beautiful *Summer Time*, and the largest collection of Andrew Wyeth of any museum in the country.

A good research library in the making contains the corpus of the Howard Pyle material, and 11,000 items, books, exhibition catalogues, and research material on John Sloan. An active art school is a part of the Fine Arts Center.

HENRY FRANCIS DU PONT WINTERTHUR MUSEUM

Kennett Pike, State 52, Winterthur, Delaware
Hours: South Wing.
Admission 50 cents, under 16, 25 cents.
Main museum open by appointment for guided tours; Tues.–
Sat., 10–4 except holidays and Spring garden tours. Ten rooms,
reception area open without appointment daily, 9:30–4.
16 rooms of main museum open without appointment during
five weeks of garden tour.

Not many early-nineteenth-century houses in America have been occupied in unbroken line by the same family, but this is true of Winterthur—or it was, until the penchant for collecting and reconstructing whole rooms forced the Henry du Ponts to turn their home into a museum and move into less historic quarters. The house was built in 1829 by a son-in-law of Eleuthère Irénée du Pont de Nemours. In 1867 it was sold to an uncle, Henry du Pont, and has remained in direct succession ever since.

Set amid gardens and meadows on a 1000-acre tract six miles northwest of Wilmington, the house was enlarged gradually through the years. As Henry Francis du Pont's collection of Americana grew into the most magnificent one in America, Winterthur acquired, in 1929, a new wing and interior architecture from old houses as far away as New Hampshire and North Carolina. Paintings, sculpture, furniture, and decorative accessories (1640–1840) were assembled in more than one hundred twenty-five rooms. A pre-Revolutionary Philadelphia room has canvases by well-known eighteenth-century American painters; a portrait of *Mrs. Wm. Morris* by Copley, 1772; a group portrait of the *Gore Children*, done when Copley was fifteen. Charles Willson Peale is represented by two portraits of the *Lloyd Family of Maryland*. Elsewhere in the museum there's John Hesselius, John Wollaston, the Hudson River Valley limners, and the important, small, full-length portrait of *Washington* painted by John Trumbull for Mrs. Washington in 1790. Of great historical moment is the sketch by Benjamin West of the American commissioners' meeting in Paris to arrange the peace treaty with Great Britain. But in spite of the museum's size, an air of intimacy pervades, probably because the Du Ponts and their children lived in the house until 1951, when it became a museum. In what is possibly the largest and richest assemblage of American decorative arts in the country, we can see the life and spirit of our forebears—in both elegance and simplicity—through a great collection displayed in a great country house.

BALTIMORE MUSEUM OF ART

Wyman Park, Baltimore, Maryland
Hours: Wed.–Sat., 11–5; Tues., 11–5 and 8–10; Sun., 2–6;
closed New Year's Day, Good Friday, Fourth of July,
Thanksgiving, and Christmas.
Library.
Café.

Rodin's *The Thinker,* as if he were their mascot, guards the entrance to four museums—Detroit's Institute of Arts, San Francisco's Legion of Honor, the Cleveland Museum, and, in an especially beautiful cast, Baltimore's Museum of Art.

The building, planned around a skylighted garden, is refreshingly simple, and seeing the collections that make up this effective museum is refreshingly easy.

Baltimore has received many private collections as gifts, some of which must be displayed as units—a provision that can be disadvantageous, but which is minimized here because the collectors were fortunately single-minded and each group has its own homogeneity.

The central orientation of the museum is around ten areas of collecting, as follows: American, especially Maryland art, past and present; old masters since 1500; the decorative arts since

1500, except where they are amply represented by the neighboring Walters Art Gallery; art of the twentieth century and contemporary art; Oriental art; prints and drawings since 1500; sculpture since about 1500; and sporting art of the past and present.

A joy of the Epstein collection is a great Northern baroque painting, *Rinaldo and Armida* by Van Dyck. Voluptuous yet tender, explosively brilliant in color, it was in Charles I's and the Dukes of Newcastle's collections until 1913. In the same group is a fine Gainsborough from the artist's Bath period, *Mrs. Charles Tudway*.

Downstairs is the Wurtzburger collection of primitive art. Any amateur who wants to learn about the mysterious primitive tribes of Central and South America can conduct his own research right here. This select grouping is installed so as to give each object its own importance; divided geographically and historically, it provides an invitation to learning.

The Maryland wing not only has all sorts of reminders of the elegance with which our Southern colonials lived—their furniture, silver, portraits (including *Portrait of Charles Calvert* with his Negro slave by John Hesselius, who painted the well-known Maryland families, as had his father, Gustavus, before him)— but also fully expresses Maryland's enthusiasm for horses. In the William Woodward gallery, decorated as an eighteenth-century drawing room, are portraits of all the great race horses of two centuries ago, sires and dams of most of today's thoroughbreds. Thirteen handsome pieces of painted old Baltimore furniture have been installed in the great oval room from Willow Brook House (Baltimore, 1799).

John Hesselius (1728–1778): *Portrait of Charles Calvert* (The Baltimore Museum of Art; gift of Alfred R. and Henry G. Riggs in memory of General Lawrason Riggs)

Henri Matisse: *The Blue Nude*
(The Baltimore Museum of Art,
Baltimore, Maryland)

The reason that most of today's collectors travel to Baltimore, it must be admitted, is to see the Cone sisters' collection. These astonishing women, with tastes so far in advance of their times and of the somnolent, polite atmosphere of Baltimore, cherished their purchases in private while they lived and willed them to the city when they died. Dr. Claribel Cone's fierce independence is the key to understanding how she came to buy Matisse's *Blue Nude* of 1907. It took courage for her to enter Johns Hopkins Medical School in 1900, when contemporary ladies were content with crocheting doilies, but it took more to buy this canvas, of such rugged beauty that time and acceptance have in no way diminished its impact.

The Cones spent a good deal of time in Paris, where their friend, Miss Gertrude Stein, introduced them to the young painters. Matisse became the one whom they collected most avidly. Realizing what an important body of his work they were acquiring, Matisse let them range and choose among his favorites. The sisters consolidated their friendship with Picasso by bringing him American comic strips, in which he delighted. The ladies also bought Delacroix, Corot, and a Cézanne *Mont Ste. Victoire,* along with Picasso's *Woman with Bangs,* painted in 1902, his *Portrait of Dr. Claribel Cone,* Van Gogh's *The Shoes,* Gauguin's *Woman with Mango,* and, of course, the whole rhythmic, colorful chorus of the Matisses.

The May collection carries on through the Cubists and adds Léger, Mondrian, Masson, and Pollock. And now the newly formed Gallagher group shows the established and the controversial contemporary American painters.

The European section, though small, has some beauties: Canaletto's *Architecture in Ruins;* Rembrandt's portrait of his son *Titus;* the Frans Hals porrait of *Dorothea Berck,* who was Mrs. Coymens (Mr. Coymens hangs, separated from his wife, in the Hartford Atheneum); a superb little canvas by the eighteenth century Venetian Pittoni titled *Circumcision;* Nattier's

Baronne Rigoley D'Ogny; Hubert Robert's *The Terrace,* the letters "psl" after the signature standing for the Prison St. Lazare, where he, as a political prisoner, was awaiting execution. Happily for him, and for posterity, another unfortunate who bore the name Hubert Robert was executed in his place. Recent additions to the collections are varied and choice; a *Fire Spitter* work from the Ivory Gold Coast, a Karel Appel, a late Gorky, a 1929 Picasso head, two pair of six-fold Japanese sixteenth-century screens, *Madridscape* by Helen Frankenthaler, *Africa* by Robert Motherwell.

The Antioch mosaics (second to sixth centuries A.D.), though originally floors, have been set ingeniously into walls around the court, which has recently been roofed over. A beautiful garden setting with fountain and pool makes a handsome background for both the museum's sculpture and the mosaics.

The Allan Wurtzburger collection of sculpture will eventually be placed in a sculpture garden at the museum. Each monumental piece has been chosen with the museum's leafy acreage in mind. Deployed about will be Maillol's *Summer,* Moore's *Reclining Woman,* Epstein's *The Visitation,* Lachaise's *Standing Woman.* Zadkine, Wotruba, Lipchitz, Richier, Marcks, Arp, Minguzzi, Noguchi, David Smith, and Paolozzi are also a part of the still expanding collection.

WALTERS ART GALLERY

Charles and Centre Streets, Baltimore, Maryland
Hours: Tues.–Sat., 11–5; Mon., Oct.–May, 1:30–5
and 7:30–9:30 P.M., July and August, 11–4;
Sun. and holidays, 2–5;
closed Jan. 1, July 4, Thanksgiving, Dec. 25.
Free.

When the Civil War started, William Walters, a wealthy Baltimore produce merchant, had already begun his collection by purchasing the works of Maryland painters. Finding himself a Confederate sympathizer in a Union city, he went to Europe for the duration; and there he began collecting rare pieces of Eastern pottery and Chinese ceramics brought to Europe for international expositions in Vienna and Paris.

In the depression that followed the war, William Walters bought up "ribbons of rust" through the South and gradually evolved the Atlantic Coast Line Railroad. Meanwhile, wings were built on his house to absorb the crates of art that followed him home. One of his special interests was the work of the French nineteenth-century sculptor Antoine Louis Barye (see the Corcoran Gallery). The museum has over five hundred Barye sculptures, paintings, and drawings. From January to March, Walters opened his collection to the public, charging 50¢ admission for the benefit of the poor. Eventually his son Henry built a Florentine *palazzo* on Charles Street which he bequeathed to the city in 1931, together with the collection and stacks of unopened, crated treasures. Henry Walters, following in his father's footsteps but covering much more ground, collected so unobtrusively, threatening dealers with boycott if they spoke of him, that even today, though the museum is renowned among world scholars, few Americans are aware of its riches.

It is probably in the Byzantine and medieval fields, in illuminated manuscripts, small bronzes, enamels, and ivories, that the museum is strongest. Its collection of Renaissance enamels is the greatest in the United States. However, ancient Greece, Etruria, and Rome, Sassanian and Islamic art, as well as earlier arts of the Near East, are richly shown. Only one-sixth of the museum's collection can be on view at one time.

In the center court of Greek and Roman antiquities, treasures crowd treasures. It takes a hard look and a penetrating eye to separate not the sheep from the goats, for there aren't any goats, unless Barye did one, but the rare and the choice. Difficult to miss (and not to be missed) are seven large Roman sarcophagi

Silver Rhyton (Sassanian; sixth or seventh century) (The Walters Art Gallery, Baltimore, Maryland)

(150–210 A.D.) taken from one family burying ground. These were part of the Massarenti collection purchased in 1902 in Rome by Henry Walters. The 1,540 objects in this collection included old masters' paintings as well as antiquities. Walters chartered a ship to bring it all to Baltimore.

Many periods have their own galleries. Gallery 6 holds works of art from the Byzantine world and the Hamah treasure, the most comprehensive service of early Christian silver in existence, dating from the sixth century; a large gem carved from a single block of Chalcedonian onyx and called *The Rubens Vase* (about 400 A.D.), once in the painter Rubens' collection of antiquities. Gallery 4 could be named "Henry's Hobby," for he had a penchant for the minute, precise beauties of Persian art. The Walters has an incredible collection of illuminated manuscripts, second only to New York's Morgan Library.

Though paintings were of secondary interest to both Walters, they acquired some fine ones. Four early panels were originally part of a predella by Giovanni di Paolo. *Piazza of an Italian City* by Luciano da Laurana is one of three known canvases by this painter (the other two are in Florence and Urbino, Italy). The picture is a perfect example of linear perspective—walk along the wall from it and the broad street will converge with you. The gallery of Dutch and Flemish paintings has an especially fine one by Hugo van der Goes, an artist of the early Renaissance in Flanders: *Portrait of a Donor with St. John.* The nineteenth-century French are well represented and include Delacroix's *Crucifixion,* Ingres' *Odalisque,* and Daumier's *Second Class Carriage,* which William Walters commissioned from the artist.

The porcelain section is rich and rare. Only a few of the extensive groups of Sèvres porcelains can be shown at a time. Look for the gold vase commissioned by Catherine II of Russia and the case of Renaissance jewelry containing the sixteenth-century Spanish *Galleon,* a pendant of gold and enamel.

Be sure to see the Chinese porcelains and potteries. Walters indulged his passion for these with so choice a group that a ten-volume work, *Oriental Ceramic Art,* written in 1897 by Stephen W. Bushell and based primarily on Walters' holdings, is still a prime reference book. In several galleries are racks to hold reference books on the types of material displayed. The basement, where only scholars may trespass, is a Fort Knox of the art world. Plans are under way for a new wing to be completed in 1971 that will bring many submerged treasures to the surface.

NEWARK MUSEUM

43–49 Washington St., Newark, New Jersey
Hours: Mon.–Sat., 12–5:30; Wed.–Thurs., 7–9:30 P.M.;
July–Sept., 12–5; Sun., 2–6;
closed Thanksgiving, Christmas, July 4.
Free.

When John Cotton Dana was asked to take over the Newark Library in 1902 he immediately began to hang paintings and prints on the walls. Out of this simple beginning the Newark Museum, in two rooms of the library, was chartered seven years later. In 1926 merchant-philanthropist Louis Bamberger gave the present three-storied building which houses history, science, and works of art with a deliberate interplay between the three.

Dana insisted that the museum be "where there is movement of people." During the languid summer lunch hour, businessmen and office workers stroll the galleries, listen to symphony recordings, or watch lunchtime art and craft demonstrations held in the garden. The garden also plays host to monumental sculpture by David Smith, Tony Smith, and Jules Kirschenbaum. For fire buffs there is a fire museum on the grounds full of antique firefighting memorabilia.

The collection is primarily American, starting with John Wollaston, William Williams (the talented but little-known teacher of Benjamin West), Joseph Badger, Ralph Earl, and John Singleton Copley. The Copley was painted at the height of his mature style, around 1765. It remained with Mrs. Scott's heirs until purchased in 1948 by the museum. "Support the artist of your time and place," exhorted Dana. One summer, a trustee cabled Dana, who was in Europe, to spend $10,000 for European art. Dana answered: "We'll spend it at home." The handsome I. Rice Pereira *Composition in White* and the superb, recently installed *Jersey Meadows* by Richard Lippold, plus examples by Thiebaud, Mallary, Corbett, Bannard, Gatch, Rosenthal, Lassaw, Donati, and Martinelli are indications of how Newark continues to follow Dana's philosophy of buying the living American artists. He felt that it was wise for Newark, just across the Hudson from the Metropolitan's incomparable Old World treasures, and at a time when there was no Museum of Modern Art or Whitney Museum of American Art, to concentrate on American painting.

Through the years, gifts have given a more catholic range to

Joseph Pickett: *Washington under the Council Tree* (Collection of the Newark Museum, Newark, New Jersey)

the collection. The European painting group is growing. Mediterranean antiquities, mostly small objects, are installed with zest and distinction. Also Newark has the splendid Schaefer classical glass collection, and its Tibetan material ranks with that of the Natural History Museums of New York and Chicago. The basic group was collected by Dr. Albert Shelton, a medical missionary, during the early twentieth century. When the Chinese seized control of Tibet, the natives, desperate for money to buy back their land, trusting Dr. Shelton, sold him objects rarely acquired by foreigners. Much of the fine ceremonial silver and painting came from the rich lamasery of Batang.

It was the founder's philosophy that only by becoming critically aware of simple things about them—the shape of a teacup, the grace of a chair—could people come to an appreciation of art; accordingly, the museum has built up a matchless historical collection of things made by New Jersey craftsmen and keeps abreast with contemporary craft production.

PRINCETON UNIVERSITY: THE ART MUSEUM

Princeton University, Princeton, New Jersey
Hours: Tues.–Sat., 10–4; Sun., 2–4;
closed major holidays.
Free.

Integrating a contemporary building into a campus as mellow and architecturally dated as Princeton's was no mean accomplishment, but it has been achieved through the use of simple planes and the same pale plum-colored stone that meanders among the gray granite of other buildings. Openness is the keynote of the three-level interior of this 1966 art museum. One enters into a sculpture court with a skylight supported by travertine piers. The U-shaped gallery surrounding the court is a half-flight upstairs, and open spaces between the two levels allow the visitor to look through to the lower galleries. This arrangement distracts some, entices others. Narrow floor-to-ceiling glass column windows give the feeling of Oriental scroll paintings that change with the seasons. Dogwood time is a favorite.

The upper-level galleries house early Italians, continue into the Renaissance, Venetian, and Roman schools, and Dutch and Flemish follow. In companion space across the court, Nattier, Chardin, and the nineteenth-century artists Constable, Delacroix, Boudin, and Monet take over. Small areas adjoining the main galleries contain English and American schools. Thomas Sully's full-length *Mrs. Reverdy Johnson* is one of eighteen Sullys here. John Singleton Copley paints the American merchant *Elhanah Watson* against the background of a sailing vessel. The story goes that Copley was finishing the portrait in England when Parliament, through George III, announced the Colonies' independence, whereupon the artist painted the American flag on the ship, starting a vogue of flag painting that continues right up to Jasper Johns. A wing of old McCormack Hall incorporated on this floor provides a handsome setting for medieval and Northern Renaissance work. Princeton's greatest painting is here: Hieronymus Bosch's *Christ Before Pilate*, a picture whose strong techniques force its psychological impact at the viewer. An ensemble of stairs, balustrades, and colonnettes from Palma di Majorca (1549) lead to smaller galleries holding the museum's graphics and outstanding drawings. Fourteenth- and fifteenth-century French windows are fitted with interchangeable frames to show some of

Hieronymous Bosch: *Christ before Pilate* (The Art Museum, Princeton University, Princeton, New Jersey)

fifty to sixty pieces of stained glass. A larger panel holds sections of original glass from Chartres Cathedral.

The lower galleries are given to the pre-Columbian and other native arts, the interesting Far Eastern group, contemporary work, and galleries for changing exhibitions. A wing holds mosaics excavated by a Princeton team at Antioch. Stored for years in the basement of Nassau Hall, they have been set ingeniously in floor and fountain. Early Christian and Coptic art adjoins. The contemporary group is small but the museum stages lively exhibitions in that area.

ALBRIGHT–KNOX ART GALLERY

1285 Elmwood Avenue, Buffalo, New York
Hours: Mon.–Sat., 10–5, except Wed., 12–10 P.M.; Sun., 2–6;
closed Jan. 1, Thanksgiving, Dec. 25.
Library.
Free.

During the Civil War the third art gallery in the United States opened in the staid town of Buffalo, population 81,000. A longtime resident, artist Albert Bierstadt, donated to the museum its first gift, his painting of the *Marina Grande* in Capri.

The little collection took shelter where it could until 1900, when public-spirited John J. Albright financed the construction of an imposing neoclassic museum building. Mr. Albright was only the first of Buffalo's men of wealth to give time and money to the Albright Gallery. Indeed, it became the final social and civic accolade to be elected to the museum's twenty-six-man board of trustees. The board was and is the town's most exclusive club, with procedures more dynastic than democratic. Ordinarily, death alone changes the trustee slate.

Tradition was shattered in the case of A. Conger Goodyear, who had inherited his board membership from his father. As one of the purchasing committee, Goodyear in 1926 pushed the purchase of Picasso's *La Toilette*. Outraged trustees protested so vigorously that at the next board election Mr. Goodyear was ousted. He immediately moved to New York and became the first president of the new Museum of Modern Art. Later, when Goodyear offered to buy the Picasso for the $5,000 it had cost the Albright, the more far-seeing trustees refused to let it go.

The winds of change began to blow about the marble halls a decade ago and with the building of the Knox wing in 1962 reached gale proportions. The policy of the now Albright-Knox Gallery is to build the collection from today toward the future, reaching back into the past only in those areas that strengthen the museum's *raison d'être*, such as the Post-Impressionists, the Constructionists, the synthetic Cubists, Futurists, Surrealists, Geometricists. A few in these categories lately come to the museum are: Antoine Pevsner, Naum Gabo, Raymond Duchamp-Villon, Gino Severini, Robert Delaunay, Max Ernst, Jean Arp, Max Bill, Jean Metzinger, Albert Gleizes.

The new wing, designed by Gordon Bundshaft, flows with grace and simplicity from old conventions to space so flexible that even such outsized audacities as Lucas Samara's *Mirrored Room* are manageable. A real dazzler to walk into, it is constructed completely of highly polished square mirrored sections, with a table and chair of the same. Benjamin Townsend in his informative *Art News* article on Buffalo (January, 1967) calls it "crystal Bauhaus." Three upper sides of this wing, the auditorium and the lounge, are of glass. To seated visitors only the sky and foliage are visible, giving the pleasant back-to-childhood feeling of being in a tree house. Outdoors, a large sculpture garden bridges the sixty-one-year gap between old and new.

The contemporary sculpture collection is second only to New York's Museum of Modern Art. Maillol's *Night*, Lipchitz's *Sacrifice*, and Lachaise's *Standing Nude* are among the top-flight pieces.

Gordon Washburn, a former director of the museum, picked up in a Paris warehouse Lehmbruck's *Kneeling Woman* for $75 in storage charges. It was recently appraised at $75,000. Baskin, Marisol, Nakian, Noguchi, Wotruba, Milkowski, Tony Smith, Max Bill, Nevelson, Mallary, Penalba, and Jim Wines are but part

LEFT TO RIGHT: Marisol: *Baby Girl;* Robert Rauschenberg: *Acc;* Robert Indiana: *Star* (Albright-Knox Art Gallery, Buffalo, New York)

of a long list of other distinguished sculptors who are represented.

The small but top group of Post-Impressionists was enhanced by Conger Goodyear's bequest of Van Gogh's *La Maison de la Crau* and Paul Gauguin's *Spirit of the Dead Watching,* which complements his famous *The Yellow Christ,* also in the museum collection. Not one to hold a grievance, General Goodyear gave to Buffalo during his lifetime, and as bequests at his death in 1964, a total of over three hundred sixty works of art. The museum is indeed fortunate in her patrons. Seymour H. Knox, long-time president, who is responsible with Gordon M. Smith, the director, for the museum's present policy, has given hundreds of important works, representing artists in depth and world trends in general.

Not only are the Klines, Soulages, Francises, and Gottliebs acquired, but also the young and unknown. Buffalo keeps in close touch with the new developments in the arts around the world and reports the action in the form of avant-garde painting and sculpture shows, and happenings of an experimental nature in music, theater, and the dance.

NEW YORK STATE HISTORICAL ASSOCIATION

Fenimore House, Cooperstown, New York
Hours: Daily, 9–5; May–Sept., 9–6.
Admission $1; children, 40¢.
Library.

Fenimore House and the adjacent Farmers' Museum are concerned chiefly with the history of New York State, but many artists and artisans who recorded the epic of an emerging nation and the men who fought for, planted, and governed her along the way are represented here.

The house was built in the 1930s on the site of a cottage occupied by James Fenimore Cooper (1789–1851). At the end of the corridor to the right of the entrance is the Hall of Life-Masks, eighteen of them, done by John Henri Isaac Browere. This sculptor, poet, and painter developed a process that enabled him to go far beyond the usual technique of the medium. Eminent Americans, among them Thomas Jefferson, Martin Van Buren, John Adams, and De Witt Clinton, are displayed in telling likenesses.

The nineteenth-century landscape group includes not only that triumvirate Thomas Cole, Asher B. Durand, and Thomas Doughty, usually accepted as the founders of the Hudson River school, but other competent if lesser names, such as Robert Havell, E. C. Coates, and James D. Hart.

The portraits are outstanding. There is an especially brilliant Gilbert Stuart done in London in 1786 of *Joseph Brant,* a pro-British Indian chief of the Mohawk tribe. Another penetrating

Gilbert Stuart: *Joseph Brant* (New York State Historical Association, Cooperstown, New York)

painting is Benjamin West's *Portrait of Robert Fulton.* Fulton, an artist as well as an inventor, was a pupil of West's. Fulton's experimental work with the submarine torpedo is suggested in the canvas's background, where shoots of flame rise from the sea.

Genre paintings of course play an important part in the collection: Long Islander William Sidney Mount's *Eel Spearing at Selauket* Thomas Waterman Wood's *The Village Post Office,* and E. L. Henry's *On the Erie* represent the best.

The folk art collection shows how, in wood, metal, and stone, unknown craftsmen carved the symbol of our patriotism, the eagle, or fashioned tools for work or made weather vanes or rugs or samplers, with which to decorate their homes. One of the known pieces is by Samuel McIntire, a prominent Salem wood carver. It is the stern board from the ship *Mt. Vernon* and shows George Washington's home carved in bas-relief. This collection made by working people for their own enjoyment or use is one of the most varied and important in America.

HECKSCHER MUSEUM

Prime Avenue & Route 25A, Huntington, Long Island, New York
Hours: Tues.–Sat., 10–5; Sun., 2–5;
closed Mon., Jan. 1, Election Day, Thanksgiving, Dec. 25.
Free.

The day the Heckscher Museum, a five-winged marble building, and surrounding park was given to Huntington, virtually the whole town turned out to accept the gift. Business was suspended, the movie houses were closed, a regimental band played, and firecrackers punctuated the speeches. It was the citizens' tribute to August Heckscher, a German immigrant who made a fortune in mining. Now, a few decades since its opening, the museum is planning a new wing.

The basis of the collection is European painting from the sixteenth to the twentieth century and includes the Dutchman Caspar Netscher with *Portrait of an Opulent Dutch Lady* and Hendrick Avercamp's *Dutch Winter Sport in Holland.* Two good canvases of the French school are L. M. Van Loo's *Lady with a Hurdy-Gurdy* and Georges Michel's *Clouds and Hills.* Mr. Heckscher, like other early twentieth-century collectors, was enamored of English portraiture, and among his examples is a fine Raeburn,

Raeburn: *Adam Rolland of Gask* (Heckscher Museum, Huntington, Long Island, New York)

Adam Rolland of Gask. A recently published catalogue of the museum's American paintings shows a collection strong in nineteenth-century landscapes: Albert Bierstadt, Ralph Blakelock, Frederick Church, Homer Martin, Thomas Moran, and his brother and teacher, Edward Moran.

From the standpoint of acquisitions, the twentieth century until recently has been largely ignored, though George Grosz's satirical *American Tourists in Berlin* is in the collection. (Grosz spent thirteen of his twenty-five years in America in Huntington.) However, lively temporary exhibitions keep the citizens informed.

CORNELL UNIVERSITY:
ANDREW DICKSON WHITE MUSEUM OF ART

27 East Avenue, Ithaca, New York
Hours: Tues.–Sat., 11–5; Sun., 2:30–5:30.
Free.

High above Lake Cayuga's waters Cornell University prepares to build its new art museum. Eschewing the omnipresent "art center" idea, the building will be designed purely for the furtherance of the visual arts. Rising on a knoll overlooking the lake from the edge of the Arts Quadrangle, the museum is the gift of H. J. Johnson (Johnson wax), class of 1922 and long-time trustee of the university.

In 1952 the present building, erected in 1871 for Andrew Dickson White, Cornell's first president, was converted for museum use. Particularly strong in Asian art and graphics, Cornell holds

Edwin Dickinson: *Woodland Scene* (Andrew Dickson White Museum of Art, Cornell University, Ithaca, New York)

over four thousand prints, a collection known for the pristine quality of much of its contents. Mantegna, Dürer (including twenty-two recently acquired etchings of the *Small Passion* series), Whistler, and Toulouse-Lautrec are represented in depth. The Asian section has its own gallery in which Chinese paintings, Korean ceramics, and Japanese masters rotate. The Western section will not overpower you, but there are examples of the Dutch school and a few Barbizon and Hudson River school paintings. In the American group, Edwin Dickinson's *Woodland Scene* commands attention. Dickinson did this brooding, surrealistic landscape between 1929 and 1935; a loner, he has continued to work in a highly personal idiom. Jean Dubuffet, Georges Mathieu, Lee Bontecou, Michael Goldberg, Robert Rauschenberg are signatures on other contemporary works here. And at Willard Straight Hall (the student union), are, in addition, Ben Shahn, William Glackens, and Marsden Hartley. Near the new Olin Library, two Lipchitz sculptures punctuate the campus, monumentally.

NEW YORK CITY MUSEUMS

NON-SPECIALIZED MUSEUMS IN NEW YORK

As stated in the introduction, this book is primarily concerned with the general art museum; however, New York City has become such a center for visiting art lovers of varied predilections, that we felt compelled to list separately specialized and unspecialized museums (see page 101).

FRICK COLLECTION

1 East 70th Street, New York, New York
Hours: Tues.–Sat., 10–6; Sun. and holidays, 1–6;
June–Aug. 10: Thurs.–Sat., 10–6; Sun., Wed., holidays, 1–6.
Free.

The progress of Henry Clay Frick from a $1000-a-year clerk in his grandfather's distillery (Old Overholt) to a coke-oven operator worth a million took until his thirtieth birthday. He had set himself that goal and was a man to get what he wanted. When Frick wanted to break the famous Homestead Strike, the first great pitched battle between management and labor, he did it by steaming 300 Pinkerton guards down the Monongahela to rout the embattled strikers from the property.

There was nothing in Henry Clay Frick's Pennsylvania Mennonite background to feed a love of the visual arts but he had it, instinctively and early. At twenty-one, when he applied for a loan, the bank reported, "on job all day, keeps books evenings, may be a little fond of pictures but not enough to hurt . . . advise making loan." His first flier was with the Barbizon school —those nineteenth-century Frenchmen who turned their backs on the rigidities of the Academy to paint from nature in an intimate, bucolic style. They became "the fashion." Prices soared and bovines found verdant pasture on the walls of the palaces of America's moneyed aristocracy.

But Frick's love of painting transcended fashion. As early as 1901, four years before he moved to New York and began his serious collecting, he acquired Vermeer's *The Music Lesson*, a Monet, and a Hobbema. Rembrandt's *Artist as a Young Man* was purchased in 1899. In 1905 *St. Jerome* was the first El Greco to go into a private collection in America.

The art dealer Joseph Duveen has been credited with building the Frick collection, but Frick made a substantial beginning before that supersalesman moved in. Roger Fry, English art historian and critic, kept Frick informed of the state of the European art market. In 1910 Frick heard that Rembrandt's *Polish Rider* was for sale and sent Fry off to Poland for it: it hangs in the west gallery today.

Frick conceived of his home, begun in 1913, as his monument and an eventual public museum. The front door of the house now leads into an elegant flowered and fountained court where cham-

Frick Collection, Fragonard room; fireplace and southeast corner (Copyright the Frick Collection, New York)

ber music concerts are given regularly. The oval room, gallery, and lecture room are the only post-Frick additions. However, in these days of frenzied museum expansion, even monuments must continue to grow and the Frick is planning changes that will give added gallery and administrative space.

We owe the delectable Fragonard Room to Duveen. He had purchased eleven panels from the Morgan estate (for $1,250,000) with Frick in mind. The four largest were commissioned by Louis XV for Mme. du Barry, who, for some whim we'll never understand, refused them. The room is filled with great eighteenth-century furniture, the fireplace from Marie Antoinette's château Bagatelle, and gay figure groups by Clodion—perfect foils for Fragonard's witty and delicate paintings.

Though the Frick's arrangement is less subject to change than most museums, loans and occasional purchases make a certain amount of shifting necessary. The Piero della Francesca *St. John the Evangelist* is now seen through the arch of the enamel room. The "Piero," one of the truly great paintings in America, shows the introspective old saint standing on two bare feet, his monolithic figure wrapped in a blood-red robe, his white woolly lamb beard relieving the solemnity. Here, too, is Duccio's *Temptation of Christ,* one of three Duccios in the United States. The others are in the National Gallery and the Boston Museum. A recent

Piero della Francesca: *St. John the Evangelist*
(Copyright the Frick Collection, New York)

acquisition is a small grisaille painting by Pieter Brueghel the
Elder, *The Three Soldiers*. It graced the collections of both
Charles I and James II.

The long gallery is alive with Rembrandt, Hals, Van Dyck,
Ruisdael, Hobbema, and two large, brilliant Turners. Turner's
Cologne: The Arrival of the Packet Boat: Evening so overshad-
owed two Lawrences it hung between at the Royal Academy in
London that Turner obligingly put a coat of darker varnish on it.

El Greco's *St. Jerome* hangs over the fireplace in the living
room, separating those disparate Englishmen *Sir Thomas More*
and *Sir Thomas Cromwell* (who had almost nothing in common
except that Henry VIII had both their heads chopped off).
Holbein painted them after Erasmus introduced him to Henry's
court, and the portrait of More is thought to be his first English
work. Across the room, between two portraits by Titian, is Giovanni Bellini's *St. Francis in Ecstasy* in a gentle landscape bathed
in Italian sunlight. Of it Osbert Sitwell wrote, "Christianity
speaks through every leaf and we are back in the lost world of
simplicity and understanding." Spread through the rooms is a
fine collection of Renaissance bronzes.

Other canvases not to be missed are: Vermeer's *Mistress and
Maid* and *Officer and Laughing Girl;* and the four Goyas, of
which *The Forge* is the most compelling, the central figures a

massive block of power. Up the Avenue at the Metropolitan is a drawing of the same three men, same pose, only working out-doors.

In Frick's official biography, George Harvey pictures him on sleepless nights wandering in the long gallery, trying one chair after another to find the best light for looking at a painting he loved. He really saw paintings, and in the last years of his life, with a trained eye and relentless zeal, went after the best. No price was too high to pay for what his eye told him was good. Whatever history's final judgment of the man, the house he built on 70th Street is a noble monument.

MUSEUM OF MODERN ART

11 West 53rd Street, New York, New York
Hours: Mon.–Sat., 11–6; Thurs., 11–9 P.M.; Sun., 12–6;
closed Christmas.
Restaurant.
Adults, $1.25; children under 16, 50¢.

By setting a policy, at its inception in 1929, of forming a collection of the immediate precursors of modern art and the most important living artists, the museum assumed a formidable task, for immediate ancestors are often in disrepute and the contemporary masters are at times difficult to judge. The museum, now forty years old, has proved its policy magnificently.

The collection begins around 1875, though 97 per cent concerns the twentieth century. You can float along on a lily pad with Monet or be catapulted into a world of kinetic, frenetic sculpture wired for sound or movement by the Swiss artist Jean Tinguely, or for light by Chryssa, the Greek-American who brought neon into the museum world.

As with many museums throughout the United States, this one was started by women. One day over a luncheon table Miss Lillie P. Bliss, Mrs. Cornelius J. Sullivan, and Mrs. John D. Rockefeller, Jr., presented a full-blown plan for a museum to A. Conger Goodyear, who, fresh but undaunted from a modern-art battle in his home town (see Buffalo), became the museum's first president. Alfred H. Barr, Jr., who had been teaching art history to young women at Wellesley, was made director. The same

Alfred Barr, retiring after thirty-nine years of service, leaves a collection which is probably the best survey of modern art in the world.

Though the museum's permanent collection crosses all national boundaries, America has had the greatest representation—ever since the first purchase, Edward Hopper's *House by the Railroad.* The inaugural show was held in an office building at 730 Fifth Avenue and such crowds clogged the elevators that the landlord threatened to cancel the lease. But the address remained the same until 1939, when the museum moved to its present handsome quarters. In 1964 a large east wing and more garden space were added; then in 1966 the museum took over the entire former Whitney Museum, which had fortuitously been placed so that it forms in effect a west wing. Here, in the first study center that has all its catalogued art available, scholars may examine works not on public view. Almost a thousand paintings are placed individually on aluminum screens that slide on rollers and can be moved about for close viewing. Large sculpture stands on pallets for easy turning. Photographs, drawings, prints, design objects and architectural drawings are included as well as film stills and films. Three small projection rooms are available. The library has been enlarged and moved here thus making archival material relative to the collections accessible. The octopus is still reaching out its tentacles; the Theatre Guild west of the museum's entrance will soon be replaced by more gallery space.

No less revealing of the surging, volatile spirit that infuses the Modern are its varied services. The film library presents one of its classics twice a day. Summer jazz concerts in the garden are sellouts. The photography department, set up in its new Edward Steichen gallery, preserves the old, explores the new. The Philip L. Goodwin galleries of architecture and design take us from Tiffany glass and the Bauhaus Movement into "Now." The Abby Aldrich Rockefeller Print Room is set aside for study of its more than 7,000 original graphics by modern artists. Call for an appointment. The new Paul Sachs galleries of drawings offer quiet space for close perusal and reflection. A series of orientation galleries are being planned, where various audio-visual techniques will prepare the visitor "for looking."

Behind these activities stands the solid forest of the permanent collection. While only a small segment of approximately 20,000 works of art can be shown at one time and major upheavals in arrangement occasionally take place, we are assured that perennial favorites will be on view. Going to the museum and not finding Rousseau's *Sleeping Gypsy* would be like meeting Groucho Marx without his cigar. Others to look for: Van Gogh's *Starry Night;* Rouault's *Three Judges;* Beckman's *Departure,* which he shipped out of Nazi Germany in 1937 as *"Scenes from Shakespeare."* The rooms of Cézanne, Degas, Léger, Matisse, and Braque culminate in Monet's *Water Lilies,* set in its own gallery; one looks out from Monet's evanescent world to the play of the fountains in the garden below.

It is hard to say whether the Modern takes over Picasso or Picasso the Modern. Over forty of his works, exclusive of drawings, prints, posters, and a rug, belong to it. Some, like *Les Demoiselles d'Avignon of 1907,* presaging the rigidities of Cubism, are landmarks. *Guernica,* that threnodic protest against war and brutality, is on indefinite loan, while its antithesis, *Night Fishing at Antibes,* full of technical similarities, hums with muted color, tender and playful.

Excellent orientation maps are provided at the entrance to the second-floor galleries, which lead in historical progression from

Pablo Picasso: *Night Fishing at Antibes* (Museum of Modern Art, New York; Mrs. Simon Guggenheim Fund)

The Abby Aldrich Rockefeller Sculpture Garden, Museum of Modern Art, New York; photograph by A. Georges

Cézanne, the Impressionists, Post-Impressionists, Cubism, and Italian Futurists to early geometric abstract art. The third floor continues with the Surrealists, Realists, Romantics, and Abstract Expressionists. A series of galleries on this floor show sculpture from traditional to recent examples. In the next year or two, with the opening of more gallery space, the great sculpture collection will be able to breathe again.

The museum's garden foliage has come of age. Tall trees drip their leaves over Reder's *Lady with the House of Cards* and Moore's *Family Group.* The Belgian sculptor Oscar Jespers' *St. Anthony* is tempted under a white birch tree. Vargas' *Snake* leers from its ivy bed; Rodin's *Balzac* is aloof, while Maillol's *Nude* plays eternally in the moss-green pool. The upper terrace holds the more optically assaulting examples of sculpture.

If there is an overriding philosophy at work here, it is that contemporary art is a facet of contemporary life, that frenetic painting is the result of a frenetic age, and that the museum is a platform on which to exhibit the period we live in.

SOLOMON R. GUGGENHEIM MUSEUM

1071 Fifth Avenue, New York, New York
Hours: Tues.–Sat., 10–6; Tues. to 9 P.M.; Sun., holidays, 12–6;
closed Christmas, July 4th.
Restaurant.
Admission 50 cents.

Lacking the skill of Lewis Mumford, the temerity of art-critic Emily Genauer, the *savoir-faire* of that arbiter of taste Russell Lynes, I shall not spend much space describing the Frank Lloyd Wright building which houses the Guggenheim Museum. So much has already been said about it that anything more is likely to be a cliché.

The building is a stunner and I defy anyone to step into its swirling rotunda and not be lifted by the daring of the concept. The happiest way to enjoy both the building and its paintings (after an initial look at the great dome from below) is to take the elevator to the top and walk down the sloping ramp. Almost all exhibitions are hung to be seen specifically in this order. Freed of the restrictions of conventional galleries, the paintings shout or murmur across the large perspective of the open court. They live in what is in fact a single, continuous gallery, unwinding as it descends and letting each canvas make its point in

Interior view of main gallery, The Solomon R. Guggenheim Museum, New York

relation to all the others in a complex total harmony. Bays scalloping the outer walls succeed in establishing an intimacy between individual painting and individual viewer.

Although the museum presents four or five major exhibitions a year, such as the popular Calder, Van Gogh, and Klee retrospectives of recent years, universal favorites from its own vast permanent collection, like old friends, keep reappearing—Chagall's *Green Violinist,* Rousseau's *Football Players,* Cézanne's *Clockmaker,* Modigliani's *Nude,* or Brancusi's seal-like sculpture *Miracle.* This is to mention only a few of the approximately four thousand works in a collection that includes the largest group of paintings by Vasily Kandinsky to be seen in any of the world's museums, as well as many important paintings by Delaunay, Klee, Léger, and Marc.

Solomon R. Guggenheim was one of seven sons of mining magnate Meyer Guggenheim. The sons, continuing their father's investments in the good earth, went from Canada to the Congo making fortunes even greater than "Papa's." Solomon, in the tradition of the time, became a collector of old masters, and it was not until 1926 that a painter friend, Baroness Hilla Rebay, introduced him to the delights of nonobjective works. Over the next two decades, on many trips to Europe, a collection of modern masters was built. The new collection was first displayed in

1939 in a gallery at 24 East 54th Street under the direction of the Baroness. This gallery, known popularly as "The Museum of Nonobjective Painting," was the conversation piece of its day. The rather mystical atmosphere featured heavily draped walls, recordings of Bach and Brahms, and silver-framed paintings hung at what critic Aline Saarinen described as "ankle level." Despite these eccentricities of installation, the museum had a considerable impact on the art public, and when Solomon died in 1949 he had already approved Frank Lloyd Wright's plan for its permanent quarters on upper Fifth Avenue.

In 1952, when James Johnson Sweeney succeeded the Baroness as director, the museum's exhibition policy was broadened to include the full range of contemporary art. This change was brought about by the trustees, feeling that the earlier, rather rigid adherence to the nonobjective idiom implied the possibility of a finality of artistic expression which was out of keeping with the museum's original revolutionary educational objectives. To give formal recognition to its new format, the museum's name was changed to the present, stylistically neutral designation as the Solomon R. Guggenheim Museum. The newly christened museum actually moved into its permanent home in Wright's visionary structure in 1959. There, under the leadership of its present director, Thomas M. Messer, the museum has continued to enlarge the scope of its exhibitions and of its permanent collection.

Several recent additions to the permanent collection have been of monumental scale: Léger's *Grand Parade,* Dubuffet's *L'Hourloupe, Nunc Stans,* and Francis Bacon's *Crucifixion* triptych. Also of imposing dimensions is Miró's *Alicia,* a ceramic mural commissioned by Harry F. Guggenheim in memory of his wife, Alicia Patterson Guggenheim. Dedicated in 1967, this work is now on permanent display at the top of the first ramp, where it is often

Fernand Léger: *The Great Parade* (The Solomon R. Guggenheim Museum, New York)

seen with its earlier sculptural counterpart, Miró's 8-foot ceramic *Portico.* Recently acquired works of smaller size, though equal artistic merit, have included Klee's *In the Current Six Thresholds,* Jawlensky's *Helene with Red Turban,* and Giacometti's *Statue of a Headless Woman.*

Perhaps the most eloquent testimonial to the museum's broadened interests is the Justin K. Thannhauser wing, with its seventy-five Impressionist and Post-Impressionist masterpieces. This special gallery, which forms a level oasis in the visitor's spiral journey, houses works by Gauguin, Cézanne, Van Gogh, and, perhaps most notably, thirty-four Picassos, a selection covering chronologically the total *oeuvre* of this century's greatest artist. Vuillard's *Place Vintimille,* Modigliani's *Young Girl Seated,* and *Woman Ironing* of Picasso's Blue Period are among the works which may be contemplated in this intimate setting.

Not only the collection, but the building itself, is undergoing expansion. A two-story annex designed by Frank Lloyd Wright's leading disciple, William Wesley Peters, was recently completed on the northeast corner of the museum's lot. This annex, by permitting the relocation of certain administrative functions, will increase exhibition space by nearly one-third, and free the top ramp to flow in ribboned harmony with the whole.

WHITNEY MUSEUM OF AMERICAN ART

945 Madison Avenue, New York, New York
Hours: Daily, 11–6; Sun., 12–6; Tues., 11 A.M.–10 P.M.;
Restaurant.
Admission 50 cents, children free.

Gertrude Vanderbilt Whitney, great-great-granddaughter of the railroad tycoon Cornelius Whitney, was the founder of the present Whitney and also a serious sculptor. In 1908 she opened her MacDougal Street studio to struggling young artists who had no place to exhibit. By 1918 the Whitney Studio Club had been formed with Juliana Force as director. Mrs. Force, a small, amber-haired dynamo from Doylestown, Pennsylvania, had no background for her job (she had run a secretarial school) but she was an organizational genius. The two women working in tandem for thirty years did much to give the American artist a showcase.

The club, center of fun and accomplishment (Edward Hopper, John Sloan, and the sculptor John Flannagan were the first shown

Night view, Whitney Museum of American Art, New York; sunken sculpture garden and entrance bridge into street-level lobby; Marcel Breuer and Associates, architects.

there) grew so rapidly that a row of houses on West 8th Street was remodeled to form the Whitney Museum, which opened November 18, 1931. Here the Whitney matured into the country's major sponsor of American art and here it remained, except for an interlude of twelve years on West 54th Street, until it opened in triumph in 1966 on upper Madison Avenue. The new Whitney, designed by architect Marcel Breuer, sits on its corner wrapped in smoky gray granite. The interior blends rough concrete walls with smooth teakwood, enormous "wall-to-wall slate" galleries with deeply carpeted enclosures for intimate viewing. A sunken sculpture court at the entrance allows passersby to look down and enjoy the works of art. Standing within, one feels the true monolithic relationship between the sculpture and the building.

In 1949 the Whitney, to the astonishment of the art world, sold all its holdings in American art executed prior to 1900. The living artists' pressing need for help seemed to justify the decision, but now, almost twenty years later, the museum is going back to its old policy of collecting and showing all facets of American art. Would that its Eakinses and Homers could be recalled as easily as its decisions (see Clark Museum). More than any other museum in the country, the Whitney has been the artists' museum. In the beginning, Mrs. Force, aware of her own

Jack Levine: *Gangster Funeral*
(Collection of Whitney Museum
of American Art, New York)

limitations, turned to the artists to put on exhibitions. She asked
Alexander Brook to seek new talents he felt worth exhibiting. He
did this for four years, along with other assorted duties such as
hanging exhibitions. From every show Mrs. Whitney bought
artists' work and the Whitney carries on that policy today. Instead
of giving medals and awards for its big annuals, it purchases
works of art from them. The Whitney's holdings in twentieth-
century American art are the largest in the country. Through the
years certain paintings have become so identified with the museum they could justifiably be called "Whitney masterpieces":
Charles Demuth's *My Egypt,* Walt Kuhn's *The Blue Clown,* Alexander Brook's *The Sentinels,* Edward Hopper's *Early Sunday
Morning,* George Bellows' *Dempsey and Firpo,* Jack Levine's
Gangster Funeral, Ben Shahn's *The Passion of Sacco and Van-
zetti,* Yasho Kuniyoshi's *Deliverance,* and Charles Sheeler's *River
Rouge Plant.* A few late acquisitions are from the studios of Mark
Rothko, Kenneth Noland, Les Levine, Conrad Marca-Relli,
Gregory Gilespie, William Wiley, Robert Mangold, Dan Flavin,
Jim Dine, and Harold Paris. The Howard and Jean Lipman Foun-
dation gave important sculpture by such artists as Durchaneck,
Irwin Judd, Trova, Snelson, Von Heune, Weinberg, Kiessler,
Chamberlain, and Schmidt, along with a continuing yearly gift.

Not only has the Whitney acquired a new home, it has also
acquired a new image. As the founder intended, its openings
attract both established and young artists; its Tuesday evening
series of avant-garde and classical music have packed the galleries; its Art Research Center in a refurbished warehouse on
the Lower East Side (185 Cherry Street) brings the museum to
the people in exhibitions of the Whitney's original work, plus
providing them with studio workshops for youngsters as well as
serious artists.

SPECIALIZED MUSEUMS IN NEW YORK

ASIA HOUSE GALLERY

112 East 64th Street, New York, New York
Hours: Daily, 10–5; Sat. & holidays, 11–5; Sun., 1–5;
closed summer months.

The object of the gallery, which is an adjunct of the Asia Society founded by John D. Rockefeller III in 1957, is to bring the finest works of art from ancient Asiatic cultures to the New York public.

Three major exhibitions are held between September and June, with material gathered from museums and collections around the world. A few samples: The Art of Nepal, The Art of the Han Dynasty, 7,000 Years of Iranian Art. Acoustiguide (recorded) lectures by the gallery director are available to visitors.

The building (designed by Philip Johnson) is a seven-story shaft of smoky gray glass between two brownstones. Exhibitions are strikingly presented in the second-floor galleries. A pleasant lounge and library on the main floor level lead to a tranquil garden and one of the contemporary sculptor Nagare's most important works.

It is wise to call, as the gallery is closed between exhibitions.

COOPER HEWITT MUSEUM FOR THE ART OF DECORATION

Cooper Square at 7th Street, New York, New York
Hours: Mon.–Sat., 10–5;
closed major holidays and Saturdays from June 1–Oct. 1.
Free.

The museum occupying the fourth floor of Cooper Union, a tuition-free college founded by philanthropist Peter Cooper, is concerned with decorative arts both past and present. Its large central gallery holds small groupings of furniture integrated with *objets d'art*, drawings, or prints. Galleries and study rooms fan off. It is difficult to departmentalize this storehouse of riches, only a small portion of which can be shown, but the drawing collection and the textile design section are among the strongest in the country. Other groupings include wallpaper, ceramics, glass, metal, and woodwork.

Now a part of the Smithsonian complex, Cooper Hewitt Museum contemplates a move to the former Carnegie mansion at 91st Street and Fifth Ave. The additional space will allow for much material, hitherto rotated or seen by appointment, to be constantly on view.

FINCH COLLEGE MUSEUM OF ART

62 East 78th Street, New York, New York 10021
Hours: Tues.–Sun., 1–5.
Free.

Founded in 1900 by Mrs. Jessica Finch, a fighting suffragette, Finch College is now located in a cluster of brownstones, a step from some of Madison Avenue's most important galleries. There is a small old master section, and distinguished exhibitions are held, usually of challenging but lesser-known aspects of art history.

However, it is in the contemporary field that the fighting spirit of Mrs. Finch lives on. Trends are explored with daring and verve. Thought-provoking, scholarly exhibitions showing the creative process of some of our most avant-garde artists are given. When the museum is not spinning with one of these shows, the modest but good contemporary collection is on view.

HISPANIC SOCIETY OF AMERICA

Broadway between 155 & 156 Streets, New York, New York
Hours: Tues.–Sat., 10–4:30; Sun., 2–5;
closed major holidays.
Library.

America is indebted to Archer M. Huntington for that island of Spanish culture anchored on upper Broadway in Manhattan. Huntington was the son of Collis P. Huntington, railroad and shipbuilding magnate. Instead of throwing his considerable creative energies toward industry, the son, with a thoroughness known to few, decided to explore Iberian culture.

In a museum built on land that once belonged to John James Audubon, one can find, in miniature, a cross section of every facet of Spain's art heritage: Iron Age artifacts and examples from the Roman period on the peninsula; the sophisticated pottery and ironwork from the Hispano-Moresque period; gold, silk brocades, ivories, tiles, silver, painting, and sculpture from Spain's great age under Ferdinand and Isabella; Renaissance liturgical objects; richly carved furniture of the sixteenth and seventeenth centuries.

The sculpture group begins with early Phoenician-style ivories, pre-Roman and Roman bronzes. The pottery dates from historic times but the Hispano-Moresque and Spanish lustre pottery, as well as the sixteenth-century enameled glass from Cataluña, is most important. Spain's national pastime, bullfighting, its history, art, and appurtenances from the thirteenth century to modern times are on display in a separate gallery.

There are important paintings by Louis de Morales, El Greco, José de Ribera, Francisco Zurbarán, and Velásquez. The Goyas include the sketch for scenes of the *Massacre of the Third of May,* a portrait of the *Duchess of Alba,* and a stunning one of *Don Manuel Lopena.* There are a few paintings of the twentieth century, but those early Picassos so thoroughly Spanish in feeling are missing.

A monumental sculpture of *El Cid* done by Anna Hyatt Huntington, the founder's second wife, stands before the museum.

The library contains over 100,000 books relating to the history and culture of Spain, Portugal, and colonial Hispanic America.

JEWISH MUSEUM

1109 Fifth Avenue, New York, New York
Hours: Sun., 11–6; Mon.–Thurs., 12–5; Fri., 11–3;
closed Sat.
Adults 50¢, children 25¢.

The gargoyled French Renaissance home of the Felix Warburgs (built in 1908) was presented to the Jewish Theological Seminary, which in 1947 established a museum to hold what is the most comprehensive collection of Jewish ceremonial objects in existence.

In 1962 the Albert A. List wing was added, giving the museum a new entrance and a modern front. Changing exhibitions of contemporary art, so new they are sometimes pace-jumpers rather than pace-setters, are on the first floor. The other two floors hold the traditional material, including a sixteenth-century synagogue wall of faïence mosaic from Iraq. In a gallery apart is a large black box sculpture, *Homage to 6 Million* by Louise Nevelson.

A rethinking of the institution's role will, according to director Karl Katz, enlarge the Judaic collection to encompass everything from the patriarchs to the present. The museum will also attempt to interpret the world of scholars for the general public, transforming learned treatises into visual three-dimensional gallery experiences.

MUSEUM OF AMERICAN FOLK ART

49 West 53rd Street, New York, New York
Hours: Tues.–Sat., 10:30–5:30.
Admission: Adults 35¢, children 25¢.

Opened in 1963, the museum is devoted to the folk tradition in American art and design. A portrait done by an itinerant artist, a Pennsylvania Dutch chest, a carved weather vane, a rubbing from a New England gravestone, or a *santos* (see Santa Fe)—whatever the subject, one is assured of seeing excellent examples of the work of many of America's gifted though untutored artist-craftsmen.

MUSEUM OF THE AMERICAN INDIAN

Audubon Terrace, Broadway at 155th, New York, New York
Hours: Tues.–Sun., 1–5;
closed Mondays and holidays.
Free.

These collections form the largest assemblage of American Indian material in the world. The life of the Indian is interpreted through everyday objects, dress, ceremonial and religious pieces. The Creek, Cherokee, Iroquois, Algonquin, Navaho, Hopi, Seminole—all the old tribal names are here. Ethnology and archaeology dominate the second-floor galleries. The third floor contains a number of examples of Middle American art and archaeology.

MUSEUM OF THE CITY OF NEW YORK

5th Ave., between 103rd and 104th Sts., New York, New York
Hours: Daily, 10–5; Sundays and holidays, 1–5;
Closed Mondays, Christmas.
Free.

Gracie Mansion, now the official home of New York Mayors, housed the museum from 1923 until 1932 when it moved to its present spacious Georgian building.

The Museum documents its political, social, and economic history in an engaging manner.

In a "please touch" area children are invited to handle many objects. Dioramas which bring a dramatic impact are used extensively with small ladders provided for tiny viewers: model rooms show interiors from 1690 to the late Victorian effulgence of John D. Rockefeller's house on West 54th Street. A Duncan Phyfe room offers fine examples from America's master cabinet maker's workshop.

For a chronological viewing, start in the Dutch Gallery on the first floor. Here the history of New York City, or Nieuw Amsterdam as it was called, is re-created from the silver and pewter of the patroons to the tools of the working people. A replica of the fort that guarded the harbor is also on display. Some fine American portraits hang on the first floor. Special events ranging from concerts for adults to puppet shows for children take place from October through May. This is definitely a family museum.

MUSEUM OF CONTEMPORARY CRAFTS

29 West 53rd Street, New York, New York
Hours: Mon.–Sat., 11–6; Sun., 1–6.
Admission 50¢, children under 12 free.

Aside from being a viewing platform, through group exhibitions and one-man shows, for the best craftsmen in the country, the museum has a library and keeps up-to-date files on craftsmen and craft schools throughout the country. These are open to the public, in the offices of the American Craftsman Council on the fourth floor; the council is the museum's parent organization. First- and second-floor galleries show changing exhibitions, about five a year. One-man exhibitions are held in a small gallery on the second floor.

MUSEUM OF PRIMITIVE ART

15 West 54th Street, New York, New York
Hours: Tues.–Sat., 12–5; Sun., 1–5;
closed holidays.
Admission 50¢, students 25¢.

Brain child of the governor of New York, Nelson A. Rockefeller, the museum is housed in two former Rockefeller town houses. Its collection encompasses the primitive cultures of Africa, Oceania, and the Americas, carvings of deities or demons, ceremonial masks, religious fetishes, instruments of war, household pots and ornaments, all the expressions of primitive, and surely not so primitive, people sparingly and dramatically displayed. Three to four exhibitions are held each year of different facets of the splendid collections. The large reference library is open to art students and scholars.

THE NEW-YORK HISTORICAL SOCIETY

170 Central Park West, New York City
Hours: Daily, 1–5; Sat., 10–5;
closed Mon.
Free.

In an exciting new installation covering the entire fourth floor and gleaming with clustered spot lighting instead of former dingy skylights, some 260 paintings from a collection of 2,000 oils, watercolors, prints, and miniatures have been hung.

Founded in 1804, the society exhibits here its rich repository of figures from our historical past: the Stuyvesants, Van Alens, Schuylers, Ten Eychs who settled New York, along with Washington, Adams, Hancock, Franklin, Jefferson, and others who brought the nation into being. Some are painted by artists whose names are lost to us, others by men who, in recording that past, acquired their own fame.

Portraits of George and Martha Washington by Rembrandt Peale are guarded by two enormous and fierce carved American eagles. The society boasts one of the finest, largest groups of nineteenth-century genre and landscape painting in the country. Those old favorites Thomas Cole's *The Course of Empire* shine forth in new splendor along with less grandiose but more satisfying canvases such as J. F. Kensett's *View from West Point.* The new installation gives one a chance to reappraise former acquaintances and to meet the newcomers in this far-from-static institution.

PIERPONT MORGAN LIBRARY

29 East 36th Street, New York, New York
Hours: Mon.–Sat., 9:30–5;
closed Sun., holidays.
Free.

Pierpont Morgan, a lordly, astute collector and financial genius, erected the present Renaissance-style *palazzo* in 1905 to house his collection of rare manuscripts and works of art. Today the main entrance is through the annex next door, formerly the site of Morgan's home. A gallery to the left is used for rotating exhibitions from the library's holdings: manuscripts, illuminations, prints, or drawings. A long corridor, also used for exhibitions, leads to the West and East Rooms of the older edifice. The West Room, or study, is opulent with red damask walls, heavily carved furniture, majolica, Limoges, faïence, and alabaster pieces much the same as it was in Morgan's day. Here he entertained princes and churchmen, intellectuals and writers and, of course, art dealers. Among the paintings are: Memling's *A Young Man with a Pink,* Tintoretto's *Portrait of a Moor,* Perugino's *Virgin and Two Saints Adoring the Christ Child,* and Cranach the Elder's small circular wedding portraits of Martin Luther and his wife Catherine.

The East Room houses one of the great libraries of the Western World, including the Constance Missal (*circa* 1450), believed to predate the Gutenberg Bible, and works from the press of the first English printer, William Caxton. While the three-tiered stacks are not open to the public, rare manuscripts are always on display. Wherever the eye rests there is an object of beauty. An ornate vestibule with a mosaic ceiling, and four marble columns on which rest delicately carved alabaster lamps separates the two rooms.

(*MIDDLE ATLANTIC MUSEUMS CONTINUED*)

VASSAR COLLEGE ART GALLERY

Taylor Hall, Raymond Avenue, Poughkeepsie, New York
Hours: Mon.–Sat., 9–5; Sun., 2–5;
June 10–mid Sept., 2–4 daily.
Free.

In an outsized portrait by Charles Loring Elliot, Matthew Vassar stands against the typical nineteenth-century classical pillared and balustraded background, pointing to the impressive new Vassar Female College painted in the distance (the word "female" was eliminated from the college name in 1867). In 1861, the year the college was incorporated, the James Renwick building must still have been on the drawing board, for the architect was busy working on St. Patrick's Cathedral in New York at the time and the college did not open until 1865. However, Matthew Vassar had an art gallery in mind from the beginning, for in 1864 he purchased an entire collection of oils, watercolors, and drawings, a few of which have survived, from the chairman of the art committee, Dr. Elias L. Magoon. The painter and inventor S. F. B. Morse was one of the original committee members.

The off-campus visitor will find the museum conveniently located in Taylor Hall just to the right of Taylor Gate. The Charles M. Pratt collection of Far Eastern pottery and porcelains contains objects from China, Southeast Asia, Korea, and Japan from the Han Dynasty to the nineteenth century. Much of the jade collection is richly carved and ornamented. Boys ride buffalos, willow trees spread their branches over stream and pagoda. The group is divided into utilitarian, ornamental, and symbolic objects, none earlier than the seventeenth century.

Paintings begin with the school of Giotto and the fourteenth-century Taddeo Gaddi, proceed to baroque and Dutch. The Italians range from the fifteenth to the eighteenth centuries and represent what Agnes Rindge Claflin, long-time distinguished professor of art, called "The Berensonian enlightenment" (see Gardner Museum, Boston). The French are represented by Jean Léon Gerôme's *Camels at a Watering Place*, Gustave Courbet's *Boy with Jumping Jack,* and Hubert Robert's *The Octavian Gate*

Giovanni Francesco Barbieri ("Il Guercino," 1591–1666): *The Circumcision* (Vassar College Art Gallery, Poughkeepsie, New York)

and Fishmarket, a rollicking view of the life of the common man under Louis XVI.

It is refreshing to come upon the Hudson River boys, those masters of the grandiose, in beautiful small examples. The twentieth century is well represented and growing. Ben Nicholson and sculptors Henry Moore and Barbara Hepworth speak for the English. Hartigan, Rothko, Mac Ivor, Rice Pereira, and Joan Mitchell are but a few in the American section. But it is in its drawing and print collection that Vassar distinguishes itself. Shown in a well-lighted gallery where close scrutiny is encouraged, the prints number, in the Felix Warburg donation alone, seventy-five Rembrandts, including a superb impression of *Portrait of Jan Six*, and over fifty Dürers. Thirteen major Rouaults are included in over two hundred twentieth-century prints.

While Vassar is specifically a teaching institution, it is hoped that some day more space will be available in which to show to student and public alike many fine objects which are at the present in storage.

MEMORIAL ART GALLERY OF THE UNIVERSITY OF ROCHESTER

490 University Avenue, Rochester, New York
Hours: Mon.–Sat., 10–5; Sun., 2–5:30;
closed Sundays, July and August.
Free.

Beginning in 1913 with two paintings, four plaster casts, and "a lappet of lace," the collection has become, especially with Buffalo's Albright Gallery going all-out for the twentieth century, the most important general museum in the state, New York City excepted. The building, with its classical lines and columned fountain court, proves an admirable setting for the medieval treasures which distinguish Rochester among smaller museums of America in that field.

In 1926 a wing doubling the original space was added, and in 1968 a commodious, clean-lined, west wing opened.

Ancient art emphasizes the Egyptians, Mesopotamians, Greeks, Etruscans, and Romans: a strange little figure from Babylon (1900–1500 B.C.), a sphinx from Karnak, two rare jars from the Aegean decorated with happy warriors are but a few examples. The primitive art section is strong in fine examples from North America, Africa, Colombia, Guatemala, Yucatan, Mexico, and Peru. A great Mayan stele from Yucatan has just come to the museum. Eastern art ranges from Persian to Japanese. The Indian carvings and a Cambodian head are outstanding. But as mentioned before, Rochester's pride is her rich medieval collection, sarcophagi, capitals, ivories, illuminated manuscripts, Limoges, a frescoed apse from a chapel in Auvergne, sculpture, stained glass, tapestries; a highlight among many objects is a thirteenth-century French limestone capital, *Doubting Thomas, Christ and Apostles*. That St. Thomas' head is missing merely sharpens the wonder. The Renaissance includes panel paintings like *Madonna and Child Enthroned* by the Master of the St. Ursula Legend and *St. Margaret with Donor* by another fifteenth-century artist, Vrancke van der Stockt. This panel is the right wing of a triptych; the left is to be found at the Allen Memorial Museum in Oberlin, Ohio. The painting schools of the seventeenth to twentieth centuries give us Magnasco, Philippe de Champaigne, Boucher, Delacroix, Constable, Courbet, two splendid Monets, Degas, Braque, Léger, Matisse, and Picasso. The Americans start with

The Legend of St. Thomas: Doubting Thomas, Christ and Apostles, figural capital (French, thirteenth century) (Permanent Collection of the Memorial Art Gallery of the University of Rochester)

primitive painters and the Colonials. A stern portrait of Nathaniel Rochester, the city's founder, is here, together with an engaging canvas by George Catlin which was commissioned by the Colt Firearms Company as an advertisement. It shows Indians pinging away at a skyful of flamingoes with Colt's best. Homer, Eakins, and Ryder are shown, along with "The Eight"—those recorders of the homely side of American life—and later twentieth–century old masters, Max Weber, Hans Hofmann, and Stuart Davis. The sculpture section is continually being enriched. Maillol, Moore, Nadelman, Noguchi, Lachaise take their place with new talents such as local sculptor, Bill Sellers.

The visitor to Rochester should also stop at nearby Eastman House, which is now part of the University of Rochester. Though primarily a museum of photography, and a great one at that, the ornate entrance hall, library, and drawing room hold some of the important paintings Eastman assembled. Portraits by Tintoretto, Van Dyck, Rembrandt, Hals, Reynolds, and Raeburn embellish the walls.

EVERSON MUSEUM OF ART

Community Plaza, Corner of Harrison & South State, Syracuse, New York
Hours: Tues.–Sun., 12–5 P.M.;
closed Monday.
Free.

The recently opened Everson Museum is one of the most distinguished museum buildings in the country. Designed by I. M. Pei, it is situated within the stunning urban complex that Pei is creating for Syracuse. Galleries overlook a two-storied central court which contains a poured-concrete spiral staircase, itself a piece of sculpture. In fact, as *Progressive Architecture* stated, "the building is quite consciously a piece of abstract sculpture . . . to house sculpture one might say, a work of art for other works of art."

The Everson's roots go back to 1896 and the Syracuse Museum of Fine Arts, which it succeeded. It has been well known on the national scene since 1932, when it established a National Ceramic Bi-Annual that continues to bring together the leading ceramicists in America.

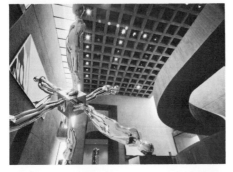

TOP: Ernest Trova: *Six Figures on a Cube* (Everson Museum of Art, Syracuse, New York; photograph by George Leavens; copyright © 1968 by TIME Inc.) BOTTOM: Exterior of Everson Museum of Art, designed by I. M. Pei with cantilevered galleries (photograph by George Leavens; copyright © 1968 by TIME Inc.)

Paintings tend to be American and range from primitive to the current. The heaviest holdings are probably in the early twentieth-century school; Arthur B. Davies, Childe Hassam, William M. Chase, Robert Henri, John Sloan, and a few offbeats such as Louis Eilshemius. Reginald Marsh and Charles Burchfield introduce the contemporary, which is gaining momentum and becoming more international, as the handsome Barbara Hepworth *Curved Form with Inner Form (Anima)* attests. Many of our best print-makers are represented, such as: Pozzatti, Margo, Yunkers, Blaustein, Bishop, Crawford, and Frasconi. The collections, doubled since 1960, are seen for the first time in ensemble in the new building. The Cloud B. Wampler Oriental collection of ceramics, bronzes, and jades is well displayed.

SYRACUSE UNIVERSITY: LOWE ART CENTER

309 University Place, Syracuse, New York
Hours: Mon.–Sat., 9–5; Sun., 2–6; Mon.–Fri., 7–10;
closed national holidays. Free.

The university's main collection is housed in the Lowe Art Center on campus, yet since 1960 the Center has embarked on an ambitious plan of commissioning murals for its various buildings.

Among the artists participating are Jean Charlot, Marion Greenwood, Anton Refregier, Kenneth Callahan, Adja Yunkers,

Robert Goodnough, Fred Conway, John Rooney, and Ben Shahn. Shahn's work is a mosaic based on the famous Sacco-Vanzetti case. A gift to the university of Rico Lebrun's massive moving triptych *The Crucifixion*, which in the library, sparked the project.

The spine of the collection at Lowe is in the American painting, sculpture, and craft field. An exception is the recently acquired John R. Fox collection of Korean ceramics, which range from the Silla through the Yi Dynasties. Another enviable gift is the Cloud Wampler print collection of over six hundred prints ranging from the sixteenth-century Albrecht Altdorfer to the twentieth century. There are complete editions of Boris Margo and Fredrico Castallon's prints. A fine catalogue provides a glossary of print terms.

Many of the paintings reflect the 1930s—Marsh, Curry, McFee, Burchfield—though Motherwell, Pousette-Dart, Knaths, and Gottlieb are also represented. One of the popular paintings is Samuel F. B. Morse's *Gallery of the Louvre*, a 6-foot-high assemblage of paintings within a painting, including the *Mona Lisa*. Morse exhibited it in America, charging a fee, but the monetary results were disappointing. Art's loss was science's gain.

Sculptors Zorach, Duckworth, Lipchitz, Bertoia, Kaish, Chaim Gross and Meštrović, long-time sculptor in residence at Syracuse, are shown in monumental examples.

MUNSON–WILLIAMS–PROCTOR INSTITUTE

310 Genesee Street, Utica, New York
Hours: Tues.–Sat., 10–5; Wed., 10–10; Sun., 2–6;
closed Mon. and holidays. Library. Restaurant.
Free.

Not-so-old-timers will remember the two stately nineteenth-century houses on Genesee Street that comprised the Munson-Williams-Proctor Institute. It all started when the Williams sisters married the Proctor brothers and established homes side by side. With an assist from Munson money (the sisters' mother was a Munson), they started traveling and collecting. The museum, chartered in 1919, opened in 1935 as a community cultural center. Several years ago one house was razed to make way for a new museum. The other, Fountain Elms, separated by a terrace and grove of honey locust, has been restored to its 1850 splendor. Rooms are done in period, and galleries of America's early decorative arts installed, plus memorabilia of the Erie Canal's heyday.

The new museum built in 1960 is an exciting contrast. Its architect, Philip Johnson, raised an austere granite block on concrete piers sheathed in bronze, and set the building into a slope which reveals its full five stories from the back, while the entrance is reached directly from the street over a short bridge of stairs. A skylighted court is visible through the glass façade. The hanging double stairway, audaciously simple, gives an elegantly baroque feeling of space against teakwood walls and travertine floors. Wide balconies, from which the galleries flow, are suffused with natural light, plunging from the glass dome.

The building lends itself to innovations. On the roof a microwave device makes it possible for TV shows to be broadcast from any of the galleries.

The institute collections are primarily of American art, decorative arts from the eighteenth century, and European twentieth-century art. There are also old master prints, Japanese woodcuts, and a collection in process of the ancient, primitive, and archaic cultures. But the emphasis is on today, as even this random selection makes clear. There are major sculptures by Baskin, *Angry Angel;* Duchamp-Villon, *The Horse;* Maillol, *Ile de France;* Lachaise, Marini, Zorach, and by Henry Di Spirito, a Utica bricklayer who became a sensitive and successful sculptor. Calder's *Three Arches,* an enormous stabile that looks like a praying mantis, is installed on the museum grounds. Major paintings are by Picasso, Mondrian, Kandinsky, Klee, Gris, Nicholson, Rouault, Luks, Henri, Stuart Davis, Pollock, O'Keefe, Dove,

Alexander Calder: *Three Arches* (Munson-Williams-Proctor Institute, Utica, New York)

Marsh, Weber, Kuhn, Sheeler, Palmer, Gorky, Stamos, Tomlin, Rothko, Okada, Baziotes, Marca-Relli.

Over the past twenty years the contemporary section gained impetus from Edward Wales Root. His concern with American artists helped build the extraordinary twentieth-century group. From nearby Clinton, where he lived in The Homestead, house of his grandfather, Oren Root, he acted as consultant on purchase. By the time he died in 1956, he had enriched the institute with over two hundred important canvases, plus drawings and prints. Today The Homestead has fittingly become the Edward W. Root Art Center. It is situated in nearby Clinton.

In spite of the play on this century, the collection constitutes a survey of all American art, based, as usual, on Earl, Copley, and Stuart. Four Hudson River school paintings by Thomas Cole are handsomely installed. This *Voyage of Life* series was commissioned for St. Luke's Hospital in New York, where they hung for decades over four radiators, getting darker and darker every year. The museum bought and restored them to their original sumptuous, if muted, colors. They epitomize the period influenced by England's lake poets and our own Nathaniel Hawthorne. Winslow Homer's Virginia visit is summarized in *Upland Cotton*. The institute owns a body of Arthur B. Davies' work. A native of Utica, Davies was president of the revolutionary Armory Show Group (1913) and he also advised Miss Lillie Bliss, a founder of New York's Museum of Modern Art, on the building of her collection. The museum has just acquired a room Davies painted for Miss Bliss's New York house.

ALLENTOWN ART MUSEUM

Fifth and Court Streets, Allentown, Pennsylvania
Hours: Mon.–Sat., 10–5; Sun., 2–5;
closed August, Jan. 1, July 4, Labor Day, Dec. 25.
Free.

Allentown is the only city in the United States that boasts a Kress collection but not a Kress store, a regular stipulation for the gift. Rush Kress made this possible. Returning to his native hearth in the Lehigh Valley (the Kress home was in nearby Cherryville), he promised the city fathers a group of Kress pictures. With this impetus, the art center, which was established in 1939, raised the money to purchase and convert a Presbyterian church to museum use.

Through its Greek-temple façade, one comes directly into a large, flexible, well-lighted gallery for changing exhibitions. What the museum lacks in the way of a permanent collection is made up for by its scholarly program. Whether it's "The Gothic to Baroque World" or "17th-Century Haarlem" or "Sources for Tomorrow," the visitor is bound to encounter a thoughtful, challenging exhibit whose installations are on a par with major museums. Beyond this area, through inviting wide glass doors, is the Kress collection. Two spacious galleries hold the main group, two smaller ones the drawing and print shows. The Kress Northern European paintings are especially fine, with Hans von Kulmback and two portraits by Jan Gossaert (called Mabuse). There's an incisive *Portrait of Anton Flugger* of the famous Augsburg banking clan by Hans Maler. There are Jan Steen, Jacob van Ruisdael, Adrian van Ostade, and Frans Hals' breezy, vibrant *The Young Fisherman*. A sparkling Rembrandt called *Portrait of a Young Woman* in the catalogue has lately been identified as a *Portrait of Saskia*, Rembrandt's young wife. Two other stunning canvases are *Portrait of a Man* and *Portrait of a Woman* by Palus Moreeles. Dressed in their stiff black brocades and lacy white ruffs, this pair traveled to England where one of their owners, eager to acquire such substantial ancestors, had the family's coat of arms painted on the left-hand corner of the canvases. Recently, cleaning removed the newer paint and the escutcheons.

The refreshing policy in twentieth-century collecting is to acquire young and relatively unknown American artists. A few are: John Cannon, Ivan Vial, William S. Becker, Jr., Shozo Nagano, Ed Ruda, Dean Fleming, George Buehr, Laurel Wagner, Robert Nel-

Frans Hals: *The Young Fisherman* (Allentown Art Museum, Allentown, Pennsylvania; Samuel H. Kress Memorial Collection)

son, R. C. Morris, Eileen Pendergast, Bernard Arnest, Michael Gloeckner, and Penelope Naylor.

Whether it's the latest art balloon ascent or "The World of Benjamin West," one can rely on seeing a good show in Allentown. It was William Allen, founder of Allentown, who was Benjamin West's first patron.

THE BARNES FOUNDATION

300 N. Latch's Lane, Merion, Pennsylvania
Hours (Sept.–June): Fri. & Sat., 9:30–4:30;
closed legal holidays, July & Aug.
Visitors limited to 100 a day with reservations, 100 without.
No children under 15.
Admission $1.

Much has been written about the self-made Argyrol King, Dr. Albert C. Barnes. Stories of his taste and testiness are legion. Though he amassed one of the great collections in the world of French nineteenth-century art, he let only those few favored by his whims see it. Museum personnel were anathema to him. Embittered when he moved to suburban Merion only to be ignored by the "Mainliners," he spent much of his time taking pot shots at socialites, especially if they collected art. The real cause for a lifetime of venomous behavior probably stemmed from the public's reaction to the first exhibition of his collection shown at the Philadelphia Academy of Art in 1921. Cézanne and, especially, Matisse with his flat planes and shocking juxtaposition of colors were too much for Philadelphians. Barnes, mingling in the crowd, heard himself categorized as a freak and Matisse a hoax. As for the press, they went down for the count when they looked at Soutine. After that the Barnes door closed. Nevertheless, remembering his own lean school days, Barnes established an art school in conjunction with his gallery and was most generous to the few students he admitted.

It was William Glackens, the painter, a friend of Barnes from grammar school, who introduced him to the world of art. When Barnes had successfully launched Argyrol he packed Glackens off to Europe with $20,000 to spend on paintings. But Barnes was soon self-propelled and became a familiar figure in the galleries of Europe and America.

After the doctor's death in 1951, the doors, though it took a

Cézanne: *Nudes in Land-scape* (The Barnes Founda-tion, Merion, Pennsylvania)

court order, opened ever so slightly. (The Barnes Foundation is tax exempt, and restive Philadelphians decided it was time to share the collection they were helping to pay for.)

The impact on entering the first gallery is terrific; Cézanne's great *Cardplayers, Nudes in a Landscape,* and the unsurpassable *Woman in a Green Hat,* along with twenty Renoirs, hang in a rectangular gallery two stories high. Between tall windows is a three-part mural of wonderfully convoluted dancing nudes by Matisse, who after a great deal of persuasion came to Merion to do them. Twelve smaller galleries fan out on either side. The paintings in almost every gallery are stacked two or three tiers high. Each picture has a small plaque with the artist's name on the frame, but canvases hanging over the doorjambs are for the farsighted only. Period furniture and *objects d'art* have no labels. The doctor's method of arrangement in the galleries was auda-cious. No attempt to place works of art in periods or schools was made. One small room contained Titian, Juan de Flandres, the American Milton Avery, El Greco, a large antique soup ladle, an Italian primitive, and a Pennsylvania Dutch chest. But such was the doctor's eye that no matter what the mixture of style, period, medium, color, the whole thing comes off. Other unlikely companions were Tintoretto, the primitive Horace Pippin, Cour-bet, some New Mexican *santos,* and Soutine. Barnes, with his prophetic eye, is said to have purchased sixty Soutines at $50 each long before the artist's recognition in the art world. One small gallery overflows with African sculpture, an infinite variety of American and European drawings, and a jack for changing a wagon wheel. Another holds a case of Egyptian pots, and Navaho jewelry, over which, assembled in two straight lines, are French and German miniatures from the twentieth to fourteenth centuries. The doctor liked hardware: every gallery has its quota of antique locks, flanges, bolts, knobs, scissors, nutcrackers, andirons, hinges, all so felicitously placed that they weave into the total hanging without distracting. Even two ancient meat saws that crown a group of small Picassos, Klees, Demuths, and Pascins seem to belong. In the big upstairs gallery the Matisses bloom alongside El Greco's *St. Francis and Brother Rufus* and Van Gogh's *The Postman,* purchased with a fraction of the original $20,000 Glackens had been given to spend.

Don't go to see this fabulous lode of 100 Cézannes, 200 Renoirs, 60 Matisses, and staggering Blue and Rose Period Picassos with a preconceived idea of lighting. You may find one small ceiling light bulb in smaller galleries, but that will change in time and, after all, the small Monet I saw was so luminous it would have stood out in a coal bin . . . a solitary figure in a houseboat, floating along the backwaters of a stream, all silvery gray-green and whites and aloneness.

INSTITUTE OF CONTEMPORARY ART

Fine Arts Building, 34th Street at Walnut
University of Pennsylvania, Philadelphia, Pennsylvania
Hours: Daily, 10:30–5:30; Sun., 12–5;
closed summer.
Free.

The aim of the institute is to present, through scholarly but lively exhibitions, the latest national and international trends in art. Five to six exhibitions are held a season. There is no permanent collection.

PENNSYLVANIA ACADEMY OF THE FINE ARTS

Broad and Cherry Streets, Philadelphia, Pennsylvania
Hours: Tues.–Sat., 10–5; Sun. and holidays, 1–5;
closed major holidays and month of August.
Library.
Free.

"When I see my boys bungling in the carving of a hand, I tell them, 'Look at your own hands . . . imitate them and you must be right.'" So instructed William Rush, America's first sculptor and possibly its most skillful composer in wood. With Charles Willson Peale, he was on the teaching staff of the Pennsylvania Academy. Established in 1805 as a combination art academy and museum, it became the first American institution to hold regular public exhibitions. To insure that females would not have to look at nude statues in mixed company, Monday was set aside as "ladies day." Its *American Annual of Painting and Sculpture* goes on year after year, and the romantic old Victorian building comes alive with stringent current art forms. The permanent collection starts with the great names in early American art: John Vanderlyn, Benjamin West, Gilbert Stuart with twenty-four canvases and, of course, the sculpture of Rush and the paintings of Peale, who stated as one aim of the academy: ". . . to unfold, enlighten, and invigorate the talents of our countrymen."

Unfortunately, space is so limited that little of the permanent collection, including some great nineteenth-century work, can be on view except during the months of June and July.

UNIVERSITY OF PENNSYLVANIA: UNIVERSITY MUSEUM

33rd and Spruce Streets, Philadelphia, Pennsylvania
Hours: Tues.–Sat., 10–5; Sun., 1–5;
closed Mon. and holidays.
Restaurant.
Library.
Free.

As no study of mankind can be made without including the arts as well as the artifacts of a civilization, the University Museum of the University of Pennsylvania—while primarily concerned with archeology and ethnology—is so rich in the arts that it demands inclusion in this book of "art museums."

On December 6, 1887, a proposal was put to the trustees of the University of Pennsylvania by a group of public-spirited Philadelphians to send an expedition to Babylon. The gentlemen would finance the endeavor with the stipulation that "all finds which can be exported are to be brought to the city and to become the property of the University of Pennsylvania, provided said University furnish suitable accommodations for the same in a fireproof building." Thus was born the famous University Museum.

As Percy C. Maderia wrote in his excellent book on the history of the museum, *Men in Search of Man,* "The time and the place were right for both scholars and dollars."

The first unit of the present museum was completed in 1899, and high time too, for a note from the board of managers dated 1898 states that cases of objects from Nippur, Etruria, and South America were being delivered faster than they could be unpacked.

Since its beginning the university has sent out over two hundred expeditions. They were the first to excavate in Nubia and have trekked from Thebes, Ur, Memphis, and Crete to the Amazon Basin, Alaska, Peru, the rain forests of Guatemala, Tikal, Piedras Negras.

The collections assemble by areas. On the main floor: North, South, and Middle America. Our own North American Indian culture covers three galleries, from a ritual carved wooden deer mask from a prehistoric site at Key Marco, Florida, to twentieth-century Indian pots. A great mine of gold works from Panama, Ecuador, Peru, Colombia, and Costa Rica glimmers in the central hall. The rotunda holds some of the rare and most beautiful Chinese art in any private museum: huge frescoes from the Moon Hill Monastery, Buddhist sculpture of the Wei and T'ang Dynasties, bas-reliefs unmatched outside China from Emperor T'ang T'ai Tsung's tomb.

The magnificent Egyptian holdings were mainly excavated by the museum, though some of the best prehistoric pieces came from British expeditions that the museum helped finance. The Upper Egyptian gallery has great sculptures: one room is filled with Nubian materials, other galleries with alabaster, faïence, pottery, stone, and bronze sculpture.

The African material, gathered long before the present "discovery" of African art, features fine pieces from the Belgian Congo and West Africa. The Near East spans fifth century B.C. to the Islamic period. The Mediterranean Basin is represented by the arts of Italy, Mycenae, Crete, Cyprus, and Greece. Few corners of the ancient world are not represented in the University Museum. With it and the Philadelphia Museum of Art, which by general agreement concentrates primarily on post-Christian art of the Western world and Oriental art since the year 1000 A.D., Philadelphians are witness to much of man's creative endeavor.

The paperback guide to the collections, with its charts, maps, and histories, is not only instructive but engrossing.

CARNEGIE INSTITUTE: MUSEUM OF ART

4400 Forbes Avenue, Pittsburgh, Pennsylvania
Hours: Mon.–Sat., 10–5; Tues., 10–10 in winter; Sun., 2–5.
Library with own entrance.
Restaurant.
Free.

The Carnegie International Triennial causes such a stir one forgets that this is a museum of art, with a representative section of European painting, including a recent gift of twenty-six old masters plus other bequests of Goya, Hals, Monet, Matisse, Degas, Renoir, Gauguin, and Bonnard. A small jewel box of a room displays a few decorative art objects at all times—perhaps a sumptuous Renaissance reliquary, a Byzantine textile, a Chinese ivory.

Despite these legacies it is the great International Triennial painting and sculpture exhibition that gives the Carnegie world stature. At a time when every other art-minded American millionaire was plunging in old masters, Andrew Carnegie told the trustees of the museum he founded in 1896, "The field for which the gallery is designed begins in 1896." And with surprising catholicity he said, "Let us hope that the pictures exhibited here . . . will be of all schools." That same year the first International was held.

As a man so astute he bobbed up from a $1.25-a-week job as bobbin boy in a cotton mill to a $175,000,000 fortune, he was clearly venturesome, and far more daring than many subsequent Pittsburghers. As recently as 1939, when the museum purchased Rouault's powerful *The Old King*, the *Sun-Telegraph* compared it unfavorably to the work of a twelve-year-old.

The Carnegie International reflects the taste of its director. But in the matter of purchases from the International, he is subject to the approval of his board. However, an occupational trait of a good director is wiliness. What he cannot get by direct approach he manages through channels. Some gold-medal winners, turned down by the Carnegie board, have found their way through private gifts into the collection. In spite of passing up some master painters such as Manet and Sisley in 1896, Renoir in 1897, Matisse in 1921, the first recognition our own Thomas Eakins won was at the 1907 show, and the German Expressionists were represented extensively and early.

Winslow Homer's *The Wreck* was the first purchase for the permanent collection, and Whistler's *Sarasate*, his first picture to be acquired by an American museum. Another extraordinary canvas is Oskar Kokoschka's *Thomas Masaryk*, a telling portrait as well as a historical document of special interest to Pittsburgh. Visiting there in 1918, Masaryk signed the pact prerequisite to the proclamation of the Czechoslovakian Republic. Behind Masaryk lies Prague, St. Vitus' Cathedral, and to the left the shadowy figure of John Amos Comenius, seventeenth-century editor whose political writings were the foundation stone of Masaryk's ideology.

David Blythe, self-taught genre painter, produced witty and satiric work in and around Pittsburgh, that has stood the test of time, as did John Kane, miner, carpenter, house painter, and a true primitive.

Pissarro's *Great Bridge at Rouen,* Jean Bazaine's *Dawn,* Alfred Manessier's *Crown of Thorns,* Ensor's *Temptation of St. Anthony* are all outstanding in the European field, while American gold medalists have included Alfred Maurer, Abbott Thayer, Ernest Lawson, Arthur B. Davies, Leon Kroll, George Bellows, Franklin Watkins, Alexander Brook, and Peter Blume. The contemporary collection grows on with Ubac, a Belgian; Alan Davie, a Britisher; Asger Jorn of Denmark; Soulages of France; Saura, a Spaniard; the Germans Jan Müller and Nolde; and the Americans Kline, Diebenkorn, Yunkers, Arp, Penalba, and David Smith. Since 1961, 150 important paintings from the fifteenth to the twentieth century have come to the museum. Highlights are: Perugino, Hals, Tintoretto and forty works by Monet, Renoir, Matisse, Cézanne, Pissarro, Gauguin, and others.

Andrew Carnegie's gift to the city of Pittsburgh is a four-headed French Renaissance monster of a building which houses the library, music hall, natural history museum, and art institute.

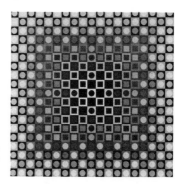

Victor de Vasarely: *Alom* (1966) (Museum of Art, Carnegie Institute, Pittsburgh; shown at Carnegie International, 1967)

Marisol: *Sun Bathers* (1967) (Museum of Art, Carnegie Institute, Pittsburgh; shown at Carnegie International, 1967)

However, the upstairs galleries have been delivered from their original overornamentation and form spacious, light, and flexible backgrounds for painting and sculpture.

The Internationals of recent years have been challenging. If the cherubic face of Andrew Carnegie is peeking around a pink cloud, he will see that the present regime is not going to be caught short, as were the custodians at the turn of the century when the Fauvist and the Cubist treasures went begging.

CORCORAN GALLERY OF ART

17th Street at New York Avenue N.W., Washington, D.C.
Hours: Tues.–Fri., 10–4:30; Sat., 9–4:30; Sun. & holidays, 2–5;
closed Jan. 1, July 4, Thanksgiving, Dec. 25.
Free.

William Wilson Corcoran, founder of this gallery, was born in 1798, reached maturity before Gilbert Stuart and Charles Willson Peale died, and outlived Sully and Neagle. As a banker he was famous for having taken up the entire loan called by the U.S. government during the Mexican War of 1847–1848. As a collector he believed in the native art of his time, and in 1859 started a museum. Before the museum could open, artists put down brushes for Civil War muskets, and the Quartermaster Corps took over the building.

Corcoran did not get his building back until 1869, and the museum opened in 1871 with a gala ball attended by President and Mrs. Grant. "The halls were hung with garlands and cages of singing canaries," reported the Washington *Daily Patriot.*

Post-bellum rejoicing gave way to serious business, and Corcoran, whether from prescience or faith, began buying American paintings again. One of his few excursions into alien fields was when, through William Walters of Baltimore, he acquired a cast of every known sculpture by the Frenchman Barye.

The collection spilled, three years after Corcoran's death, into its present building (the old one two blocks away will become a museum of contemporary American crafts). There are some dozen pre-Revolutionary canvases. The earliest by a known artist is *Peter Faneuil* by John Smibert. Copley's *Jacob Fowle* is in the painter's direct American style before he moved to London. The Hudson River school, following the tradition of romantic painting long established in Europe, became the vogue early in the nineteenth century, and Corcoran collected its painters, chiefly Thomas Cole.

One of the most popular paintings in the museum is Samuel F. B. Morse's *The Old House of Representatives.* A drawing hangs beside the painting and serves as a key to the eighty-six portraits in the glowing, complex composition. Hiram Powers' *The Greek Slave* nostalgically reminds one of the museum's beginnings; the piece (one of six copies) was in Corcoran's home. One of the few nudes Victorian America took to its heart and hearth, it was approved by a committee of Cincinnati clergymen. Small replicas, under glass bells, were requisite for the well-dressed drawing room, and even Henry James was moved to write that the statue was "so undressed, yet so refined."

The Corcoran is a unique bank of America's past in paintings of the events and people which shaped her. Here are portraits of Presidents by Gilbert Stuart and George Healy, and a vital likeness of *Benjamin Franklin* by Joseph Wright; also one of the great documents of the Western saga painted by Albert Bierstadt, who left the Hudson Valley to set down the drama enacted on the Western plains as the Indian killed the buffalo and the white man killed the Indian. *The Last of the Buffalo* is a moving report.

The painters who bridge the nineteenth and twentieth centuries are Winslow Homer and his strong *A Light on the Sea;* Eakins, represented by *The Pathetic Song;* John Sloan with *Yeats at Petitpas;* Marsden Hartley with *Berlin Abstractions;* and George Bellows with his appealing *Forty-two Kids.* Mary Cassatt's *Woman with a Dog* was painted in Paris while she was working with the French Impressionists.

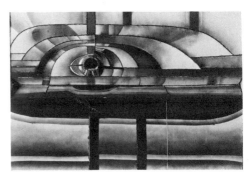

LEFT: Hiram Powers: *The Greek Slave* (Collection of The Corcoran Gallery of Art, Washington, D.C.) **ABOVE:** Lee Bontecou: *Untitled* (57) (Collection of the Corcoran Gallery of Art, Washington, D.C.)

In 1928 a new wing was opened to house a bequest by the Senator from Montana, William A. Clark. Among its treasures: a large group of Corots and Monticellis and some fine Degas sketches. The stamp of the Corcoran is, nevertheless, indelibly American, continuing its founder's original intention to the present day. American drawings range from Copley to Calder. The ever-expanding contemporary section includes MacIver, Lebrun, Anuszkiewicz, Bontecou, Jimmy Ernest, Diller, Stephen Greene, Olitski, and Gene Davis. The Corcoran's Biennial Exhibition is one of the oldest and one of the most important surveys of contemporary American painting.

CORCORAN GALLERY, DUPONT CIRCLE

1503 21st Street, N.W., Washington, D.C.
Hours: Tues. 10–5; Wed.–Fri. 10–10; Sat. & Sun. 11–5

Formerly the Washington Gallery of Modern Art, this institution has recently merged with The Corcoran Gallery of Art, and its lively exhibitions—usually experimental in character—add another dimension to the already impressive Washington art scene. In various visual forms and happenings, the *now* is emphasized, both artistically and sociologically, for it is one of the Corcoran-at-

Dupont-Circle's aims to involve the people of the surrounding area in creative work. Thus, some of the institution's exhibits will move into nearby storefronts in the hope that the neighborhood as a whole will actively participate in the excitement of the gallery's multi-faceted programs.

DUMBARTON OAKS COLLECTION

1703 32nd Street N.W., Washington, D.C.
Hours: Tues.–Sun., 2–5 P.M. Gardens daily, 2–5;
closed holidays, and July through Labor Day.
Library.
Free.

The prim Georgetown brick entrance of Dumbarton Oaks gives no hint of the staggering treasures it holds. The collection was formed through a lifetime of searching by Mr. and Mrs. Robert Woods Bliss and given in 1940 with the library, house, and gardens to Harvard University. Dumbarton Oaks is administered by the trustees of the university.

The body of the collection represents the full play of the Byzantine Empire (fourth–fifteenth centuries) and the lands adjacent to it. The foundations of Byzantium are stressed by the inclusion of the arts of classical Greece and Rome. In fact, all nations that encroached on this dominant culture are represented.

The scale is generally intimate—manuscripts, wares, jewels,

The Riha Paten (Constantinople, 565–578 A.D.) (The Dumbarton Oaks Collection, Washington, D.C.)

liturgical appurtenances, enamels, painting, and textiles. Each piece is of the highest quality. As one art critic succinctly put it: "There are no shards here."

Another facet of the Bliss collecting which the public was generally unaware of was pre-Columbian art. Though Mr. Bliss purchased a handsome Olmec sculpture in 1912 and added occasionally through the years, the main body of the collection was assembled between 1940 and 1950. Before Mr. Bliss's death in 1962, the collection was given to Dumbarton Oaks, with Philip Johnson designing a setting for it. The building which flows from the Dumbarton proper is a rich, imaginative, small wonderland. A series of glass drums forming small galleries look outward to the woodland and inward to a simple center fountain—a single cascade of water falling to a slate-edged floor. The inner pillars are of agate marble, the floors a patterned teakwood bound by green Vermont marble. Lucite drums or pedestals give even such solid objects as a limestone mask (Teotihuacan, 300–600 B.C.) a look of suspension in air. Objects are arranged according to cultures, primarily that of Meso-America, the best known of which are the Aztec, Totonac, Zapotec, Mixtec, and Mayan—the Andean area comprising parts of Ecuador, Peru, and Bolivia.

The Music Room, a handsome section in the original house, contains an El Greco, *The Visitation;* a late Gothic *Madonna* by the German sculptor Tilman Riemenschneider; Flemish tapestries; Italian and Spanish furniture from the sixteenth and seventeenth centuries. In this room in 1944 were held the important political conversations that led to the establishment of the United Nations the following year.

FREER GALLERY OF ART OF THE SMITHSONIAN INSTITUTION

Jefferson Drive at 12th Street S.W., Washington, D.C.
Hours: Daily, 9–4:30;
closed Dec. 25.
Library.
Free.

No visitor to Washington should miss the Freer Gallery. Its simple—at least in Renaissance terms—building houses one of the great Oriental collections of the world, as well as a large body of the work of the American artist James McNeill Whistler, and his contemporaries.

The donor, Charles Lang Freer, spent a considerable part of his adult life studying, traveling, and collecting the arts of the Near and Far East. Resigning from the Peninsular Railroad Car Works at forty-four, he dedicated himself to building and refining his collection. He was aided by Ernest Fenollosa, a great Orientalist, professor at both Harvard and the University of Tokyo. The Oriental section includes works of art from the Far East—China, Japan, Tibet, Korea; from Indo-China and India; from the Near East—Iran, Iraq, Asia Minor, Byzantium, and Egypt. Every facet is included, sculpture, painting, ceramics, metalwork, lacquer, glass, bronze, and jade. Outstanding Christian manuscripts are fourth- and fifth-century Gospels according to the Evangelists and third-century Greek (Egypt) papyrus manuscripts of the Minor Prophets.

Freer's inclusion of his friend Whistler's work is not incongruous, as Whistler, who was deeply involved with the arts of the Orient, played an important role in forming Freer's taste. The whole span of Whistler's work—oil paintings, watercolors, drawings, etchings, and lithographs—is covered here by over a thousand objects. The famous "Peacock Room," done for the London house of shipowner F. R. Leyland, is installed at the Freer. The room became a *cause célèbre,* and the stories of Whistler's difficulties with Leyland are legend. The sales desk at the museum supplies a booklet on the subject that is more compelling than a "who-done-it." Whistler's painting, a portrait known as *Rose and Silver; the Princess from the Land of Porcelain,* hangs in the room. In fact, it was for the setting for this portrait that Whistler was commissioned to alter the room slightly. His audacity led to fights, lawsuits, and the mental derangement of the man who had first done the room for Leyland. Mrs. Gardner, when she was

Kuang (Chinese, Shang dynasty) (Freer Gallery of Art, Washington, D.C.)

building Boston's Fenway Court, asked her friend Sargent to try to buy the room for her but it had already passed into Freer's hands.

Only a part of the collections can be on view at any one time, but objects in storage may be seen by appointment.

JOSEPH H. HIRSHHORN MUSEUM

The Mall, Washington, D.C.
To open 1971

Everything that architect Gordon Bunshaft of Skidmore, Owings and Merrill does is touched with elegance, and the cylindrical marble museum which opens on Washington's Mall in 1971 will surely be no exception. The building, windowless from the outside except for a large opening looking into a sunken sculpture garden, rests on four supports that reach out like Gothic arches. The glass interior of the circle encloses yet another circle of foliage and sculpture. Garden-level galleries are slated for changing exhibitions, the first and second floors for the permanent collections. An auditorium, library, and restaurant are also on the agenda.

The collection, which has lived a great deal of its life in warehouses awaiting this exposure, is mainly American contemporary. Paintings, however, start in mid-nineteenth century and include Europeans of the stature of De Staël, Bacon, and Dubuffet. Sculpture, for which Mr. Hirshhorn has a passionate affinity, starts with antiquities—the Hittites, Etruscans, archaic Greeks—but goes into depth from the mid-nineteenth century to today. Presumably the monumental works now resting on the windswept hilltop of the Hirshhorn Connecticut demesne will come to the Mall.

At the age of six, the begetter of this, one of the world's largest private collections, emigrated in 1905 from Latvia with his impoverished family. Self-supporting from the age of twelve, Hirshhorn used $225 in savings to establish himself at seventeen as a curb broker. He made $168,000 the first year. But it was a plunge in the forties and fifties in uranium mining that rocketed his fortune.

Collecting has obsessed him since the early thirties. His art-buying methods, like his business transactions, are quick and to the point, and woe to the dealer who tries to influence him. His mistakes and triumphs are his own.

The collection was given to the U.S. government in 1966 with the proviso that the Joseph H. Hirshhorn Museum be established. Although it enters the growing family of the Smithsonian Institution, the museum will operate with the same autonomy as the Freer and the National Gallery.

MUSEUM OF AFRICAN ART

316 A Street N.E., Washington, D.C.
Hours: Mon.–Thurs., 11–5:30; Sat.–Sun., 2–5:30;
closed Fri. and holidays.
Free.

The story of this new museum (1964) is necessarily and fittingly related to the heartening American success story of Frederick Douglass. Born a Negro slave in Maryland, Douglass, through personality, integrity, and intellect, became an advisor to Lincoln and was appointed to high office in the administration of five Presidents—Grant through Cleveland. He served as Marshal and Recorder of Deeds in the District of Columbia and as the first U.S. Minister to Haiti.

The typical Victorian brick townhouse that the museum occupies was Douglass' home. The other half of this double dwelling was occupied by his son. It is the museum's hope to incorporate it with the present structure. A walled garden in the rear creates a harmonious exhibition space for sturdy little tribal figures or an elegantly carved house post from Nigeria.

The brain child of Warren Robbins, former State Department

Fertility doll (Ghana, Ashanti) (Museum of African Art, Washington, D.C.)

and USIA cultural attaché, the museum takes in both traditional and contemporary Africa and seeks to show the great influence African sculpture has had on the development of twentieth-century Western art. While it is the hope to have representation from every country in Africa, the concentration will be mainly in the west and central region. Present holdings speak for eighteen countries and thirty-five tribes. Soon, a gallery will be devoted to the work of gifted American Negroes. Embellishing the excellent small permanent collection are indefinite loans from some of America's leading aficionados of African art. Adjacent is the Frederick Douglass Institute for Inter-Cultural Understanding, its mission to demonstrate the social meaning of art.

NATIONAL COLLECTION OF FINE ARTS

Smithsonian Institution,
8th Street between F and G Streets, Washington, D.C.
Hours: 9–4:30 daily; April–Aug., 9–10 P.M.;
closed Dec. 25.
Library, tea room.
Free.

To most Americans the Smithsonian is a huge octopus whose tentacles reach all about The Mall in Washington and whose innards are dressed in inaugural ball gowns and envigorated by Lindbergh's *Spirit of St. Louis.* If they think of the place in terms of "fine arts" at all, it's in terms of cowboys and Indians. And why not? The Smithsonian's National Collection of Fine Arts owns 445 paintings by George Catlin alone, a stupendous, staccato record of Indian tribes of the Great Plains and the far northwest. Long housed in a crack of space between totem poles and stuffed elephants at the Museum of Natural History, the collection has at last been moved into a home of its own. The old Patent Office building, remodeled neoclassic, provides the new address.

English scientist James Smithson, piqued at being denied a hereditary title because he was the illegitimate son of the first Duke of Northumberland, willed his fortune to a country he had never seen, the United States. An ungracious Congress quibbled. Senator John C. Calhoun declared it, in 1835, "beneath the dignity of the United States to receive presents of this kind from anyone." Only after three years of senatorial wrangling did a clipper ship bearing 105 bags of English gold sovereigns sail into port. Cast into American coins, they produced $508,316.46—a fine sum, indeed, in those days. Smithson's desire was that an institution be formed for the increase and diffusion of knowledge. Congress established that institution in 1846 to, among its aims, collect and show works of art.

The collection gained impetus in 1906 through an important bequest by Harriet Lane Johnston, niece of President James Buchanan.

A New York merchant, William T. Evans, donated a long and impressive list of American paintings, among them Winslow Homer's *High Cliff, Coast of Maine,* painted in 1894 and sold to Evans in 1903. Homer had complained to his dealer: "Why do you not sell that *High Cliff* picture? I cannot do better than that. Why should I paint?"

In 1929 a colorful New Yorker, John Gellatly, donated 1,640 objects, from Egyptian mummy masks to European and American paintings, among them: seventeen canvases by Albert P. Ryder, including *Jonah and the Flying Dutchman,* plus twelve by John Twachtman, fifteen by Childe Hassam, twenty-three by Abbott Thayer.

In 1938 Congress passed a bill for the National Collection of Fine Arts (its official name since Andrew Mellon's National Gallery of Art made off with its original name) to be housed in its own building. War and other priorities postponed the realization until now. Americans finally have a national museum whose main concern is. to collect and exhibit the arts connected with America's heritage. But its activities go far beyond being a showcase. Its lending service places hundreds of works of art in government buildings, the White House included. A traveling exhibition service will include "artmobiles," an archive and study center, a conservation department for all art belonging to the government.

The past status of American art here, or lack of it, had not exactly encouraged collectors to deposit their treasures in its indifferent arms. However with the 1968 opening of the noble space within the Patent Office walls, the collections, seen in proper perspective, prove to be far richer than one suspected.

The first painting acquired is a portrait of Washington's biographer François P. G. Guizot by the painter George P. A. Healy. Another oldster who shared the collection's nomadic existence is a monumental marble, *Dying Tecumseh.* A British Brigadier General in the war of 1812 commissioned a popular German-American sculptor Ferdinand Pettrich to do the famous

Stuart Davis: *International Surface No. 1* (1960) (Courtesy of The National Collection of Fine Arts, Smithsonian Institution, Washington, D.C.)

Shawnee Indian chief. The estate of the nineteenth-century American sculptor Hiram Powers, as left complete in his Florence studio, has come to the Smithsonian.

No longer cautious, the museum plans to present all important contemporary trends. The S. C. Johnson and Sons (Johnson's wax) collection of 102 current paintings assembled by dealer Lee Nordness have come to the NCFA. Containing many works by well known artists the beauty of the gift still lies in its flexibility. Any painting can be exchanged at any time for a better example of the artist's work.

The two block building was completed in sections, the F Street part in 1842, the East Wing in 1853, the West in 1864. Meanwhile, its wide corridors were used as a military hospital, and for a while the first Rhode Island Militia was quartered in its halls. The last link around a large central courtyard, the North Wing, was added after the Civil War. Although the interior is Greek Revival, arched and vaulted, clever reconstruction has made some galleries appear intimate, others grandiose. One 6,000 square foot room had been a warren of small offices, its granite piers and gracefully arched ceiling hidden. Today, the unsheathed piers form handsome backgrounds for sculpture. The ballroom where Lincoln danced at his second inauguration has had its marble columns scrubbed of coats of government-green paint. The Lincoln gallery runs from G Street to F Street with a survey of American art from the Colonials into the turn of this century. While the Colonial and late eighteenth century period is rather sparingly represented, it is hoped that now that our National Collection of Fine Arts has been given a home in an historic building in our Nation's capital, art minded citizens will come to the aid of their country and fill the gaps.

The library, a vast room of tiered balconies that formerly displayed new inventions, has been left a fetching Victorian oddity made more fetching by the latest library devices and lighting.

NATIONAL PORTRAIT GALLERY,
SMITHSONIAN INSTITUTION

F Street at 8th, Washington, D.C.
Hours: 9–4:30 daily;
closed Christmas.
Library.
Tea room.
Free.

"Aaron Burr would be just as welcome as Alexander Hamilton or John Wilkes Booth as Abraham Lincoln. For though the contribution of these men, who were more than common assassins, was far from constructive no one can doubt that the direction of the country's history was changed by what they did." So stated Charles Nagel, first director of the new National Portrait Gallery. Gathered together here for the first time in our history are likenesses of the great, the near-great, and the infamous; men and women whose lives and deeds have shaped our country.

Situated in the old Patent Office building, the gallery shares space with and is under the same protective arm of the Smithsonian Institution as the National Collection of Fine Arts. Its portrait concern encompasses all media: painting, sculpture, drawing, prints, daguerreotypes, miniatures, bas-reliefs. Even that latest form, the photograph, will have its place. Small as yet (about three hundred examples), the collection harbors prizes. The earliest likeness, one of Pocohontas, done in 1616 by an unknown painter, shows our Indian maid with an Elizabethan lace ruff around her sweet, inscrutable face. Another fine canvas is one by John Elliott of Julia Ward Howe, the indomitable abolitionist and composer of the stirring "Battle Hymn of the Repub-

John Singleton Copley: *Henry Laurens* (1782) (National Portrait Gallery, Smithsonian Institution, Washington, D.C.)

lic." When Lincoln was introduced to Mrs. Howe, he is said to have remarked, "So you're the little lady who started the big war."

The gallery is hampered by the fact that starting at this late date it has missed many fine historical portraits that long ago found their way into museums, private collections, and state-houses throughout the land. However, a nucleus of 350 paintings and 15 sculptures, including Gilbert Stuarts and a Copley, is not bad, and it is to be hoped that treasures that rightfully belong in a National Portrait Gallery will now find their way to Washington.

PHILLIPS COLLECTION

1600–1612 21st Street, N.W., Washington, D.C.
Hours: Mon., 11–10 P.M.; Tues.–Sat., 11–6; Sun., 2–7;
closed July 4, Labor Day, Dec. 25.
Free.

The Phillips Collection is distinctly personal. Even in his under-graduate days at Yale, Duncan Phillips' interest in art ran parallel to his interest in literature. Later he and his wife, painter Mar-jorie Phillips, decided to form a collection in this rambling, pleas-ant house where he grew up. It was incorporated as a museum in 1918, though the Phillipses continued to live there until 1930, when their avidity as collectors finally forced them to seek an-other home. Though stressing the contemporary, the collection goes back to El Greco and some of the roots of modern art.

Mr. Phillips has stated his aim succinctly and lucidly: "It is the collection's diversity and its unity as a personal creation which gives to our institution the special character that makes it some-thing of a novelty among the public galleries of the world . . . ours is an unorthodox gallery with a way of its own in not segre-gating periods and nationalities, the better to show the univer-sality of art and the continuities of such ancient seeing habits as realism, expressionism and abstraction."

The new wing of nine galleries has been brought into harmony with the spacious old house. The same "invitation to linger" pervades. For a first visit it is perhaps better to enter through the new wing at 1612 21st Street. Seymour Lipton's *Ancestor* guards the stairwell and a gallery of smashing Braques sets the key for the museum, whose resolute aim is to show only works of the highest quality. A Maurice Prendergast may hang between a

Berthe Morisot and an early Picasso, on the assumption that certain paintings have a natural affinity which is not necessarily intellectual. Two that challenge the imagination are El Greco's and Goya's interpretations of the same theme, *The Repentant Peter*. They adhere precisely to the subject yet differ utterly in spiritual content. The *Peter* of Goya is an earthy peasant overcome by the enormity of his betrayal, beseeching forgiveness. The *Peter* of El Greco, expressively sorrowful, is already forgiven and lifted into a mystical union with God.

Another fascinating pair, this time by the same artist, Van Gogh, are the *Entrance to the Public Gardens, Arles*, where trees are softly swirling brush strokes, and *Street Pavers*, whose trees literally writhe their way through the pavement, seeming to be made of sinew rather than wood.

Standing before Thomas Eakins' portrait of the tired, introspective *Miss Van Buren*, one is puzzled that it took this American painter so long to be recognized. Renoir's glowing *Luncheon of the Boating Party* is surely the greatest Renoir in America. The delectable young woman with the poodle in the left foreground became Mrs. Renoir shortly after the picture was painted.

But to isolate paintings in the Phillips Gallery is to court frustration. Duncan Phillips acquired anywhere from five to twenty examples of the work of many artists and his collection of Bonnards is the largest in this country, the first bought thirty-five years ago before Bonnard was well known here. Some of the Americans represented voluminously are Hartley, Gatch, Burchfield, Knaths. The aggregation of Arthur G. Dove is truly enviable. Mark Rothko has a small gallery all to himself. De Kooning, Joan Mitchell, Pollock, Guston, Sam Francis are represented. Recent acquisitions include Loren MacIvor, Morris Louis,

LEFT: Thomas Eakins: *Miss Van Buren* (ca. 1889–1891) (The Phillips Collection, Washington, D.C.) **RIGHT:** Renoir: *Luncheon of the Boating Party* (1881) (The Phillips Collection, Washington, D.C.)

Georges Braque: *The Philodendron* (1952)
(The Phillips Collection, Washington, D.C.)

Mathieu, Ken Noland, Adolph Gottlieb, Jack Tworkov, and several more Karl Knaths.

It is a temptation to go on about the Soutines, Klees, Rouaults, about Weber, Marin, and Matisse, about André Derain's *Summer Day*, evoking memories of southern France and almond trees in bloom. In fact, it is a temptation just to stay in the Phillips. Music is almost as much a part of the gallery life as is painting. Every week, except in summer, there are concerts, and many a young composer has had his first hearing in the gallery. A program of activities is available at the desk.

SOUTHEASTERN ART MUSEUMS

BIRMINGHAM MUSEUM OF ART

Eighth Avenue & 20th Street, N. Birmingham, Alabama
Hours: Mon.–Sat., 10–5; Thurs. 10–9; Sun., 2–6.
Free.

Art in Birmingham, on the move since 1908, finally came to rest in 1959 in a handsome home, the Oscar Wells Memorial Building. The museum, small but imposing in Italian travertine and dark green Vermont marble, incorporates engaging technical devices: a television system that permits live broadcasts, zoned temperature controls, closed loading docks, and the latest lighting ploys in the fifteen galleries that fan out from a two-storied court. When the Birmingham Art Association was formed in 1908, exhibits were hung wherever sympathy and space were available —mostly in stores. Later, the library housed them, then the new City Hall, where in 1951 the venture received an official kiss and the name "Birmingham Museum of Art."

In the fifteen years since it has been gathering a permanent collection, the emphasis has been placed on a general art museum concept. The Kress collection encompasses all major schools of Italian painting from the thirteenth to late eighteenth centuries. One of the treasures is *Madonna and Child* attributed to Lorenzo Veneziano, a fourteenth-century Venetian painter. Another Kress gift is a large panel by an unknown Flemish artist depicting *The Battle of Pavia* (1525), where the French were defeated and Francis I captured. There are Flemish, Dutch, and German old masters. A unique group of Palestinian artifacts and sculpture stretches from paleolithic prints to Byzantine pottery. The Far East section holds ancient Japanese and Chinese pottery as well as modern ceramics and textiles. Pre-Columbian art includes outstanding examples of Chimú gold. Artifacts of American Indian

The Battle of Pavia (Flemish, ca. 1525) (Birmingham Museum of Art, Birmingham, Alabama; Samuel H. Kress Collection)

culture include fine material of the Northwest Coast and Plains. The decorative arts section quarters British silver, French and German ceramics, and an almost complete sampler of Sandwich glass goblets. In the contemporary painting department artists of the Southwest region mingle with other American and foreign artists.

The pattern of burgeoning industrial cities sprouting cultural centers is being repeated in Birmingham. The museum is a part of a tremendous, ambitious plan for expanding the center. Two new galleries have already been added and more are in blueprint.

UNIVERSITY OF MIAMI:
JOE AND EMILY LOWE GALLERY

3301 Miller Road, Coral Gables, Florida
Hours: Tues.–Sat., 10–5; Sun., 2–5;
closed holidays.
Free.

The Lowe Gallery not only serves a large student body but the whole Greater Miami community. The simple, pleasant 1952 building is at the edge of the campus, easily accessible from U.S. 1. Since the collections have outdistanced the space, plans are afoot for a complex of similar structures to circle the present one. An adjoining high tower will hold the art school.

Dr. Virgil Barker, revered historian of American art and author of *American Painting: History and Interpretation,* was the gallery's first director—this accounts for the distinguished and catholic group of American paintings, primitive through contemporary. Other strong points: the Kress collection of European old masters, the Alfred Barton collection of American Indian artifacts (including a renowned group of Southwest Indian textiles), and choice Oriental objects, T'ang through Ming Dynasties. The two Kress galleries are always on view. Among the jewels: *Madonna and Child with Donor* by Adriaen Isenbrandt; *Portrait of a Man,* Giovanni Bellini; and a small charmer by Francesco Guardi, that oft-painted church *Santa Maria Della Salute,* in Venice.

Right now, space prevents the primitive, classical, and Asiatic holdings from being on permanent display. But these and art from outside sources appear in changing exhibitions in the large central gallery. One wall of the lecture hall is taken up by Washington Allston's *Jason Returning to Claim the Throne.* Rolled up since 1807 when Allston worked on it in Rome, it is an unfinished work, interesting primarily in showing how that master of the grand scene built up his canvases. He used the square patch in the lower right-hand corner as his palette. When the additions are finished and the permanent material permanently installed, the museum will become an even more important center in this important area.

Adriaen Isenbrandt: *Madonna and Child* (Joe and Emily Lowe Art Gallery, University of Miami, Coral Gables, Florida; Kress Collection)

CUMMER GALLERY OF ART

829 Riverside Avenue, Jacksonville, Florida
Hours: Tues.–Sat., 10–5; Sun., 2–5;
closed major holidays.
Library.
Free.

The inviting entrance foyer here, a fetching meld of marble and polished wood, looks directly through a loggia to the St. John's River beyond. The gardens once graced the old Cummer mansion, on whose site the museum went up in 1961, a simple symmetrical building whose galleries flow around three sides of the central loggia. The art ranges through painting from the fifteenth to twentieth centuries, sculpture, tapestries, furniture, and *objets d'art*. Seek out *Avarice*, a penetrating canvas by Paulus Bor, a little-known master, a Rembrandt follower; three remarkable portraits by unknown Elizabethans who obviously clung to the pattern set by Holbein at the Court of Henry VIII; a sixteenth-century Spanish writing desk-chest, embellished with Limoges enamels depicting the life of the Virgin. Some portraitists are Gilbert Stuart, Benjamin West, John Neagle, John Hoppner, Sir Henry Raeburn. The nineteenth-century American group has a small but choice Thomas Cole and a dreamy little Martin Heade, *St. John's River*, the same river that laps along the museum's gardens.

No knowing pilgrim leaves the Cummer Gallery without seeing the Wark collection of Meissen china, the largest group of Meissen tableware in the country and one of the great collec-

Paulus Bor: *Avarice* (Cummer Gallery of Art, Jacksonville, Florida: photograph by Charles Smith Studio, Jacksonville)

tions of the world. Mr. and Miss Wark assembled not only this earliest of European china, but the first pieces done by its innovator, Johann Friedrich Böttger, the man who discovered the Chinese secret of true porcelain. These unsophisticated early pieces of red sandstone date from 1708 to 1710, the year Böttger produced his first white porcelain. Many exquisite and well-documented examples come from celebrated collections—from the Japanese Imperial Palace, from Elizabeth of Russia's collection in the Hermitage, from Marie, Queen of Hanover. They captivate both aesthetes and students alike.

JACKSONVILLE ART MUSEUM

4160 Boulevard Center Drive, Jacksonville, Florida
Hours: Mon.–Fri., 9–5; Sat.–Sun., 2–5.
Library.
Free.

Set in a cypress grove, this 6-acre haven for artists and art students and art watchers is now primarily a teaching institution. Painting, ceramics, sculpture, photography, and print-making studios join a cinema room, a gallery for changing exhibitions, a members' lounge, and a library in the new studio building. In time such amenities are proposed as rental studios, artist–in–residence houses, an art library building for the permanent collection, and a tea house, all rural and serene in planning. Off a large garden court with sculpture pool, landscaped paths with sketch platforms will finger through the cypresses.

SOCIETY OF THE FOUR ARTS

Four Arts Plaza, Palm Beach, Florida
Hours: Mon.–Sat., 10–5; Sun., 2–5.
Open Dec.–mid Apr.
Free.

As it has no permanent collection, the Four Arts does not fall into the pattern of this book. However, distinguished exhibitions are held in its sumptuous galleries through the winter months. The annual American painting show usually stresses the Southern seaboard states. A large auditorium is used for an active program of music, the dance, films, and lectures on art and other topics.

MUSEUM OF FINE ARTS

225 Beach Drive N., St. Petersburg, Florida
Hours: Tues.–Sat., 10–5; Thurs., 10–9; Sun., 1–5;
closed Christmas.
Library.
Free.

A newcomer to the art scene, this sprightly museum opened in 1965. The curving entrance façade is classical in design, while the rear of the building, overlooking Tampa Bay, with its tiled courtyard and lush planting can only be described as Florida Mediterranean. Though the collection is understandably modest, there are good beginnings in early Chinese sculpture, European prints from the seventeenth to nineteenth centuries, and English silver. American paintings include an impressive Frederick Church, *Falls near Tequendama*; an engaging landscape by John H. Twachtman; and one of Thomas Moran's Florida series, *St. John's River*. The entrance hall, 24 feet of dark marble height, is elegantly embellished by enormous carved and gilt twin mirrors from Blenheim Castle. A century ago one of the Dukes of Marlborough, more interested in agriculture than art, sold these handsome pier glasses to raise money for his agrarian needs. Blenheim Castle now has copies of the mirrors.

Three of the museum's nine galleries are period rooms, Jacobean, Georgian, and French Provincial. One tranquil gallery, a reflecting pool in the midst of the museum's busy life, forms a setting for specimens of Indian, Southeast Asian, and Chinese art,

Vishnu the Preserver, detail (Bengal, India; twelfth century) (Museum of Fine Arts, St. Petersburg, Florida)

including a full-standing limestone figure of a T'ang Dynasty bodhisattva and an immense, elaborately carved wood household shrine from the west of India.

St. Petersburg, a favorite spot for retirement, offers built-in advantages which the museum's director wisely taps. From talents in the town he has assembled a volunteer staff on a par with professionally staffed museums. The head librarian, a former librarian of Radcliffe, enjoys the assistance of five graduate librarian volunteers. A retired dean of architecture from Pratt Institute has given and services his large collection of architectural slides. The *Bulletin* is edited by an ex-editor of *The Columbia Encyclopedia*. Even the chief guard was recently retired from Washington's National Gallery. The museum thus brings services to its public far beyond the dream of the average small institution.

JOHN AND MABEL RINGLING MUSEUM OF ART

5401 Bayshore Road, Sarasota, Florida
Hours: Mon.–Sat., 9–5; Sun., 1–5;
closed Thanksgiving, Christmas.
Library.
Admission $1.

As a young man traveling the circus circuit, Ringling visited museums and art galleries and began buying the lesser Barbizon painters. Disillusioned when he took six of them to Chicago's Art Institute for appraisal and found them worth little more than the price of the frames, he resolved never to buy another painting until he could afford masterpieces. On one of his trips he asked Julius Boehler, European art dealer, to help him pick out statuary for a grandiose real estate venture he planned for Sarasota. From Venice to Naples they went, buying up marble doorways, columns, and statues by the dozen. They ordered an 18-foot copy of Michelangelo's *David* cast in bronze. The real estate scheme never saw daylight. The idea of a museum as a monument to the Ringling name did. Ringling commissioned a building in the style of late Renaissance Florence, with wings enclosing a long, formal garden court. *David* stands now between the lengthy loggias that flank the wings.

When he died in 1936 the museum became an orphan. Bereft of patron or taxpayer, it stood for ten years waiting for the

Cast of Michelangelo's *David* (Ringling Museum
of Art, Sarasota, Florida)

estate's settlement. Only then could the Florida legislature accept
the donor's gift. A. Everett Austin, former director of the Wadsworth Atheneum in Hartford, took over. An authority on baroque
and rococo art, he refined the collection and gave it direction.
Today it is probably the greatest repository of baroque art in the
country.

In the big gallery to the right of the entrance are four of a
series of eleven Rubens tapestry cartoons, designed for the sister
of Philip III of Spain. (For any such great cartoons, Rubens
made small sketches; then his workshop executed them, and
Rubens only applied the finishing touches.) Put up for auction at
Christie's in London, they were so massive there were no takers
until the "King of the Big Top," intrigued with their gigantic
scale, took them home. They set the baroque style of much of the
collection.

The galleries flow on, each with a background color to set its
mood. Gallery V introduces the Venetian school with Bassano's
Christ Kneeling in the Garden of Gethsemane and Veronese's
Rest on the Flight into Egypt. The latter is exuberant. Above the
little family under the palm trees, angels spiral, procuring food
and doing the laundry. The concept is naïve, but the richness of
the colors and the exotic landscape give sumptuous overtones.
The last gallery on the right is given to Dutch paintings, among
them Rembrandt's *Portrait of a Lady*, De Heem's *Still Life with
Parrots*, and one of Hals' most penetrating portraits, a likeness of
Pieter Olycan. Just after Ringling unpacked the Hals in his New

York office, Lord Duveen came in and saw it. As a dealer, he was piqued that so important a canvas could have left England without his knowing it. He examined the painting quietly, then offered Ringling $300,000 in cash for it—just twice what he had paid. The offer was rejected.

Across the garden court is Rubens again, and his portrait of the *Archduke Ferdinand.* At the time this was painted, Ferdinand had just succeeded his aunt, the Infanta Clara Eugenia, as Governor of the Netherlands. (A portrait of her by an unknown Spaniard hangs in the next gallery.) The Rubens belonged for a time to Sir Joshua Reynolds, later hung in J. P. Morgan's London house. Another great Rubens in the collection is *The Departure of Lot and His Family from Sodom.*

Even Lord Duveen, with his matchless gift for turning art into gold, was defeated by the size of Gainsborough's largest painting, *General Philip Honywood,* and let Ringling have it at half-price. Gainsborough managed to combine his commission from the pompous general, whom he portrayed with a countenance uncorrupted by thought, with the landscape he loved to paint but could find no market for.

Poussin's *Ecstasy of St. Paul* is a little gem. The artist fell in love with this small work and hated to give it up to Dr. Chanteloup, who had commissioned it. He put his patron off by telling him it was not quite finished and, when forced in time to admit that it was, he still insisted it needed "a few caresses." Eighteenth-century Venice contributes Canaletto's *View from the Piazzetta* and Tiepolo's *Two Allegorical Figures,* a stunning transferred fresco in grays and gold, probably painted for a Venetian *palazzo.* Though baroque and rococo art dominate the collections, with the opening of additional space, art objects of a more general nature are shown and galleries of contemporary art have been added. As a state museum, the Ringling does much to encourage and exhibit Florida artists.

A ceiling painting of the Tiepolo school overlooks the enchanting small theater. Built inside a great castle hall in Asolo, Italy, this is the only eighteenth-century Venetian theater in America. Opera and concerts are given all year around and a talented resident theater company puts on plays—from Shakespeare to avant-garde. Wide corridors outside the boxes are hung with fifteen rare paintings of Harlequin in his various guises by Giovanni Domenico Ferretti. They were for years in Leopoldskron, Max Reinhardt's Salzburg castle.

The Ringling residence, Ca'D'Zan—Venetian dialect for Home

of John—is approached just north of the museum and through a patch of exotic landscaping. (Guided tours 5 minutes past each hour; $1.) The interior shows how the Ringlings lived in the opulent twenties, when they furnished it with objects from all over Europe. The exterior cheerfully mixes the Doge's Palace in Venice with several other architectural styles. Note the tower, similar to the one on the original Madison Square Garden, built by Sanford White and owned by Ringling.

The Ringling Circus Museum, on the drive to the residence, recreates the nostalgic, magic spell of the sawdust ring, with "Big Top" memorabilia gathered from all over the world: costumes, documents, rare prints, posters, ornate animal cages, circus wagons. (Guided tours; 75¢ admission, children free.)

NORTON GALLERY AND SCHOOL OF ART

Pioneer Park, West Palm Beach, Florida
Hours: Tues.–Sat., 10–5; Sun., holidays, 1:30–5:30.
Library.
Free.

Few collectors, after reaching the upper echelons of collecting, admit that their original motive was merely to decorate their living room walls. With refreshing candor, Mr. and Mrs. Ralph Norton confessed just that. In the course of filling a big house in Chicago, where he was president of Acme Steel, they explored the good New York and Chicago galleries and gradually became serious collectors, interested in the quality of the paintings themselves rather than in how they would look over the sideboard.

When the collection reached the hundred mark, something had to give. Not all of the Nortons' collection was of museum caliber, but they had some fine American Impressionist paintings by men like Childe Hassam and Ernest Lawson and pictures from The Eight. So the Nortons, by then living largely in West Palm Beach, built a museum. Norton invited the lively Palm Beach Art League to manage the institution for the benefit of the public. He provided building money for the museum, a clean-lined, simple structure enclosing a patio, and till his death was deeply absorbed in broadening its scope. More than twenty-five years now since the opening, activities and acquisitions overflow the original area and a matching wing with another interior courtyard is projected to give breathing space.

A forerunner of the "art center" complexes cropping up all over America today, the 1941 museum is in four parts; an art school, an auditorium, and galleries for both permanent and temporary exhibits form a square around an open court. Four large orange trees at the corners of the patio lift their branches above the low-slung roof. The entrance looks down a long mall to Lake Worth. Among the European masterpieces, the earliest is a strong thirteenth-century Tuscan *Madonna,* in the Byzantine tradition. The greatest treasures are in the French gallery, where there are three Braques, including *The Mantel* and *Still Life with Red Tablecloth;* Juan Gris' *Le Journal; Au Café,* which Picasso painted during his first trip to Paris in 1901; and a large 1924 Picasso canvas, *Still Life with Printed Foulard,* a stunning and authoritative work in pinks and berry browns. In *The Artist's Son,* Cézanne has painstakingly built up his paint as a sculptor builds up clay, to give a three-dimensional force to the canvas. Gauguin's *Agony in the Garden* dates from shortly after his stormy and tragic interlude with Van Gogh. The deeply suffering face of Christ is Gauguin's own.

The American selection is distinguished by paintings of Hopper, Avery, Dove, Brook, Kuniyoshi, Knaths, Marin, and Shahn. Walt Kuhn's *Morning,* painted for the famous Armory Show of 1913, is in the style of the Fauves. Charles Sheeler's *Shadow and Substance* masses fleecy white clouds about a substantial white barn. One gallery is reserved for watercolors. A large gallery is devoted to Oriental art. Archaic jades and ritual bronzes are the outstanding pieces. The sculpture, usually shown in a glassed-in area of the patio, features powerful pieces by De Creeft, Flannagan, Moore, Lipchitz, Arp, Duchamp-Villon, Roszak, Noguchi, and Constantin Brancusi's shining bronze *Mlle. Pogany,* the last of several versions, carried from marble to metal.

Head of Buddha (Chinese; Northern Ch'i dynasty, 570 A.D.) (Norton Gallery and School of Art, West Palm Beach, Florida)

UNIVERSITY OF GEORGIA:
GEORGIA MUSEUM OF ART

Jackson Street, Athens, Georgia
Hours: Mon.–Fri., 9–5:30; Sat., 9–12;
closed Sun.
Free.

When New York lawyer Alfred Holbrook retired, he and his growing collection of nineteenth- and early twentieth-century American paintings settled in Athens. The University of Georgia offered a museum. Established in the old library in 1948, it sports "early post office and library" architecture. Its undistinguished façade is mellowed by its site in a soft enclave of the oldest buildings on campus.

There is a small Kress study collection, but the principal excitement is American—the Holbrook canvases by George Caleb Bingham, Asher B. Durand, Childe Hassam, John Twachtman, Preston Dickinson, Arthur B. Davies, and by each of The Eight, those young rebels who in 1908 refused to go along with the rigidities of the academicians or the dreams of the American Impressionists. Ben Shahn, Lamar Dodd, Karl Zerbe, Milton Avery punctuate the contemporary action. New gallery space will expedite the display of the important nineteenth-century group and current, changing shows.

Drop by the university art department just across the street from the rear of the museum. Wide corridor galleries present faculty and student work as well as contemporary exhibitions. Something lively is always going on.

ATLANTA ART ASSOCIATION

1280 Peachtree Street, N.E., Atlanta, Georgia
Hours: Sun., Mon., 1–5; Tues.–Sat., 10–5;
closed national holidays.
Library.
Restaurant.
Free.

The new Atlanta Memorial Cultural Center, with its peristyle around three sides, its great fountain, its Peachtree and Lombardy Gardens, brings another dimension to an old town, gathering up under one roof a theater, a major concert hall, an art school, an art library, a restaurant, and the art museum. The present museum is the pivotal point, for all the rest of the grand design has literally been folded around it. Interconnecting public areas include a promenade, a galleria, and lounge space. The same address on Peachtree Street is about all that will be left of the old High Museum.

New galleries will provide more exposure for the increasing contemporary holdings and the decorative arts. The Kress collection will remain on permanent view. Of its over thirty examples of Italian art from the fourteenth to the eighteenth centuries, a favorite is a late Giovanni Bellini, *Madonna and Child,* done when the artist was over eighty, its universal appeal attested by the prevalence of old copies of it in European galleries. Annibale Carracci's *The Crucifixion* is dramatic and original in concept, the central figure overshadowed by the sign painter and his sturdy little apprentice who arrived tardily to nail "INRI" on the head of the cross. Tiepolo painted the splendid *Offering by Young Vestal Priestess to Juno Lucina* in rich dusky colors to decorate the Palazzo Barbaro-Curtis (which served Mrs. Gardner as model for much of her Fenway Court in Boston). The great German sculptor Tilman Riemenschneider is represented sparingly in America, but Atlanta has his strong *St. Andrew.*

A "Great Painting Fund" has been established to bring more masterpieces to the museum. Two purchases: *Boy with Flowers* by Michelangelo da Caravaggio; *Cherries, Iris and Lupin,* said to be the earliest painting by the Spaniard Blas de Ledesma in America. The graphic section, strong and growing, offers Renoir, Goya, Manet, Kollwitz, Lyonel Feininger, and Picasso's *Frugal Repast.* An ingenious feature of the gallery, the large print file, allows visitors to slide open the drawers, study prints protected by acetate or glass. The museum's gathering of American paintings is graced by a charming Copley, *Elizabeth Deering Wentworth,* companion in style to the portrait of her sister in the New York Public Library. Charles Willson Peale's portrait of *Senator W. H. Crawford,* a Georgian contender for the presidency in 1824, is from Peale's late period. A minute Mary Cassatt, *Girl Reading,* Thomas Doughty's *Lake Scene,* and a moonlight canvas by Blakelock are favorites in the nineteenth-century group. Among authors of contemporary painting and sculpture here: Zorach, Moore, Doris Caesar, Kuniyoshi, Bellows, Burchfield, Hopper, Hultberg, Gottlieb. The museum sponsors an eight-state annual regional exhibition.

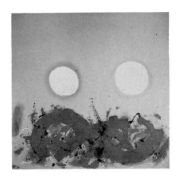

Adolph Gottlieb: *Duet* (1962) (The Atlanta Art Association, Atlanta; gift of Governor Nelson A. Rockefeller)

On the grounds are the McBurney Art Memorial building, which sets forth in historical sequence major styles in the decorative arts, 1670–1920; and Thornton House, moved from Union Point in 1960, one of the few eighteenth-century houses left in Georgia.

TELFAIR ACADEMY OF ARTS AND SCIENCES

121 Barnard Street, Savannah, Georgia
Hours: Mon., 12–5; Tues.–Sat., 10–5; Sun., 3–5;
closed Aug., national holidays.
Free.

Situated across from Telfair Park, one of those charming green squares that grace downtown Savannah, the museum built as a home for the Telfair family in 1815 became, with additions, a public institution.

The two-storied, domed entrance hall and twin stairway is part of the original home, as is the dining and sitting room on one side and the long drawing room on the other. Parts of the permanent collection, late Renaissance and baroque painting, colonial and Federal portraits hang here. A distinctive feature of the drawing room is two beautifully carved marble mantels signed by John Frazee, the only stone carver to become a member of the National Academy.

The rest of the collection and rotating exhibitions are shown in spacious galleries upstairs and down at the rear. It consists mainly of the American Impressionists and American scene painters out of the thirties and forties. One of George Bellows' best works, *Snow Capped River*, is here. There is a small print and

Robert Henri: *La Madrileñita* (Telfair Academy of Arts and Sciences, Inc., Savannah, Georgia; photograph by Taylor & Dull, New York City)

drawing collection, including twenty-eight Childe Hassams and a complete edition of Holbein's *Dance of Death.*

In the entrance hall are two handsome third-century B.C capitals dating from Alexander's building spree in Egypt. They were brought across the ocean to Savannah as ballast and dumped on Ballast Island in the Savannah harbor at the end of the trip.

The Owens-Thomas House, an authentically furnished English Regency house at 124 Abecorn Street is also administered by the museum.

ISAAC DELGADO MUSEUM OF ART

Lelong Avenue at City Park, New Orleans, Louisiana
Hours: Tues.–Sat., 10–5; Sun., 1–6;
closed Mon., national holidays.
Library.
Free.

What dreams Isaac Delgado had for the museum he gave to New Orleans no one knows, for the sugar magnate died shortly before the building opened. Chicago architect Samuel Marx, himself an art collector, designed the classical Greek structure, which is approached down an *allée* of white oaks and magnolias.

The simple, beautifully proportioned interior embraces a center sculpture court dominated by sculptors Rodin, Lipchitz, Penalba, Butler, Consagra, and David Hare. The treasure room holds classical and Oriental wares, Sung and Han ceramics, jade, late Chinese porcelains, a fine six-fold Japanese screen, and early Roman and Persian glass. The Samuel H. Kress collection is set up chronologically, thirteenth through eighteenth century. Not to be missed is *The Last Supper,* a small Italian primitive. Scholars do not agree on the painting's origin. Artists painting solely for the medieval Church did not sign their work. Thus, art historians can only surmise through technique and appurtenances in which school to place a picture. Paolo Veronese's *Sacra Conversazione* and Lorenzo Lotto's *Portrait of a Bearded Man* are other distinguished Kress paintings. European masters, fifteenth through the eighteenth centuries, are rotated in other first-floor galleries.

Two upstairs galleries hold Arts of the Americas—specifically those countries in Central and South America for which New Orleans is a gateway. The charming, semi-primitive, semi-sophisticated Cuzco and Quito colonial schools are in one gallery; sculpture from the Inca and Mayan cultures is in the other. No heterogeneous collection of pots and fragments these, but distinguished sculptures of Chimú and Mochica culture of Peru and both early and late classical Mayan periods.

The nineteenth- and twentieth-century French room holds real gems: a pair of doors painted by Paul Gauguin in Tahiti in 1893. Gauguin was driven to painting the doors because his landlady was always peeking in to be sure only models were there. Until recently the museum had but one bronze race horse to remind citizens of New Orleans of their ties with the French artist Degas. Degas' mother was born here and one of his brothers married a New Orleans cousin. During a visit of some months in 1873, he did many portraits of his large family and painted his important *The Cotton Office in New Orleans* to commemorate his trip (it hangs in the Municipal Museum of Pau, France; a smaller version is at the Fogg Museum at Harvard). Most of the portraits have been lost, but recently when the portrait of Estelle Musson Degas, *Jeune Femme Arrangeant un Bouquet,* came on the market, New Orleans rose to the challenge and in a dramatic city-

Edgar Degas: *Portrait of Estelle* (1872) (Isaac Delgado Museum of Art, New Orleans)

wide drive raised $190,000 to bring the painting back home. Another acquisition is *Pesthouse at Jaffa* by Baron Antoine Jean Gros. It shows Napoleon visiting his men in a plague-ridden Jaffa hospital. The final version is in the Louvre; a tapestry based on the same subject enjoys the hospitality of the Baltimore Museum. On another wall a large Utrillo, *Montmartre*, showing Sacré Coeur and the Moulin de la Gatte, reminds New Orleanians of their own flatter Vieux Carré.

Works related to fluorescent aesthetics are crowned by *Oeuvre Cinétique*, the accomplishment of Julio le Parc, a member of a French group known as the *Groupe de recherche d'art visuel*. This piece, set in its own darkened room, brings all the mystery of movements through light into play. It was purchased in 1960, before neon sculpture and other electronic compositions took over in 57th Street galleries. Another important work is Victor Vasarely's retinally disturbing canvas of brilliant oranges, reds, and blues. Other contemporaries include Baziotes, Hans Hofmann, Lipchitz, Max Ernst, Kandinsky, and Juan Joseph Tharrats.

The Southern genre painters are also represented. While these artists did not succeed in immortalizing the cotton fields, as George Caleb Bingham immortalized the Missouri River, many are worth more than regional attention. Certainly William A. Walker and Richard Clague belong in the mainstream of genre paintings, along with the North's E. L. Henry and William S. Mount.

The city has pledged monies for a very much needed new wing. Work will begin shortly.

UNIVERSITY OF NORTH CAROLINA: WILLIAM HAYES ACKLAND MEMORIAL ART CENTER

South Columbia Street, Chapel Hill, North Carolina
Hours: Tues.–Fri., 2–5; Eves., 8–10; Sat., 10–5; Sun., 2–5 during academic year.
Free.

The Ackland Art Center is possibly the only museum in the United States where the donor's remains actually lie within the building his bounty made possible. Like the Renaissance patrons of old, Ackland's sculptured, recumbent figure rests on a marble sarcophagus. Done in bronze by Milton Hebald in baroque undertones, it is an imposing and awesome piece of sculpture. Ackland's interest in the arts led him to set up a trust to benefit students and public alike in the pursuance of the visual arts. His stipulation was that the institution be in the South. The front of the building holds three exhibition galleries and two English period rooms in which paintings and *objets d'art* are displayed. The rear part of the structure, forming a three-floor T shape, is now occupied by the art school, but will soon be taken over by the museum.

Though the collections are formed primarily for the needs of art students, their quality is far above that of most institutions of like size. There are a few Egyptian and Cypriot pieces, a fine first-century Greek or Roman torso, and a fifteenth-century Flemish stone carving of a Madonna and child still resting in the stone niche that must have been cut from some cathedral pillar. Among the prides of the painting collection: Jacopo del Sellaio's *Madonna and Child with Saints*, Rubens' *Imperial Couple*, and a magnificent Delacroix, *Cleopatra and the Servant*. A darkly brooding Courbet, *Roe Deer in the Snow*, is a gem. Recent acquisitions comprise an important 1910 Max Weber and a gleaming Arp: *Sculpture—Seuil*. The print and drawing portfolio contains over five thousand pieces. The silver cache has rare examples of Russian silver, more than thirty delicately wrought small cups which enable Carolinians to see with what elegance the Russian aristocrats tossed off their vodka. The shifting contemporary scene is shown in changing exhibitions. This program has many scholarly shows to its credit, and the art explorer roaming through the tall scrub pine of North Carolina would do well to check in at Chapel Hill.

Eugene Delacroix: *Cleopatra and the Servant* (William Hayes Ackland Memorial Art Center, Chapel Hill, North Carolina)

MINT MUSEUM OF ART

501 Hempstead Place, Charlotte, North Carolina
Hours: Mon.–Fri., 10–5; Sat., Sun., 2–5;
closed holidays & May 20.
Free.

Few museums have been erected by Act of Congress or put to such varied uses as the attractive Mint Museum, designed in Federal classical style in 1835. Before the California gold fields opened, this North Carolina region was a major gold-mining area. The government needed a mint nearby, so up went their building. During the Civil War it was turned into conference headquarters, then became a hospital. From 1900 to 1903 Thomas Edison used it for experiments. Removed to its present site, it opened as a museum in 1936. A new wing, adroitly placed so as not to detract from the purity of the Federal façade, has just been added. Its center is a theater-in-the-round, galleries on the periphery. It also houses a fine ceramic collection, major emphasis on eighteenth-century Wedgewood.

The permanent collection, though small, consists of Italian Renaissance, baroque, Dutch, and some American paintings. Among the latter: Inness, Cropsey, and a beautiful little John La Farge. An Allan Ramsey portrait of *Queen Charlotte,* for whom the town was named, hangs in the English gallery along with Turner watercolors and an eighteenth-century sedan chair done after designs of Robert and James Adam.

A rental and sales gallery offers works of artists from an eleven-state region.

NORTH CAROLINA MUSEUM OF ART

107 East Morgan Street, Raleigh, North Carolina
Hours: Tues.–Sat., 10–5; Sun., 2–6;
closed national and state holidays.
Library.
Free.

North Carolina was the first state to set aside public funds to found an art museum. In 1947 it voted $1,000,000 for works of art and $350,000 to refurbish a large building, originally headquarters for the Highway Department. This historic gift resulted from the drive of Robert Lee Humber, a Carolinian who wrung a promise of a million dollars' worth of paintings from the Kress Foundation, then pressed the state to match it. William Valentiner, long-time director of the Detroit Museum, was persuaded to take over the new museum. He assessed the paintings earmarked for purchase, and in 1956 the museum opened. When Valentiner died two years later, he left a good part of his own contemporary trove, mostly in the German Expressionist field, to the museum. His fine art library came, intact, to Raleigh.

Get the excellent floor plan of the galleries before beginning. A block from the capitol and a step from the street, the museum entrance leads, appropriately, straight into America's heritage. Here is *Sir William Pepperell and His Family* (descendant of the only New Englander ever created a baronet) painted by Copley after both painter and sitters had turned their backs on the American Revolution and settled in England. Copley, who became a Royal Academician, shows in his canvas the elaborate composition characteristic of the English portrait school. A poignant footnote: Lady Pepperell died during the voyage back to England. When her husband commissioned the portrait, Copley, who had painted Lady Pepperell before her marriage, drew on his memory and used his own wife as the model for the figure. Also at Raleigh: Gilbert Stuart's portraits of the king and queen during whose reign America won independence, George III and his wife Charlotte.

The museum's emphasis is on painting, though there is a small group of Egyptian, Greek, and Roman antiquities. The Kress Italian collection starts with Giotto and his school, Tintoretto, Veronese, and Botticelli's beautiful *tondo, The Adoration of the Child,* and includes the Northern Europeans. The room to the

John Singleton Copley: *Sir William Pepperell and His Family* (The North Carolina Museum of Art, Raleigh)

Jean Marc Nattier: *Madame de Vintimille* (The North Carolina Museum of Art, Raleigh)

right of the entrance is rich in Rubenses, including his portraits of *Philip III* and *Dr. Theodore de Mayerne,* court physician to James I and Charles I of England. Rubens' *The Bear Hunt* is a fierce picture of plunging horses and plumed gallants wrestling with the bear. The animals are the work of Paul de Vos, a painter attached to Rubens' workshop, whose forte was animal portrayal. Several canvases of Van Dyck, Rubens' great pupil, include a full-length portrait of *Mary, Duchess of Lennox,* with her young son in the habiliment of Cupid beside her. The French rooms have a *fête galante* air about them, with bouncing Boucher cupids romping about on clouds and five Beauvais tapestries depicting carefree life in pre-revolutionary France. Nattier has painted Madame de Pompadour's daughter-in-law, *Madame de Vintimelle,* splendidly alive, adjusting the Grecian headdress which the artist liked his sitters to wear. Chardin's handsome *Kitchen Table with a Ray Fish* brings us back to reality. *St. Jerome in His Study* is the only example outside Europe of the fifteenth-century German master Stefan Lochner. The museum has two splendid Rembrandts, *Young Man with a Sword* and the richly expressive *Esther's Feast,* painted when the artist was only twenty. Another accomplishment of a twenty-year-old here is Raphael's *St. Jerome Punishing the Heretic Sabinian.*

In every one of the fifty-six galleries there are treasures: Teniers the Younger's *Armorer's Shop,* probably dating from the years when he was painter and curator for the Governor of the Spanish Netherlands, Archduke Leopold William; Hendrick Terbrugghen's *Young Man with a Wine Glass by Candlelight;* and Frans Pourbus the Elder's *God Creating the Animals*—Pourbus was one of the first artists to paint animals from life. To Raleigh Dr. Valentiner left nineteen canvases by Morris Graves, three Diebenkorns, three

Beckmanns, paintings by Baziotes, Gottlieb, Miró, Klee, Kandinsky, and a group of German Expressionist works. Perhaps Valentiner's concentration on this group was due to the fact that his sergeant in the German army, World War I, was Franz Marc, a member of the Blue Rider movement.

A fascinating innovation here is a gallery for the blind. A layout of the exhibits in raised forms is at the door. Sculpture, fabrics, and artifacts have been chosen for their tactile as well as their aesthetic elements. Each piece is easily accessible, its label written in Braille. In a reading corner is an art library in Braille.

CAROLINA ART ASSOCIATION, GIBBES ART GALLERY

135 Meeting Street, Charleston, South Carolina
Hours: Mon.–Sat., 10–5; Sun., 3–6; closed holidays.
Library. Free.

Though the Carolina Art Association was formed a couple of years before the booming across the bay at Ft. Sumter sparked the Civil War, its real expansion began when the group moved into its present home, the Gibbes Art Gallery. Erected in 1905, in the days when architects vied with each other in the game of more cupolas, taller windows, and fancier pilasters, its grandiose space is better adapted to Hiram Powers marble sculptures than to the hanging of paintings. The association was not responsible for the architectural style. A large gallery on the second floor holds splendid early American portraits of South Carolinians by such well-known painters as Jeremiah Theüs, Benjamin West, Gilbert Stuart, Rembrandt Peale, Samuel F. B. Morse, and Washington Allston. Arriving in Charleston in 1791 at the age of eight, when his father became manager of the Charleston Theater, Thomas Sully painted both affluent and picturesque Charlestonians. The museum has ten examples.

Charleston has the distinction of harboring what is probably America's first artist, at least as far as signed works are concerned. Henrietta Johnston and her husband arrived in Charleston from Ireland in 1705. (According to American art scholar E. P. Richardson, Justus Engelhardt Kuhn came to Maryland in 1708 and Gustavus Hesselius settled in Philadelphia in 1711.) It was thanks to her improvident husband, who fell into the Atlantic on the crossing, that Mrs. Johnston became an artist. Though retrieved, Mr. Johnston understandably never recovered from the

Henrietta Johnston: *Mary du Bose* (Collection of Carolina Art Association, Gibbes Art Gallery, Charleston, South Carolina)

experience and his wife turned to delicate pastels as their means of support. The museum owns five.

Another pride of the Gibbes Gallery is its collection of miniatures. The largest group, three generations of Charlestonians from the Revolution to the Civil War, is by Charles Fraser, a native son. Fraser's notebook, with a watercolor on every page, shows him to be a sensitive landscapist as well. Edward Greene Malbone was another fine native miniaturist. His descendant, Leila Waring, who died in 1917, was the last of the line in this precious, succinct art form. A small gallery holding a growing collection of Japanese prints adjoins. In the contemporary field the museum, wisely chauvinistic in the light of their history and budget, encourages, through exhibition and purchase, mainly South Carolina artists. But the first-floor galleries hold many traveling exhibits. Peggy Guggenheim's collection had its first airing outside New York in Charleston in 1937, and Joseph Albers showed as early as 1944.

The visitor interested in American art should not miss the paintings just down the street at City Hall, where hangs a trio of portraits of famous men by famous artists: George Washington by John Trumbull, Andrew Jackson by John Vanderlyn, and James Monroe by Samuel F. B. Morse.

COLUMBIA MUSEUM OF ART AND SCIENCE

Senate and Bull Streets, Columbia, South Carolina
Hours: Tues.–Sat., 10–5; Sun., 2–6; closed Mon.
Library, planetarium, nature garden. Free.

Few art museums are as felicitously located, for native and visitor alike, as Columbia's. In the heart of the city, it is two blocks from the state capitol, one block from the university, and one from U.S. 1. The museum opened its doors in 1950 with high hopes, $5,000, and an old house. Even this modest beginning didn't take place overnight, but was the outgrowth of the Columbia Art Association started in 1916. The "old house" is a commodious mansion whose great hall and broad stairway lends itself to the flow of traffic engendered by one of the liveliest programs a museum could undertake. Ample wings have been added and an ambitious urban renewal plan is enlarging the museum, the art school, and bringing a science museum and theater into the complex.

There are small pre-Columbian and Chinese clusters, examples of such masters as Van Dyck and Rubens, and such fine American paintings as Washington Allston's *Coast Scene on the Mediterranean,* and a good contemporary showing. But the museum's true distinction lies in its Kress collection. Purchase a catalogue of the Kress paintings, an illuminating companion on a visit; all scholarly attributions are listed, and the detective-story aspect of tracing origins makes fascinating reading. The Kress assemblage is divided into three groups; early Christian, High Renaissance, and late Baroque. A star among the early Christian works, placed in a small, chapel-like gallery with wide brick flooring, is Matteo Di Giovanni's heavy-lidded *Madonna and Child with St. Catherine of Siena and St. Sebastian.* The other two Kress galleries, their ambiance set by soft gold-green fabric-covered walls and appropriate furniture, are rich in treasures. For instance: Andrea Solario's *Madonna and Child;* Botticelli's *The Nativity,* a fresco transferred to canvas set to preserve and bring out the quality of the original; Tintoretto's imposing *A Gentleman of the Emo Family.* For years the background of this painting was black, but after 1948, when it came into Kress possession, careful

Washington Allston: *Coast Scene on the Mediterranean* (Columbia Museum of Art, Columbia, South Carolina; posthumous gift of Dr. Robert W. Gibbes III)

cleaning brought out a clear view of the Papal fortress, Castel Sant' Angelo.

A recent museum purchase is a painting of one of South Carolina's first Chief Justices, *Peter Edgarton Laigh,* painted by John Singleton Copley in 1756 when Copley was nineteen. Though Copley never visited the Carolinas, a search into South Carolina's archives revealed that the Chief Justice had made a trip to Boston at that time. Lost for years, the picture was discovered at Stratford-on-Avon. It will hang either in the museum or in the Governor's office. Wherever he comes to rest the return of the native was a coup for Columbia.

BOB JONES UNIVERSITY ART GALLERY AND MUSEUM

Greenville, South Carolina
Hours: Tues.–Sat., 10–5; Sun., 1:30–6;
June–Aug., and Christmas vacation, Tues.–Sun., 2–4;
closed Monday, Christmas, New Year's Day.
Free.

"Unique" is the word most often used to describe the Bob Jones University collection and I can't find a more accurate adjective. To fully savor the aura of the museum, one must understand the orientation of the university itself. It was founded forty years ago by the Reverend Bob Jones as a fundamentalist school, preaching with no apologies "the old-time religion" and the absolute authority of the Bible. The tradition is being carried on by Bob Jones, Jr., and Bob Jones III. Keeping up with the Joneses, who are sometimes referred to as "the Holy Trinity," means no smoking, drinking, gambling, or dancing on campus.

The collection of Christian religious art was begun a mere fifteen years ago by Bob Jones, Jr. In 1965 a sumptuous new museum opened in a remodeled campus building. Wood-paneled Gothic and Renaissance rooms have been reinstalled. Truly distinguished furniture—*cassones,* commodes, chairs, a Gothic *dressoir* from Avignon—grace the painting galleries. As the museum's new brochure stated: "A red carpet has been placed over the sawdust trail." Actually, the boldly colored carpets and walls in some galleries almost lead to visual indigestion. However, the heady High Renaissance and ebullient baroque paintings manage to hold their own against yellow walls and purple carpets or purple walls and yellow carpets. John Coolidge of the Fogg

Joachim Beucklaer: *The Holy Family* (1565) (Bob Jones University Collection, Greenville, South Carolina)

summed it up as expressing "a marvelous lack of timidity." After the first dozen galleries, the decor falls into a more tranquil pattern. The twenty-eight galleries follow in numerical sequence and are arranged by country and period.

The overall strength here probably is in the major works of minor masters and in its fourteenth- to eighteenth-century Italian paintings. However, the Spanish, French, German, Dutch, and Flemish schools are well represented. The range is from a monumental Sienese crucifix, *c.* 1370, to a rather spectacular nineteenth-century Gustave Doré *Christ About to Take Up the Cross.*

Even within the restricted framework, the fare is so rich and varied that one must choose at random: *Salome with the Head of John the Baptist* by Lucas Cranach the Elder; the enchanting *Madonna of the Fireplace* by Jan Mabuse (Gossaert); *Pentecost,* is said to be the only work of Juan de Juanes in America. Also in the Spanish section is *St. Catherine Appearing to the Family of Bonaventura in Prison,* one of a series of four paintings, two in the Louvre, the other at the Prado. The scope of the Italian pictures is staggering. They include three recently acquired magnificent sections of a great altarpiece by Paolo Veronese, a set of *Four Evangelists* by Guido Reni, *Procession to Calvary* by Giovanni Antonio Bazzi (called Sodoma), and *Holy Family and St. John the Baptist* by the sixteenth-century Venetian Vincenzo Catena. Among the Dutch paintings, *The Holy Family in the Carpenter Shop* by Gerard Van Honthorst is a gem. This work is sometimes attributed to a French artist influenced by Georges de La Tour.

The War Memorial Chapel, a short distance from the museum, is a must for students of eighteenth- and nineteenth-century American art. Seven grandiose canvases by Benjamin West—their theme, fittingly enough, "Revealed Religion"—are part of a series commissioned by West's patron George III for Windsor Castle. Before the project could be completed, the king's mind had deteriorated and West was left with the canvases. The posthumous sale of his work in 1829 included many from this series. They hung in an English country house until 1962, when they were auctioned at Christie's in London. Six were acquired at the sale for the university and a seventh was presented as a gift. They are particularly suited for the chapel of the world's most unusual university, standing for the "old-time religion."

GREENVILLE MUSEUM OF ART

106 Dupont Drive, Greenville, South Carolina
Hours: Tues.–Sat., 10–5; Sun., 2–6; closed Mon.
Free.

This is a museum to watch. Because the Greenville Museum has at present little in the way of a general permanent collection, it does not fall within the purview of this book. But its exhibition and activities program and future expectations are spirited enough to warrant its inclusion within these pages and within a traveler's itinerary. Established in 1958 in a mansion whose architecture can best be described as odd (the mistress of the house was its architect, but she was no Isabella Stewart Gardner —see Boston), the forty-room redesigned interior affords airy galleries, a lecture hall, a two-story music room, a print cabinet, an attractive shop where regional artists' prints and drawings are on sale. Some good contemporary canvases have been donated and, thanks to the museum purchase fund, prints by Chagall, Calder, Lichtenstein, and Giacometti are on hand. The building rests on a large wooded rise of ground, ideally suited for monumental sculpture. Such is the confidence and enthusiasm of the staff, that the monumental will probably shortly materialize.

NORFOLK MUSEUM OF ARTS AND SCIENCES

Yarmouth Street and The Hague, Norfolk, Virginia
Hours: Tues.–Sun., 12–5; closed Mon., national holidays.
Library.
Free.

Yet another museum is sprouting and doubling its size. The present building will house chiefly science and history, the new brick

Charles Willson Peale: *Mary O'Donnell* (ca. 1787) (Norfolk Museum, Norfolk, Virginia)

and limestone wing an attractive theater and art museum. One great main-floor gallery is given over to changing exhibitions, its counterpart on the second floor to some of the permanent holdings. Another gallery tells, through art and artifacts, the history of Norfolk and the Tidewater region.

For a small museum, the displays are fairly diversified: Roman, Persian, European, early American glass, and English silver. Jewelry from the fifteenth to eighteenth century is unique in character, as is a small trove of pre-Columbian gold-working tools. European paintings ramble from pre-Renaissance to baroque, with a gallery's worth of sixteenth- and seventeenth-century Flemish and Dutch masters. The early American painting section is probably the richest, especially with the advent of three Charles Willson Peale portraits to supplement his *George Washington: Mrs. Thomas Elliott;* a beguiling child's likeness, *Mary O'Donnell;* and *Mrs. John O'Donnell,* who holds in her hand a miniature, presumably of her husband—thus giving the museum yet another Peale portrait. Some of the good drawing collection, Renaissance to present, will appear in the wide stairwells.

The museum also administers two charming historic houses, the Thoroughgood and The Myers. Visitors in Norfolk should not miss the Hermitage Foundation museum, where emphasis is on religious arts and crafts of European and Oriental cultures, with special stress on the ritualistic arts of the Far East.

VIRGINIA MUSEUM OF FINE ARTS

Boulevard at Grove Avenue, Richmond, Virginia
Hours: Mid–Sept. to mid–June, Tues.–Sat., 1–5, 8–10; Sun., 1–5;
Summer, Tues.–Sun., 11–5.
Library.
Restaurant.
Admission weekdays 50¢, under 16 free.

Richmond burned for three days after it fell to Grant at the end of the Civil War. For decades thereafter the city concentrated on rebuilding. But it wasn't until 1936 that the Old Dominion could gather together its rich cultural heritage and an international art collection under the roof of a museum. Today, just some thirty years later, two wings are projected. The north wing, an entrance pavilion, will take visitors to a large entrance foyer from which stairs will go down to the theater and up to the galleries. In front, a terraced sculpture garden will glimmer with fountain and reflecting pools, reminiscent of baroque water gardens. Building funds are privately donated, but the institution is maintained by the Commonwealth of Virginia, whose schools and art centers it serves. Four artmobiles—big motor coaches with built-in galleries, air conditioning, and sound equipment—make the Virginia rounds with some hundred exhibits each year.

In a setting reminiscent of the great days of czarist Russia, the Pratt Collection of Imperial Crown Jewels nestles in embrasures suggesting draped rococo opera boxes. Carl Fabergé's unbelievable fantasies in crystal, gold, and gems take the form of Easter eggs, icons, a whole garden of bejeweled potted plants, cigarette cases, snuffboxes. These endearing baubles, like everything else in the museum, are exhibited with a lively sense of theater. Incandescent lighting sets each treasure apart from its neighbors. Each air-conditioned room is provided with appropriate music. The harpsichord may accompany an exhibition of eighteenth-century English silver. A flute plays delicate arpeggios in the French gallery in deference to Watteau's *The Ogler,* a beautifully succinct little ballad in blues, pinks, and moss green. Among favorites in the European section: a fourteenth-century stained-glass window, a rare example of Austria's Gothic glass in America, in such superb condition that it has needed almost no restoration. A small panel for an altar by Signorelli, *The Presentation of the Virgin,* sharply recalls his great frescoes in the Cathedral of

Francesco Guardi: *Piazza San Marco* (The Virginia Museum of Fine Arts, Richmond, Virginia)

Orvieto, Italy. Francesco Guardi's *Piazza San Marco* is an especially fine example of Guardi's absorption in the Piazza, and Constable's *Ponds at Hampstead Heath* is a felicitous picture with its sensitive use of light.

A series of portraits, primitive and relatively sophisticated, evokes colonial Virginia. The tobacco boats plying between England and America carried planters to London on business. While there, they often seized the opportunity to sit for portraits. Those who didn't make London might send detailed descriptions of how they looked, or wished to look, and in a matter of months "portraits" were returned, presenting later historians with problems. Fortunately, it is known that the portrait of *William Byrd the First* was painted from life while he was a schoolboy in England, before he returned to his James River house, Westover. Even children didn't escape classicism then: young Byrd is decked in the toga and trappings of an embryo emperor.

Richmond has a remarkable cluster of canvases known as the Ambler portraits, the coats of arms attesting that they were painted before 1775, when family escutcheons went out of style, at least for a while.

In few museums is the ambiance of a period more dramatically created than here. No walking into a gallery just to look at Flemish pictures. Lucas Cranach and Jan Brueghel are there, but so is the long refectory table, the bowl of fresh fruit, the candle, the book, the spectacles, the pushed-back chair. The nineteenth-century room has a Victorian settee, palms, and plush Indian maidens holding crystal gas lamps—and Hiram Powers and Thomas Doughty and Samuel F. B. Morse. The pre-Columbian, Oriental, and Egyptian offerings call forth these civilizations

Elizabeth Jaquelin (unknown American Artist, ca. 1722) (The Virginia
Museum of Fine Arts, Richmond, Virginia)

faithfully. The contemporary galleries contain works by Stuart
Davis, Edward Hopper, Philip Guston, Ben Shahn. Paintings by
Virginian artists are always on view.

A radio-guide comments on the art of each period, while stereo
viewers elucidate further facets of the times. The theater, one
of the best-equipped in America, offers concerts, plays, and ballets
during the season. Visitors can phone for tickets. There's a
members' lounge and restaurant, and an Everyman's cafeteria and
tea room takes in a walled sculpture garden. In the Virginia
Museum, art is meant to be enjoyed in comfort.

ABBY ALDRICH ROCKEFELLER
FOLK ART COLLECTION

Williamsburg, Virginia
Hours: Tues.–Sat., 10–9; Sun., 12–9;
closed Mon.
Library.
Free.

Any trip to Williamsburg should include this museum—and for
this museum alone any student of primitive American art should
go out of his way to Williamsburg. Not that the museum lies
within the Restoration. Because most of the collection represents
the early part of the nineteenth century and cannot be considered
a part of eighteenth-century colonial Williamsburg, its stately
brick repository sits just outside the Williamsburg enclave, between the Inn and the Lodge. The scale is that of a roomy private

William B. Gleason: Ship's figurehead—*Minehaha* (ca. 1856) (Abby Aldrich Rockefeller Folk Art Collection, Williamsburg, Virginia)

home, the intimate wainscotted galleries and low benches compatible with the unassuming painting and sculpture.

In the stairwell, a great shipshead figure of Minnehaha sails out proudly and boldly. It is believed to have been carved in 1856 in Boston for the ship named for our romanticized, victimized Indian maiden. A stern, outsized Andrew Jackson—the work of William Rumney, another master figurehead carver of Boston—greets one at the top of the stairs. Across the hall, the charming early-nineteenth-century room was taken from a house in Wagram, North Carolina. It was probably done by an itinerant portraitist and decorator. Over the mantel is a horizontal skyline *View of New York*. Some folk artists here: Edward Hicks, Erastus S. Field, John Brewster, Edbury Hatch, William Gleason. The collection rotates, and occasionally this is the address of important exhibitions of other American folk material.

MUSEUM OF CONTEMPORARY ART

237 E. Ontario, Chicago, Illinois
Hours: Tues.–Sat., 11–6; Wed., 11–10 P.M.; Sun., 12–6.
Admission 50¢, students and children half price.

Chicago's first museum of contemporary art opened in the fall of
1967 in a severe rectangular white box more than half of whose
façade is covered by a stunning copper relief sculpture by the
Hungarian-Swiss artist Zoltan Kemeny. An 8-foot moat filled with
washed anthracite coal (surely a new use for the ore) separates
the museum from the sidewalk. Originally a bakery and recently
the home of Playboy Enterprises, the building has 10,000 square
feet of unencumbered exhibition space. The interior is white on
white—walls, ceiling, floors.

For the present, a permanent collection is being eschewed.
This is an action museum—ideas in action, objects in action,
people in action—a veritable happening box.

As director Jan Van Der Mark says, "The museum's role is to
seek out new trends rather than cater to established values. I think
of a museum·as a place of experiment, a proving and testing
ground, a laboratory . . . I want to show what is living in the
minds of the artists today."

UNIVERSITY OF CHICAGO:
ORIENTAL INSTITUTE MUSEUM

1155 East 58th, Chicago, Illinois
Hours: Tues.–Wed., 10–12, 1–5; Thurs.–Sun., 10–5;
closed national holidays.
Free.

Since its founding, in 1919, by the Egyptologist James Henry
Breasted, the institute has been sending expeditions forth to

excavate in Iran, Iraq, Palestine, Turkey, Egypt, and Syria. Though its interest is primarily archaeological, the results displayed are more often than not of deep aesthetic value, whether it's a small Luristan bronze or the colossal *Portrait of Tutankhamen*, Egyptian XVIII Dynasty.

UNIVERSITY OF ILLINOIS: KRANNERT ART MUSEUM

Sixth and Peabody Drive, Urbana, Illinois
Hours: Daily, 9–5; Sun., 2–5.
Free.

In 1947 the university held its first Biannual Survey of Contemporary American Art. It remains today the oldest and most distinguished biannual in the country. Not only current trends and leading artists are given a platform, but many young painters are shown and some have made their reputations here. Wisely purchasing from each exhibition, the museum has through the years built up an enviable collection—examples of the highest quality by such artists as Shahn, Rosenthal, Baziotes, Roszak, Lebrun, Jenkins, Motherwell, Morris, Hofmann, Burchfield, Stuart Davis, Loren MacIvor, Karl Knaths. The list is long and impressive.

In 1961 the Krannert Art Museum, a simple, functional, elegant little building, was erected. Commissioned for the entrance and crowning a long reflecting pool is a large bronze by the sculptor Mirko. It is appropriately entitled *Initiation*. Except for the exhibition galleries where the biannuals are held, the building is paneled in warm walnut wood.

The works of art in the first gallery, the Trees Gallery, range from the fifteenth- to nineteenth- and twentieth-century landscape paintings. Through a series of bays, this good but diverse collection is brought into order. Except during the period of the biannual, it is a permanent installation. Some high points are a Frans Hals portrait, François Clouet's *Madame De Piennes*, landscapes by Inness and Blakelock, and *French Farm*, a little gem by Winslow Homer.

The Krannert's aim is to build a good historical collection while continually holding important contemporary exhibitions. As the only general art museum in that vast prairie country of Illinois, except of course for the Chicago Art Institute, the Krannert brings to the student body and the general public exhibitions which are

John Hultberg (1922–): *Arctic Cabin* (1955) (Krannert Art Museum, University of Illinois, Urbana)

enjoyed by New Yorkers at the Guggenheim, the Whitney, or the Museum of Modern Art, sometimes showing them prior to New York openings.

Some late purchases for the museum are Murillo's *Christ after the Flagellation;* a fourteenth-century Sienese panel painting, *Madonna and Child; La Famille de Bourbon-Conti* by Nicolas Lancret; *The Drover's Cart* by Thomas Gainsborough; a distinguished Gandharan stele of the second century A.D.; Ming porcelains; and the beginning of a pre-Columbian collection. A huge Mathieu, *Homage to Charlemagne,* usually hangs in the broad stairwell.

A print gallery, the auditorium, and some beautifully recessed cases in which ceramics by major potters are shown, are on the lower floor. The museum follows the same pattern with the crafts as with its painting and sculpture biannuals, holding important national craft exhibitions and purchasing top works from them.

After only six years, the collection has outgrown its new home and plans are under way for an additional wing.

INDIANA UNIVERSITY MUSEUM OF ART

Fine Arts Building, Bloomington, Indiana
Hours: Daily, 9–5;
closed Sun.
Free.

The fine arts program of the second oldest major state university west of the Alleghenies camped out, after World War II, in slightly remodeled military structures. Their only saving grace was that a few more feet of lumber could always be tacked on for burgeoning needs. A small fireproof art gallery was nailed together and probably, as its exhibitions overflowed into corridors and classrooms, pointed to the need for the present attractive cultural complex that went into business in 1962. The same foundation and mechanical paraphernalia take care of two separate buildings, one for the performing arts, the other for the visual. The entrance faces the Plaza and Showalter Fountain, a large oval basin with a bronze sculpture by Robert Laurent, long-time instructor of I. U.

Statue of a Youth, a second-century Roman marble, sets a tone of quiet elegance in a red marble niche on the entrance stairwell. Warm travertine walls backdrop other Greek and Roman pieces. To the right in a gallery of antiquities, a succinct little museum in itself, the pure and sparse display of each piece or fragment induces one to linger and study. The second-floor sculpture court and other galleries shine with vital exhibitions so scholarly that other institutions often borrow them. The primitive art, especially its African delegation, defies in size most college collections. In the Oriental and Far Eastern section, heads from India, Java, Cambodia, Thailand, and China were mounted so aesthetically for comparative study by students that they have become part of the permanent exhibit. Only the Cleveland Museum has a Haniwa horse as large.

Appropriate rugs and furniture soften the terrazzo floors in the permanent painting galleries. Admire the big Limoges processional cross and the Vigary reliefs, a series of eight *Scenes from the Life of the Virgin* in brilliantly polychromed high relief, many with intricate architectural backgrounds. Although Vigary was born in France, he arrived in Burgos, Spain, in 1498, in time to introduce to Spanish sculpture the stylistic concepts of the Italian

Attributed to Praxiteles: *Torso of Leaning Satyr with Panther Skin* (Roman copy; original ca. 320 B.C.) (Courtesy of the Indiana University Art Museum, Bloomington)

Renaissance. The series is unique in university collections. Paintings include a good little cache of Renaissance from the Kress collection and a growing assemblage of important contemporary works, one a large mural that Stuart Davis did in his W.P.A. days.

Each departmental art historian acts as a curator within his specialty in this museum, which reflects largely the creativity of Dr. Henry Hope, long-time fine arts chairman.

EVANSVILLE MUSEUM OF ARTS AND SCIENCES

411 South East Riverside Drive, Evansville, Indiana
Hours: Tues.–Sat., 9–5; Tues. eve., 7–9; Sun., 12–5;
closed Mon., national holidays. Library.

The Evansville Museum—a combine of the arts, history, and science—doesn't fall within the spectrum of this book. But visitors to Evansville should stop by its clean-lined contemporary building on the banks of the Ohio. Indian arts and crafts and Civil War weapons are among the attractions.

FORT WAYNE ART MUSEUM

1202 W. Wayne Street, Ft. Wayne, Indiana
Hours: Tues.–Sun., 1–5; Wed., 1–8;
closed Mon., national holidays. Free.

Though its roots go back to 1886, when both the art school and the Ft. Wayne Institute of Arts were founded, the museum proper had its beginnings in 1922. It moved in 1950 to the former William Mossman home on a shady tree-lined street. Monthly exhibitions, mostly on the contemporary art scene, are shown. Ancient Egyptian material is on extended loan from the Metropolitan Museum. Though working toward a general collection, the present holdings emphasize painting, sculpture, prints, and drawings by such distinguished Americans as Ivan Albright, George Bellows, Edward Hopper, John Marin, Larry Rivers. Some Europeans are: Oskar Kokoschka, Maximilien Luce, Emil Nolde, Giuseppe Santomaso, and Paul Signac. An ambitious arts center which includes the museum is being planned for downtown Ft. Wayne, masterminded by a master architect, Louis Kahn.

ART ASSOCIATION OF INDIANAPOLIS, INDIANA, HERRON MUSEUM OF ART

110 East 16th Street, Indianapolis, Indiana
Hours: Tues.–Sat., 10–5; Sun., 1–6;
closed Mon., holidays.
Library.
Free.

Except for moving the Temple of Dendur from the banks of the Nile to the Metropolitan on the banks of Fifth Avenue, no more exciting project is in the making in the museum world than the one under way at the Herron Museum. The J. K. Lilly estate, Oldfields—46 acres along the White River, landscaped in 1914 by the Olmstead brothers, whose firm laid out New York's Central Park—has been given to the museum. The grounds have the incredible beauty one has been led to expect only from Charleston and Virginia gardens. Groves of giant beeches, minute flowering orchards, broad lawns, *allées* of trees unfold in ingenious perfection. A canal wanders through the property. Built in 1830 as part of an ambitious project to join Indianapolis with the Great Lakes, it was abandoned when steam engines became numerous. Museum plans have pleasure barges for the weary floating between the grassy banks. The new museum building with adjoining art school will go up on a high rise of land in a nest of beech trees. A simple glass-walled square, it will be skirted by a wide covered atrium that admits daylight, protects from glare, and quarters sculpture and ceramics. A two-story tapestry court leads to two 100-foot-long galleries on each floor which can be broken into units.

A short meander through the woods brings one to the Lilly home, French château in character. Seventeenth- and eighteenth-century pieces, primarily French, furnish the house and important canvases hang on its walls. The great hall contains Fragonard, Boucher, and one of the most striking Nattiers in America, *Mme. Crozat de Thérèse et sa Fille*. In the music room Copley appears at his "English period" best in his tender, rollicking *Daughters of George III*. A stunning Gilbert Stuart family group and Romney's *The Horsley Children* complement Copley. Goya's portrait of *Don Feliz de Larriategue*, descendant of Columbus, dominates the library. The house's play pavilion will probably be made into a restaurant.

My enthusiasm for what will be a uniquely beautiful art

complex in the heart of the country is no cause to delete a précis of the present fine museum, which will play at the old stand for the next two or three years—into 1970. In 1883 Indianapolis had a well-organized art association pursuing a brisk program. In 1895 a farmer named John Herron, whom no one in local art circles remembered having met, died and left the association a munificent sum. Mystified and annoyed, Herron's relatives battled the will. When the art association won out after lengthy litigation, it named the museum for its unexpected benefactor.

Among the museum's most splendid possessions are two twelfth-century Spanish frescoes. From a series of six, *circa* 1150, found in the abandoned Chapel of San Baudelio in Berlanga, north of Madrid, they were brought to this country when it was still possible to spirit Spain's national treasures out from under the nose of an indifferent monarchy (see Cincinnati). Upstairs the collection begins with thirteenth- and fourteenth-century Sienese painting. Dutch and Flemish rooms display both the big-name painters and lesser but important men from both these schools. Among them is Hobbema with *The Water Mill* and Aelbert Cuyp with his fine *The Valkhof at Nijmegen*. American veterans of World War II who pushed the Germans back across their own border through Nijmegen will find little to remind them of the experience in this peaceful landscape. Most popular of the museum's several pictures by Turner, England's eminent nineteenth-century painter, is his *The Fifth Plague of Egypt*. Indianapolis also owns a delightful piece of Turner memorabilia, a painted tray. When the artist was illustrating one of Sir Walter Scott's novels, he went to Abbotsford, where Scott entertained him with a lavish picnic. As a souvenir, Turner painted on a coffee tray a charming landscape of the party, Abbotsford dominating the background. Perhaps John Singleton Copley's best-known canvas, reproduced in many schoolbooks, is *Brook Watson and the Shark* (see National Gallery and Detroit for more on this). It was his first effort outside the field of portraiture, done at a time when the grandiose and dramatic canvas was the vogue. The Indianapolis painting shows *His Honor Sir Brook Watson*, decades after his encounter with the shark, dressed in his robes as Lord Mayor of London.

The institute's aim is to cover with a few first-rate examples the most important periods rather than to emphasize one or two. Thus the Chinese pottery and bronze and the Persian pottery displays are small but choice. Masterpieces in the French field are Seurat's *Port of Gravelines*, Van Gogh's *Landscape at St. Remy*,

TOP: John Singleton Copley: *Sir Brook Watson* (1796) (Art Association of Indianapolis, Herron Museum of Art, Indianapolis) BOTTOM: Vincent Van Gogh: *Landscape at Saint Remy* (Art Association of Indianapolis, Herron Museum of Art, Indianapolis; given in memory of Daniel W. and Elizabeth C. Marmon)

and Picasso's *Ma Jolie*. Two outsized regal portraits of *George III and His Queen* by Allan Ramsey have just come from the collection of Marina, Dutchess of Kent, to the museum. Americans, from the early portrait painters through the Hudson River school and The Eight, are well represented. The avant-garde is missing but will find its place in the new complex.

ALLEN CLOWES COLLECTION

3744 Spring Hollow Road
Golden Hills, Indianapolis, Indiana

Those lucky enough to be in Indianapolis on a Thursday from 4 to 7 should not miss the George Henry Clowes collection, which is open to the public at those hours. This relatively unknown but exciting cache of paintings contains five El Grecos; self-portraits by Dürer, Van Dyck, and Hals; Titian's *Portrait of a Doge;* several succinct Corneille de Lyonses; a Fra Angelico *Nativity;* and a small canvas, a Madonna, that many scholars credit to Raphael.

UNIVERSITY OF NOTRE DAME ART GALLERY

O'Shaugnessy Hall, Notre Dame, Indiana
Hours: Daily, 1–5;
closed Dec. 25, Jan. 1, Good Friday.
Free.

In 1850, eight years after its founding, Notre Dame was given a sizable art collection. Five years later, without benefit of catalogue, the art went up in flames. Desultory collecting followed until 1917, when the Braschi group from Rome was purchased. Some acquisitions raised the eyebrows of art historians. Lately, under an enlightened administration and the scrutiny of eminent scholars, the collection is coming into proper focus. Italian, French, English, Flemish, and American paintings feature some exceptional portraits, two by the Dutch Paulus Moreeles in the Kress study collection. There are two splendid Nattiers, Romney, and Sir Peter Lely's *Portrait of Mary II of England* when she was Princess of Orange. Closer to our time is Thomas Eakins' *The Reverend Philip R. McDevitt.* The contemporaries, long neglected, now are far from it, with the likes on hand of George Mathieu, Laszlo Moholy-Nagy, Karel Appel, Ben Nicholson, James Brooks, Will Barnet, William Congdon, Joseph Cornell—many from the distinguished G. David Thompson collection.

Easily accessible to students and townsmen, the museum consists of a formal hall holding works by Ivan Meštrović, long-time artist-in-residence, and two large galleries. It is to be hoped that some arrangement can be made to keep more of the permanent holdings on view.

SHELDON SWOPE ART GALLERY

25 South Seventh Street, Terre Haute, Indiana
Hours: Tues.–Sat., 12–5; Sun., 2–5;
closed August, Mon.
Free.

No one knows why, twenty-five years ago, Sheldon Swope left his money to establish an art center, since his interest in the arts was previously confined to his jewelry business. But he did, and the unprepossessing entrance on a busy downtown street leads to pleasant, well-lighted, upstairs galleries where unabashed twentieth-century realism is the mainstay. Grant Wood's last painting, *Spring in Town*, is here. So is Hopper's *Route Six Easton* and Burchfield's *Old Houses in Winter*. So are Marsh, Benton, and Raphael Soyer. About one-third of the collection, which also includes Oriental works, Japanese prints, and nineteenth-century Americans such as Inness, Doughty, and Blakelock, can be shown at one time. One gallery is usually reserved for the contemporaries: among them Leroy Lamis, William Hopper, Martha Slaymaker, and many more of Indiana's own whom the gallery does much to encourage.

J. B. SPEED ART MUSEUM

2035 South Third Street, Louisville, Kentucky
Hours: Tues.–Sat., 10–4; Sun., 2–6;
closed Mon., holidays. Library. Free.

First and largest art museum in the Blue Grass State, the Speed conjures up Kentucky's past admirably. Take the whacking 7-foot-tall *Chief of the Mechanics' Volunteer Fire Brigade of Louisville,* carved and painted like a cigar store Indian. When the alarm sounded in the 1800s, the formidable chief was turned by crank, from his stand atop the firehouse, to point in the direction of the conflagration. Take John James Audubon, who began doing portraits to finance his birdwatching, a good deal of it in Kentucky. Two portrait drawings of *James Berthoud* and *Mrs. James Berthoud* by Audubon are here, as well as two oils of the same subject, also attributed to the artist. Mrs. Berthoud is seen in profile at a window which looks out on the site where J. B. Speed

Chief of the Mechanics' Volunteer Fire Brigade of Louisville (Courtesy of The J. B. Speed Art Museum, Louisville, Kentucky)

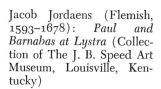

Jacob Jordaens (Flemish, 1593–1678): *Paul and Barnabas at Lystra* (Collection of The J. B. Speed Art Museum, Louisville, Kentucky)

later built a cement works and part of the fortune that founded this museum. James Peale's *Madame Dubocq and Her Family* is more sophisticated. Matthew Jouett, "Master of the Blue Grass" and pupil of Gilbert Stuart, is shown by several portraits. Chester Harding painted the *John Speed Smith Family* during 1819 and 1820 when, twenty-eight, he stopped in Kentucky and achieved local fame by doing over a hundred portraits in six months.

But, for all its Kentuckiana, this is no provincial museum. A recent bequest of fifty paintings contains fine examples of Courbet, Monet, Seurat, Degas, Picasso, Cassatt, and an excellent Kokoschka—*Nogent-Sur-Marne Viaduct 1932*. The drawing collection encompasses eleven periods. Other distinguished canvases: Paolo Veronese's *Portrait of a Young Woman Holding a Skull;* Vincenzo Poppa's *St. John the Baptist;* Jacob Jordaens' *Paul and Barnabas at Lystra*. The collective skill of Jan Brueghel the Elder and Hendrick von Balen produced the spirited *A Bacchanale*. There are portraits by Nattier and Largilliere and a great Rubens sketch. Julius Held, art historian, Rubens authority, and master sleuth (as all good art historians should be), has identified it as a sketch done for a series of tapestries depicting *The Triumph of the Eucharist*, designed for the Convent of the Descalzas Reales in Madrid. The tapestries left Antwerp for Spain July 12, 1628, and are still in the convent. Held said of the Louisville sketch, "It betrays the hand of the master in every stroke." Goya's *Fray Josquin Company, Archbishop of Saragossa*, and the polished dome of *Mlle. Pogany* by the twentieth-century master Brancusi, remain favorites. *The Flagellation*, an important Alessandro Algardi, has joined the substantial Italian bronze group.

Hattie Bishop Speed gave the museum to the public in 1925 in memory of her husband. In the Preston P. Satterwhite wing, opened in 1954, are the donor's collection of art, furniture, and *objets d'art* and a superb Elizabethan great hall shipped intact from Devonshire. An addition will open up galleries and a restaurant and auditorium. Eventually, a quadrangle will surround a circular court.

An innovation other museums might envy is the establishment of a group of friends, or patrons, or elite corps . . . call it what you will. Each pledges $2,000 a year toward the purchase of art. If a Flemish painting is needed, a seminar is given the "friends" during the year on Flemish painting. Then two or three members and the director go to the New York galleries, or paintings are sent to the museum for study. The museum benefits from the friends' money—and the friends, hopefully, benefit from the seminar and the knowledgeable sharing in building the museum's collections.

UNIVERSITY OF MICHIGAN MUSEUM OF ART

Ann Arbor, Michigan, State Street and S. University Avenue
Hours: Daily, 9–6; Wed. & Sat., 9–6, 7–9; Sun., 2–5.
Closed holidays.
Free.

The works of art that the University of Michigan started buying as early as 1855 drifted about the campus like orphans until 1910, when they were gathered together in Alumni Memorial Hall. In 1946, collections reassessed, the museum became a modern functioning entity. Among survivors of the weeding process: an 1862 gift, *Nydia*, a marble by the sculptor Randolph Rogers, a leading figure in the late stages of the classical revival; Charles Wimar's *The Attack on an Emigrant Train;* and Eastman Johnson's *Boyhood of Lincoln.* As with most university museums, Ann Arbor's is primarily a teaching museum; its collections and exhibition program tend to reflect the strength of different university departments. The extensive Oriental collection, for instance, is partially the result of excavations sponsored by the department of anthropology.

Best described as American Classic, the building has recently been smartly remodeled. The large entrance gallery is used for the permanent collection or changing exhibitions. The open construction allows a show to flow with little interruption to the

Standing Guardian with Armor (Chinese, Ming dynasty) (The University of Michigan Museum of Art, Ann Arbor; James Marshall Plumer Memorial Collection)

mezzanine gallery. A second floor holds historic Western painting and sculpture. Side galleries contain Orientalia. A new feature on the ground floor is a reference room with easily available study racks for material not on display. The drawing collection is especially strong, with some emphasis on architectural and ornamental material ranging from sixteenth to early nineteenth century. The painting section covers late Renaissance and middle baroque to the present, with beautiful entries by Conrad Marca-Relli, Robert Indiana, Roland Ginzel, James Brooks, and a stunning Hans Arp bronze. The print collection is equally rangy, some four hundred Whistlers mingling with fine Japanese holdings, the whole print scene reaching from Altdorfer to Archipenko and beyond. The Oriental group, seeded by the collection of a revered teacher, James Marshall Plumer, includes ceramics, bronzes, jades, wood and metal sculpture, and painting. An interesting small group of Iranian ceramics is being formed. Among the contemporary sculpture excitements are examples by Englishmen—Chadwick, Meadows, Caro, Butler, and Robert Adams—plus Lipchitz, Arp, Giacometti, Seymour Lipton, and David Smith.

A major catalogue accompanies each major exhibition. The biannual Museum of Art bulletin analyzes in scholarly fashion important purchases. With a remodeled building and new preservation study and exhibition techniques, the university can look forward to an expansion of its already noteworthy scholarly tradition.

DETROIT INSTITUTE OF ARTS

5200 Woodward Avenue, Detroit, Michigan
Hours: Tues., 9–9; Wed.–Sun., 9–6; July–Aug., 9–6;
closed Monday and holidays.
Library. Restaurant. Free.

Detroit is so much a symbol of Industrial-America-on-wheels that it is easy to forget it was founded by a French aristocrat, and that as late as 1830 city proclamations were made in both French and English. A fire in 1805 left less of the town than Mrs. O'Leary's cow left of neighboring Chicago. Some of the few links with Detroit's colonial past are in the museum's French Canadian provincial gallery.

The institute grew out of an art loan exhibition initiated by a newspaperman, William Brearley, in 1883. By 1889 James E. Scripps, publisher of the *Evening News,* had given seventy old masters to the museum, some of them among the best paintings in the collection.

An Italianate Renaissance building, companion to the public library across the street, was erected in 1927. Two recent wings give the museum 11 acres of coverage. (Collections are being rearranged and maps and other directional aids will be available.) The new south wing opens into a court, its three-storied roof supported by elegant brass columns. The outside marble walls of the main museum ingeniously form the inside walls of the court. Galleries on all floors lead to overhanging balconies. Windows in stairwells and at corners soar vertically, ground to roof. A thoughtful gesture is an underground garage.

The great hall with its armor and tapestries takes you to the Rivera court. When one recovers from the shock of these powerful, stridently colored Diego Rivera frescoes in an Italianate setting divided by pilasters, pylons, grilles, and baroque masks, the genius of Rivera as a muralist hits home. Somehow unity happens. The life of the auto worker from embryo to assembly line, the monster machines, everything that goes into the making of an automobile shows upon the walls; Edsel Ford made one stipulation, that the subject matter must have to do with Detroit.

The museum's objective is to show in sequence the arts of human civilization. The encyclopedic aim is modestly realized in some areas, spectacularly well in others. Dominating baroque paintings from the seventeenth and eighteenth centuries is Rubens' *St. Ives of Treguier,* a relatively early work of imposing scale and brilliant color, generally agreed to be entirely by the master's hand. Don't miss the small Rubens sketch of *Briseis Returned to Achilles,* made from one of a series of tapestries. All trace of the tapestries has disappeared and the last record of them is in an 1852 catalogue by Viollet-le-Duc, the great nine-teenth-century architect and medievalist. The surmise is that they were burned to obtain their gold and silver thread.

In one of the finest collections of North European paintings in America, an undisputed masterpiece is Pieter Brueghel the Elder's *The Wedding Dance,* equally admired by scholars and school children. Among the earlier Italian works there are three marvel-ous small Sassettas of the Passion. These Renaissance paintings were separated in the eighteenth century and finally brought back together in Detroit in 1953. The museum had bought the first of its Sassettas from Sir Joseph Duveen in 1924 and acquired the second in Assisi in 1946. Chivalry is not dead, even in the auction house. When the last of the trilogy went up for sale at auction in London, sympathetic museum directors refrained from bidding against Detroit.

It's the rare "find" that keeps art scholars happy and alert; one occurred recently in the heart of London's Piccadilly. The Mother Superior of All Saints Roman Catholic Convent sent to Sotheby's auction house a small painting which had hung in the convent parlor for years. It was recognized as a panel from a predella representing the Passion. Other panels from the same predella were discovered in the nineteenth century and are in the Vatican, the Fogg Museum, and the Philadelphia Museum. In Detroit's panel, *Resurrection,* Christ soars above the tomb in golden glory against dawn-black Tuscan hills. It is attributed to the Master of Osservanza (Osservanza is a convent outside Siena), whose fif-teenth-century work has long been confused with Sassetta's. Another panel "find" is the Sienese Giovanni di Paolo's *St. Cath-erine of Siena Dictating the Dialogues.*

There is a rich trove of small Flemish and German treasures. In Van Eyck's *St. Jerome in His Study,* that most painted of all saints in the history of the church is busy translating the Bible from Hebrew into Latin. One of the first examples of oil painting, it is as fresh and brilliant as it was when Van Eyck did it 500 years ago. Detroit has another masterpiece in *St. Jerome in the Desert* by Rogier van der Weyden.

The Dutch galleries are museum magnets. Ruisdael's *The Wind-mill* and *Canal Scene* are placid little paintings, contrasting sharply with his darkly romantic *The Cemetery.* In *The Visitation,*

Rembrandt sets and dresses this scene from the life of the Virgin in his own seventeenth century. The face of Mary is the face of Rembrandt's first wife, Saskia. *A Woman Weeping* is one of Rembrandt's smaller gems. Terborch's *Lady at her Toilet* is richly organized in color, brilliant in the depiction of satiny stuffs and textures, charming in gesture—one of Terborch's tours de force. Less brilliant but equally satisfying is this master of genre's *Man Reading a Letter.*

The Oriental section has one of the great Chinese paintings in America, *Early Autumn,* by Ch'ien Hsuan. Early European sculpture wanders from the third to thirteenth centuries, with fine examples of German and French carvings. Andrea Pisano's *Madonna and Child* looks astonishingly contemporary.

The outstanding American section goes the distance—primitive to now. Of great popular interest is Copley's 1778 *Watson and the Shark.* After he settled in London, Copley met Brook Watson, an Englishman who told him how, as a young apprentice seaman swimming in Havana Harbor, he had been attacked by a shark. He was saved by a group of men in a small boat, but not until the shark had made off with a leg. The painting, commissioned by Watson, was Copley's first ambitious excursion outside the field of portraiture. The original is now in the National Gallery, Washington; an almost identical version hangs in the Boston Museum of Fine Arts; the preliminary oil sketch is at the Metropolitan; and a fourth oil, a smaller version signed and dated 1782, is Detroit's. Nearby hangs a beautiful head, painted by Copley in a singularly free style, of the Negro sailor who stands in the rescue boat. Rembrandt Peale's *Self Portrait* was a "consolation" painting for his wife, whom he left behind when he went on a two-year

Gerard Terborch (Dutch, 1617–1681): *A Lady at Her Toilet* (Courtesy of the Detroit Institute of Arts)

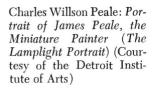

Charles Willson Peale: *Portrait of James Peale, the Miniature Painter* (*The Lamplight Portrait*) (Courtesy of the Detroit Institute of Arts)

trip to Europe. His father Charles Willson Peale's *The Lamplight Portrait* is a direct, affectionate portrayal of his brother, James Peale, the miniature painter. In this work Charles Peale was unusually preoccupied with light, using lamplight to dramatize a portion of the face much in the manner of Georges de La Tour, the French painter. Just about every great name in American Art is here, including Whistler whose *Nocturne in Black and Gold: The Falling Rocket* caused the noisy defamation suit between Whistler and Ruskin. But the strength of the collection lies in its completeness, including the lesser names that contributed so much to American art trends. The gift of the John S. Newberry collection of nineteenth- and early twentieth-century drawing strengthens an already important group of drawings and prints that begin with the fifteenth century.

The contemporary section, once something of a stepchild, has been accepted into the family. Admire Clyfford Still, Soulages, Tworkov, Kline, Moore, Arp, Vasarely, Max Bill, Morris Louis, Rothko, Baziotes . . . and watch for newcomers.

Beyond the paintings, Egyptian, Greek, Assyrian, and Persian arts are far from neglected. The prehistoric Irish gold stash is a coup and an enchantment.

Decorative arts holdings are used in proper context, whether it is to create an ambiance in the galleries of seventeenth-century French paintings or in a Renaissance room.

Besides presenting a collection skillfully chosen and documented, the Detroit Institute publishes *The Art Quarterly,* and was responsible for setting up the Archives of American Art. Now an independent organization, with headquarters in the institute and an office in New York, the archives will ultimately be a complete research center, an unparalleled sanctum for records of our whole cultural history.

DE WATERS ART CENTER:
FLINT INSTITUTE OF ARTS

1120 E. Kearsley Street, Flint, Michigan
Hours: Mon.–Sat., 10–5; Sun., 1–6; Tues., 7–9.
Library.
Free.

Eight years ago the thirty-seven-year-old Flint Institute of Arts moved to the De Waters Art Center, a bustling school with classes in almost every phase of the arts for both the young and the not-so-young.

In 1966 a new wing was added, doubling the institute's space; the result was a low-slung complex built on simple clean lines around an inner glassed-in court. In summer concerts are held in the court, but through all seasons William Zorach's handsome *Spirit of the Dance* and David Hare's *Man Learning to Fly* preside there.

At the institute's entrance is a rich panel of stained glass by Abraham Rattner. Exhibitions change in the large galleries at the left. For the opening, the first Flint Invitational Exhibition was held. Two museum directors from metropolitan centers selected a contemporary painting exhibition of the highest quality. Out of this the institute purchased paintings by Curtis Rhodes, Edward Higgins, Adolph Gottlieb, Mary Bauermeister, and Richard Anuszkiewicz—an auspicious beginning. A small Oriental collection contains jades, ivories, porcelain, and Chinese scroll paintings. A Renaissance room of grand proportions holds tapestries, furniture, and *objets d'art*. The informally named Ramp gallery contains more of the permanent collection, and beyond is what must be the most elegant and comfortable Members' Room and library in museum circles.

The collection is small but, like everything else in Flint, growing. There is a fine, atypical Cassatt, a Renoir, a Redon, an Utrillo, a Jawlensky, and works by Americans Stuart, Heade, and Cropsey. Eighteenth-century Germanic goblets and rummers, formerly in the Hohenlohe and Lubeck collections sparkle now in Flint.

However, it is in its continuing program that the institute is especially fortunate. Few museums have the financial civic backing of their exhibition program that Flint enjoys. "Realism Revisited," a show that attracted national interest, was sponsored by the Fisher Body Company, as was "American Sculpture 1900–

Mary Cassatt: *Femme à la Tapisserie* (ca. 1881) (Flint Institute of Arts, DeWaters Art Center, Flint, Michigan)

1956." The Flint Annual was made possible by the A. C. Spark Plug Company. This pattern of industrial support leaves idea and selection to the museum professionals and provides distinguished exhibitions otherwise beyond the reach of a small museum.

KALAMAZOO INSTITUTE OF ARTS

341 South Park Street, Kalamazoo, Michigan
Hours: Tues.–Fri., 11–4:30; Wed., 7:30–9:30; Sat., 9–4; Sun., 1–4;
closed Mon., holidays, and last two weeks in August.
Library.
Free.

Kalamazoo is an Indian word for "water boiling in the pot," and the pot where the art simmers here is a handsome building erected by Skidmore, Owings and Merrill. Built in the shape of a "C" around a garden court, it has an outdoors-indoors ambiance, and even its nether regions—mail and printing room, workshop, tool crib, matting room, photo printing lab—make larger museums envious. Incorporated in 1924, its first meeting in the YWCA, the art center moved about, gaining the momentum that resulted in the present 1961 structure. An ingenious removable-panel system provides space for large painting exhibitions or, when removed, reveals built-in wall cases for display of three-dimensional objects.

The institute aims to establish a distinguished collection of prints, drawings, watercolors, and small sculpture from all parts of the world, as well as twentieth-century America. Sculpture by Zorach, Armitage, Caesar, Epstein, and Gauguin are good initial ingredients, and an active, changing exhibition program keeps the spacious galleries alive with new excitement.

AKRON ART INSTITUTE

69 East Market Street, Akron, Ohio
Hours: Tues.–Fri., 12–5; Sat., 9–5; Wed.–Thurs., 7–10; Sun., 2–6.
Closed holidays.
Free.

The Akron Art Institute is a good example of how a lively museum can be created without much of a permanent collection to draw from. One gallery rotates work of artists of the region; traveling exhibitions change almost every month. Northern Ohio's excellent craftsmen hold their exhibitions here every spring. Dutch and Flemish paintings include *The Conversion of St. Paul* by Hendrik de Clerck and *The Backgammon Players* by Dirck van Baburen. Italian highlights are *Madonna and Child* by Cima da Conegliano and *The Woodcutter* by Alessandro Magnasco. Top among the French nineteenth-century paintings is *Apotheosis of William the Silent* by Eugène Delacroix, while the twentieth century is best represented by the Belgian surrealist René Magritte's brooding, ominous *Les Pas Perdus*.

CINCINNATI ART MUSEUM

Eden Park, Cincinnati, Ohio
Hours: Mon.–Sat., 10–5; Sun. & holidays, 2–5;
Tues. eves. Oct. to April, 5–10;
closed Thanksgiving & Christmas.
Free.

Cincinnati was ready for art well before this museum opened in 1886. Early settlers had carted their family portraits, spinets, and libraries across the mountains to settle on the banks of the Ohio. In 1837 Nicholas Longworth sent the young sculptor Hiram Powers abroad to study. In the 1850s the Ladies Academy of Fine Arts planned a "gallery of good taste." But the Civil War intervened. The ladies, or their daughters, made a second start in 1877 with the Women's Art Museum Association; nine years later a formidable Romanesque building, the core of today's museum, was opened.

   To the right and left of the entrance is the world of antiquity. Rare Nabataean sculptures of the first and second century from southern Jordan and Israel, the Holy Land in the time of the

Apostles, are to the left. Nowhere else outside Jordan can one see such a collection of Nabataean figure pieces. Proceed directly ahead for a resumé of Egyptian, Greek, Roman life and culture: a tense little Etruscan warrior of sixth to fifth century B.C.; a *Sacrificial Heifer,* a third-century B.C. copy of a sculpture by Myron. The original, a life-size bronze, stood on the Acropolis for centuries, then disappeared. An Athenian late sixth-century B.C. bronze *Bull,* grand and elegant, is a pet of scholars and amateurs. To the right of the entrance are the ancient Near East, pre-Persian, Persian, then Sassanian.

Many of the small pieces, monumental in their implications, cover 3,000 years of Mesopotamian history. A favorite is the bronze *Votive Calf* (Sumerian), 10 inches tall. The scale is intimate, the concept tender. Barely able to stand, he thrusts his head out inquiringly at his brand new world, the world of twenty-three centuries before the birth of Christ. A noteworthy *Libation Bowl,* which is inscribed "Darius Great King," is Persian, 522–485 B.C.

The centuries unroll from Moslem India to a still older Buddhist India, and China. *The Four Sages of Shang Shan,* largest and most important of the five paintings which survive from the hand of Ma Yuan (1190–1224 A.D.), is among the rarest masterpieces of Chinese painting in America. The transition from East to West takes place in the new (1965) decorative arts wing, where French, English, and American period rooms adjoin a Henri IV salon (1608–1610), a bijou of painted panels recounting the story of Amintas and Sylvia. With justifiable pride, Cincinnati stresses its own past. The Greek Revival hallway of the 1815 Kilgour house is set with marble busts of famous "Cincinnatians," among them Nicholas Longworth by his protégé Hiram Powers. Thomas Jefferson gave the cider jug in the wall case to John Adams in the twilight of their lives. A plate from the Mount Vernon dinner service was a present from Washington to Hamilton.

Painting galleries are upstairs, with the Alms wing reserved for changing exhibitions. The mood of the Italian room is reminiscent of a great *galleria* in a Florentine *palazzo.* Again the centuries unroll. Who better represents the Renaissance than Mantegna with his *Esther and Mordecai,* one of six Mantegnas in America. Or Botticelli with his little jewel, *Judith with the Head of Holofernes.* Or Titian's *Portrait of Philip II,* which Berenson called "a great painting, heroic without rhetoric," or Fra Angelico's tiny *tondo Madonna and Child with Goldfinch.*

To the right of the medieval sculpture hall, *not* to be passed through hurriedly, is the museum's pride—the reconstructed apse

LEFT: Andrea Mantegna: *Esther and Mordecai* (Cincinnati Art Museum) **ABOVE:** San Baudelio frescoes (Cincinnati Art Museum)

of San Baudelio de Berlanga (Spain). To fully appreciate the apse and its frescos, get the monograph (at the entrance book counter) written by the museum's director, Philip R. Adams. The story of the frescos' transfer and tribulations makes fascinating reading. Most of the secular subjects, apart from those in Cincinnati, which were at The Cloisters in New York, have gone back to Spain and the Prado. Two are in Boston's Museum of Fine Arts; two at the John Herron Art Institute, Indianapolis; three at The Cloisters. At the opposite end of the apse is a great piece of twelfth-century Gothic sculpture, the figure of Don Sancho Saiz de Carillo. The tomb portrait lies on a low, wooden casket and has been faithfully reconstructed from the site in the Ermita de San Andres, Mahamud, Province of Burgos. The noble head rests on a pillow. One hand holds gauntlets, while sword, chain, and ring, accoutrements of knighthood, can be seen.

Holland and Flanders are handsomely represented in Cincinnati by Rembrandt's *Young Girl Holding Medal,* Pieter de Hooch's precise and luminous *Game of Skittles,* works by Ruisdael, Terborch, Van Dyck, Nicholas Maes's engaging *Titus, Son of Rembrandt,* and Joos van Cleve's portrait of the connoisseur king, Francis I. It was Francis who brought Leonardo da Vinci to France and in whose hands the aged Leonardo left the *Mona Lisa.*

The Spanish galleries, adjacent to the Dutch, hold great retables (the raised surface back of the altar, usually a painted triptych) at either end of the room. One by Lorenzo de Zaragoza shows the life of St. Peter. The other, the *Tendilla Retable*, was painted when the Count of Tendilla had defeated the Moors and Spain was mistress of the New World.

Gainsborough has a room all to himself with four landscapes and seven portraits, including *Lord Greville* and a rare miniature of *Lord Mulgrave*, who commissioned *The Cottage Door*, one large version of which hangs in the gallery. The French galleries, extending back in time to Claude, celebrate the flowering of art under the Louis' with paintings by Watteau, Boucher, and Fragonard. It arrives at the classicism of Ingres, the drama of Delacroix, and culminates in that great chapter of French art, Impressionism. Cézanne's first dated canvas, *Bread and Eggs*, is wonderfully strong and rich. Octagonal galleries break the tyranny of row galleries. One full of small French treasures leads into the new Mary Johnston galleries with great Braques, Picassos, Grises, Rouaults that have come to the collection from a recent bequest. Among the prints: many rare and unique old masters, an extensive contemporary group, and the most complete single collection of contemporary Biblical and religious prints in the country.

Representing America is a large and handsome section of paintings. Two delightful portraits are Charles W. Peale's *Mr. and Mrs. Francis Bailey*. Benjamin West's *Laertes and Ophelia* fills an entire wall and must have posed an engineering problem when Nicholas Longworth had it hauled over the Alleghenies in 1819.

Anthony Van Dyke: *Portrait of Christine Bruce, Countess of Devonshire* (The Columbus Gallery of Fine Arts, Columbus, Ohio)

Frank Duveneck, born across the river at Covington and some-time director of the museum's art academy, and other native-son artists, John Twachtman, Worthington Whittredge, Henry F. Farny, painter of Western scenes, are well represented. A flag-raiser is Grant Wood's *Daughters of Revolution*. That this gently satirical canvas will take its place "in the hearts of my country-men" right alongside *Washington Crossing the Delaware* (shown as the background of Wood's painting) is a foregone conclusion. The American watercolor section is rich in works by Homer, Sargent and Whistler.

In the large center court upstairs, two enormous murals by Miró and Steinberg commissioned for the Terrace Plaza Hotel hold forth. Along with the large Calder mobile, these refugees from the Hilton chain are shown to fine advantage.

While the museum is not strong on contemporary works, the examples of sculpture by David Smith, Jacques Lipchitz, Mary Callery, Charles Cutler, and Marino Marini are important, as are recently acquired paintings by Hans Hofmann, Will Barnett, and Julian Stanczak. And the Contemporary Arts Center picks up where the museum leaves off. The three great museums in Ohio complement rather than compete with each other: Toledo with its definitive glass collection, Cleveland with its medieval treas-ures, and Cincinnati's superb Near Eastern holdings.

CONTEMPORARY ARTS CENTER

113 West 4th Street, Cincinnati, Ohio
Hours: Daily, 10–5; Sat., 10–3;
closed Sun. and holidays.

The Contemporary Arts Center is the place in town to see what's up and coming in today's art scene. The center's present quarters on the fourth floor of a downtown building will be changed for a permanent home in the core of Cincinnati's redevelopment area around Fountain Square. A shopping arcade will occupy the first floor, the center, the entire upper tier for gallery, administrative, and membership space. Given this added dimension, its exhibi-tions reflecting the current national and international arena will, we are sure, continue to be thoughtful and provocative.

TAFT MUSEUM

316 Pike Street, Cincinnati, Ohio
Hours: Mon.–Sat., 10–5; Sun. and holidays, 2–5;
closed Thanksgiving, Christmas.
Library.
Free.

The Charles Taft home, built in 1820 for Morton Baum, mayor of Cincinnati, marks the transition from Federal to Greek Revival architecture. Baum sold the house to Nicholas Longworth. Later it passed to the Tafts, who gave it to the city in 1932 to become a public museum.

Today, the lovely old edifice is virtually its original self. Tall cases in the style of the moldings and the mantels have been added to hold the decorative arts. These are rich in French Renaissance jewelry, Chinese porcelain, Italian majolica, rock crystal, and enamels. Distinguished are two Leonard Limosin's portraits one of the *Duc de Guise* and the other of *Thomas Cranmer, Archbishop of Canterbury,* and of course, a Limoges triptych of the Crucifixion.

Many paintings hang exactly where they did during the long years that the Tafts lived there. The Dutch and English schools of painting are strong, with twelve Turners and three important Hals. Rembrandt's *Young Man Rising from a Chair,* an early work, can be compared with his late *An Elderly Woman,* which is in the same room. There are two Goyas—*Toreador* and *Portrait of Queen Maria Luisa;* in the second, the artist comes as close to satire as was safe for a court painter, showing the Queen as a plump woman with a mean little mouth, vainly overjeweled, her

Goya: *Queen Maria Luisa* (Taft Museum, Cincinnati, Ohio)

crowning arrogance a foot-long diamond arrow stabbing through a mop of black hair.

Gardens around the house make a haven from the streets of downtown Cincinnati. Nicholas Longworth spent a good deal of time on the plantings. A family story tells how a tall young man leaned over the fence one day and asked Longworth, grubby in old gardening clothes, if he thought his master would mind his looking around the gardens. Without identifying himself, Longworth took the stranger around. The young man was Abraham Lincoln on his first trip to Cincinnati.

COLUMBUS GALLERY OF FINE ARTS

480 East Broad Street, Columbus, Ohio
Hours: Daily, 12–5; closed Christmas, Thanksgiving.
Library.
Free.

The museum's founding father, Francis C. Sessions, was, in the familiar nineteenth-century tradition, a wealthy private collector who left his home, his pictures, and his "statuary" to the city.

In 1931, a pleasant neo-classic building replaced the Sessions house, and into it went Ferdinand Howald's distinguished collection of contemporary American art. No one knew what led Howald, a thoughtful, reticent bachelor and owner of the town's leading furniture store, to become one of the century's most courageous and selective collectors of American art. But by 1908, Howald had begun to purchase such American Impressionists as Ernest Lawson, and works of then unknown young artists. A recluse, he never met any of the men whose paintings he collected with such taste and foresight. He did most of his buying through the small Daniels Gallery on New York's Madison Avenue, including some of the first canvases by Peter Blume, Max Weber, and Kuniyoshi. Later, he moved into the modern French field, buying Picasso and Matisse at a time when most Midwesterners were still looking for bargains in Bierstadt. The glory of Howald's gift to Columbus is one of the finest collections extant of such recognized Americans as Marin (twenty-eight watercolors), Demuth (twenty-eight), Prendergast (fourteen), and the largest group of Pascins in any museum in the country.

Another collector important in the gallery's growth was Frederick Schumacher, who made his fortune from the patent medicine Peruna. No recluse, he felt a typical nineteenth-century mission to "bring things of beauty to this new raw land." His preferences were for the English portrait school and seventeenth-century Dutch flower painting. An outstanding picture in the Schumacher gallery is the portrait of *William Robert Fitzgerald, 2nd Duke of Leinster* by Sir Joshua Reynolds, executed with all his subtle richness and elegance. The Duke sits at his desk; his hand, emerging from a lace cuff, toys with a pen. Even a neat job of restoration cannot conceal the fact that the entire lower right area, the part containing the hand, has been slashed. Robert Fitzgerald was accused of having sold out the Irish Parliament, and the slashed hand was the one that signed the dissolution. It is quite probable that some Irish patriot, visiting the country house where the painting hung, took his revenge.

The general range of the collection is wide, including Egyptian and Renaissance sculpture, Renoir's charming *Madame Henriot in Fancy Dress Costume,* and Sebastiano del Piombo's portrait of *Vittoria Colonna and Ferdinando d'Avalos,* her husband. Del Piombo caught the fine, austere intelligence of Vittoria Colonna, for it was around her that writers, artists, and the intellectuals of the day gathered. Del Piombo's own teacher, Michelangelo, was Vittoria Colonna's long-time platonic love, and of her he was to say that she perfected his character as a sculptor perfects his clay model, "by carving it in hard living stone." A magnificent portrait by Bronzino of the elderly Vittoria hangs in the De Young Museum in San Francisco.

The enormous skylighted Derby Court in the center of the museum houses the Derby collection of the masters. Of two recent additions, courtesy of the Derby Fund, *Christ Triumphant Over Sin and Death* by Rubens is a rarity. Large altarpieces completely by Rubens' hand are unusual outside European royal collections or the churches for which they were painted. Rubens did this one in 1618 at the zenith of his productivity. *Christina Bruce, Countess of Devonshire* by Anthony Van Dyck was painted about 1632 and remained in the family until its recent migration.

The town takes inordinate pride in its native son, painter George Bellows, although he disappointed many when after college he left to study art in New York instead of going into major-league baseball. In the days before we had stringent amateur rules, Bellows spent his college summers playing with national teams. But his legend grows and is cherished in his home town. Some of his choicest paintings, including *Portrait of My Mother,*

Polo at Lakewood, and *Children on the Porch,* are here in the Bellows room.

Visitors interested in archaeology should stop at the Ohio State Museum. The whole midwest basin of the Mound Builder civilization is recorded and many rare examples displayed. Plans are being drawn for a new $10 million museum scheduled to open in 1970 in the Fair Grounds.

DAYTON ART INSTITUTE

Forest and Riverview Avenues, Dayton, Ohio
Hours: Tues.–Fri., 12:30–5; Sat., 9–5; Sun., 1–6;
closed holidays.
Library. Restaurant. Free.

The Big Miami River flows sluggishly through the center of Dayton. From a lofty hill, the far-from-sluggish art institute peers down upon it. Italian Renaissance *palazzi,* above all the Villa d'Este, inspired the building Mrs. H. G. Carnell gave the town in 1929. (Lately a handsome new art-school wing has been added.) You expect a gloomy entrance into such ponderous buildings, portrait of donor downstage center. You're surprised. Comfortably furnished conversation areas becken hospitably. A broad stair takes you to a marble sculpture hall where a Matisse bronze may find congeniality with a fourth-century portrait head.

Originally, as in so many museums, the collection reflected the predilection of the donor. Mrs. Harrie G. Carnell preferred Oriental art. However, out of a sizable collection, much is reserved for study; only objects of top quality are displayed, on the theory

Hindu deity (Vaishnavi) (Tanjore district, South India; Chola period, 850–1200 A.D.) (The Dayton Art Institute)

that the average layman benefits most from seeing the best. The best includes a small silver vase of the T'ang Dynasty (618–906 A.D.) with birds and animals in exquisite gold relief, one of two such pieces in America. The other is in the Boston Museum of Fine Arts. In the last Oriental gallery, the dawn of Chinese Buddhist sculpture is exemplified by a bodhisattva head, from the temple caves (Northern Wei Dynasty, about 500 A.D.). This was carved from the living rock of a cave temple. Simple and strong, the head is a fine contrast to a sophisticated and worldly Kuan Yin head in dry clay of the Sung Dynasty, 960–1279 A.D. Some superb small Mayan pieces are in the pre-Columbian collection.

Few museums can boast a portrait of their city's founder, but here is Thomas Sully's *Elias Jonathan Dayton,* a good example of that popular nineteenth-century painter's work. The present emphasis on buying is for that exuberant period, the baroque. One fine psychological canvas, *Portrait of a Widow,* is by Ludovico Carracci. In 1848 it was put up for sale in a Paris auction room as a portrait of Mary Stuart by Velásquez. The attribution was not entirely foolish, as scholars who have lately studied Velásquez hold that he may well have been influenced by Ludovico, who, with his painter nephews, had established the first academy of painting in Bologna some years before Velásquez, young and impressionable, visited Italy. Other recent purchases are *Boy Violinist* by Hendrick Terbrugghen, the first Dutchman influenced by Caravaggio; and Rubens' painting of his friend *Daniel Nys; St. Sebastian* by Paolo Pagani; *St. Francis in Ecstasy* by Barnardo Strozzi. A superb *quattrocento cassone* panel by Jacopo del Sellaio is a recent acquisition, as is the granite, tenth-century, South Indian *Vaishnavi.*

Norman Bluhm, Sam Francis, Raymond Parker, Ad Reinhardt,

Ludovico Carracci (1555–1619): *Portrait of a Widow* (The Dayton Art Institute)

Alan Davie, and sculptors Robert Ranieri, Michael Lekakis, Fred Farr, and Richard Stankiewicz are among those represented in the contemporary collection. Eight artists of the region are chosen for one-man shows each year.

Dayton's museum was the first in America to start a rental library, in 1922, even before the present building was erected. It became known as the "Dayton plan."

A bright feature of Dayton's purchasing policy is based on a "speculative fund" set up to buy work of young artists, most of whom have not yet reached the point of having dealers handle them—a refreshing combination of confidence and venturousness.

OBERLIN COLLEGE:
ALLEN MEMORIAL ART MUSEUM

Oberlin, Ohio
Hours (Winter): Mon.–Fri., 1:30–4:30, 7–9; Sat.–Sun., 2–5:30.
Summer: Mon.–Fri., 10–12, 2–4; Sat., 2–5, 7–9; Sun., 2–6.
Closed spring holidays, July 4, Thanksgiving, Christmas holidays.
Free.

Cass Gilbert, New York architect, called upon local quarries for this buff and pink Italianate museum, the gift of Dr. Dudley Peter Allen, a distinguished Cleveland surgeon. As soon as it opened in 1917, the first college museum west of the Alleghenies, the trustees embarked upon the serious business of forming a collection. Charles L. Freer (see Freer Gallery, Washington) had previously given Chinese and Japanese paintings and ceramics. The opening of the museum stimulated more check writing. But it was the establishment in 1940 by a former graduate, R. T. Miller, of a generous purchasing fund that allowed the college to compete in the marketplace for such masterpieces as Hendrick Terbrugghen's *Saint Sebastian* and Jusepe da Ribera's *Blind Old Beggar*. The Kress Foundation added to the considerable fifteenth- and sixteenth-century Italian group. While not abounding in great names, the canvases hold unusual interest, especially the Dutch, German, and Spanish. The nineteenth-century French come off well with Cézanne, Pissarro, and two gleaming Sisleys (though English by birth, Sisley is always counted among the French). A little charmer is *The Crowd* by Felix Vallotton. Daumier, on seeing Monet's *Garden of the Princess, Louvre* in a gallery window, urged the proprietor to take the horror out. While not agreeing

Expulsion from Paradise (Netherlandish, early seventeenth century) (Allen Memorial Art Museum, Oberlin College, Oberlin, Ohio)

with Daumier, we prefer his *Wisteria,* also at Oberlin. Kokoschka, Kirchner, Modigliani, Picasso, Braque, and Matisse bring us into the twentieth century, to Jim Dine and Larry Poons.

Sculpture starts with the Sumerians and Egyptians, goes on to Etruscans and Romans, from the Copts to medieval and Renaissance. A little wild Tuscan *Mask of a Fawn* is arresting. An early seventeenth-century Netherlands ivory, *Expulsion from Paradise,* shows a coy and unrepenting Eve and Adam in a "photographers go away" stance. Rodin's *Prodigal Son,* Picasso, Maillol, Despiau, Moore, and Arp bring sculpture to the present. Those interested in American glass will find a selection from a group of 1,400 pressed goblets always on display. The 1967 catalogue of the collection, compiled by art historian Wolfgang Stechow, is a must for the serious visitor.

TOLEDO MUSEUM OF ART

Monroe Street at Scottwood Avenue, Toledo, Ohio
Hours: Tues.–Sat., 9–5; Sun., Mon., & holidays,
except Dec. 25 and Jan. 1, 1–5. Library. Free.

Understandably, one of the great collections in Toledo is glass—ancient, Islamic, European, and American. Edward Drummond Libbey, museum founder, took a personal interest in old glass as well as old masters, and the museum never passes up an opportunity to keep its glass collection among the most glittering.

Libbey came to Toledo in 1880. Its natural gas attracted him when wood for his glass-blowing works became scarce in Cambridge, Massachusetts. With him, Libbey brought Mike Owens, a labor leader with whom he fought constantly, but whose talents he respected. When Owens invented the first machine for blowing bottles, the Libbey-Owens fortune was made. This move made Toledo one of the glass capitals of the world and provided the economic base—on which all art depends—for Libbey and other citizens to develop a center for the city's cultural life. In 1901, they pooled $1,200 and opened Toledo's first art gallery in one room of a downtown office building. Unlike many other tycoons of the era, who contributed to museums but would have been just as happy building stadiums, Libbey loved the arts. He was purchasing for his home the Rembrandt and Hals which form the basis for Toledo's fine Dutch and Flemish section when "Barbizon forests" flourished thickly in most American drawing rooms. Not that Libbey eschewed the Barbizons. Toledo has some striking examples. At a time when the Metropolitan in New York allowed "groups of not more than six" children through its halls, Libbey in 1906 was encouraging every school child in Toledo to visit the museum. His concern gave Toledo its lead in art education, today over 2,000 children troop every Saturday to free classes.

Start with the many facets of the world of glass in a large gallery at the left of the sales desk. Enameling on the important Islamic piece *Toledo Flagon* (Toledo, Spain, about 1300), which to Western eyes seems a pleasing abstract design, really is an Arabic inscription dedicated to the nobility. The iridescence of some ancient glass here with its shimmering, multicolored beauty comes from centuries underground as tomb offerings, where age, decay, and chemical reaction set in. The Tiffany glass of our century was inspired by it. Certainly Wedgewood went straight to the Roman first-century blue glass for its color seed. One of the world's great Roman pieces is Toledo's *Amphora* or *Cameo Vase* (first century), which is comparable to the British Museum's *Portland Vase*. The ancient glass, whether Syrian, Sassanian, Mycenaean (see the beautiful blue necklace, fourteenth century B.C.), or Egyptian, is shown in distinguished examples. American glass commences with the work of Jamestown's eight glass blowers, members of the group who settled in Virginia in 1607. Amelung and Stiegel glass keynote Toledo's great wealth in nineteenth-century American glass, blown, pressed, and cut—with appropriate emphasis on New England and Ohio vessels. Cut glass, for which Libbey set the standard, is understandably well represented. The European entries range from cobweb Venetian (see the enameled fifteenth-century goblet from Anzolo Barovier) to sturdy Bohemian, to the brilliant clarity of the lead crystal made in England by Thomas Ravenscroft in the 1600s.

From the workshop of Anzolo Barovier: enameled goblet (late fifteenth century) (The Toledo Museum of Art)

The Book Room, first gallery of its kind in an American museum, records the history of man's communication through the written word: the birth of the alphabet in Egyptian hieroglyphics; the cylinder on which Nebuchadnezzar describes the building of the walls of Babylon; a letter of Diogenes; illuminated manuscripts; leaves from the Gutenberg Bible; rare incunabula and first editions.

A gloriously gay and light Rubens, *The Crowning of St. Catherine*, sheds an atmosphere more secular than religious. Paul J. Sachs, the Harvard art historian, called this canvas "beyond question the finest and purest large Rubens in the country." Among the Spaniards, Velásquez, El Greco, Zurbarán, and Goya dazzle. In *Christ at Gethsemane* El Greco presents an atypical and interesting study in circles—the sleeping Apostles wrapped in a womblike fold, a round of guards, and a great moon plunging through the clouds. His *Annunciation* on the same wall is a personal, tender interpretation. Italian paintings range from a severe Romanesque panel to seventeenth-century baroque canvases. Piero de Cosimo's *Adoration of the Child* is surely one of the two or three great Renaissance *tondi* in America. Two figure panels by Luca Signorelli are part of an altarpiece commissioned for the Bicchi Chapel in Sant Agostino, Siena. An important predella panel from the same altar is at the Clark Institute, Williamstown, Massachusetts. Of several impressive paintings acquired in the last few years Mattia Preti's *Feast of Herod,* the horrifying scene of Salome before the court, painted by the Neapolitan baroque master, and Pietro da Cortona's *The Virgin Appearing to St. Bernard* majestically represent the Italian seventeenth century. A masterpiece that entered the collection in 1964 is Francesco Primaticcio's *Ulysses and Penelope,* a rare easel painting showing Ulysses recounting his adventures to his wife Penelope. It is based on a fresco in the Gallery of Ulysses at Fontainebleau, Primaticcio's greatest work. Gerard David's *St. Anthony Raising the Drowned*

Francesco Primaticcio (1504–1570): *Ulysses and Penelope* (ca. 1563) (The Toledo Museum of Art)

Child is one of three altarpiece scenes here illustrating St. Anthony of Padua's miracles (the center panel is in the National Gallery). David, an artist of the early Dutch Renaissance, painted in rich, deep colors.

Libbey's last purchase was Manet's *Portrait of Antonine Proust* (Proust authored a book on Manet). The museum took it from there and has built a fine hoard of Impressionist and Post-Impressionist paintings. Don't overlook Cézanne's *The Avenue at Chantilly* or an equally fine Courbet, *Landscape Near Ornans;* or the older masterpieces—Poussin's *Mars and Venus* and a great Boucher, *The Mill at Charenton.*

There's sculpture of all times and from all places. Ancient Egyptian reliefs and statues lead into Greek and Roman. Medieval saints passively survey a grouping of cloister arcades representing three French sources from mid-twelfth century to late fourteenth century. The Renaissance shows up in the enchanting *San Donato Madonna* by Lucca della Robbia, and in fine small bronzes. The glazed terra cotta relief of the Madonna is considered by scholars as the finest Della Robbia in America. Sculpture rambling through the ensuing centuries terminates in a great Henry Moore reclining figure as monumental as the colossal Egyptian pharaoh who sets the pace for a sculpture promenade.

American paintings? Toledo's interest in American art has been, from the first, eager. Practically every outstanding painter from John Smibert to the present-day heroes is represented by top examples, such as Thomas Cole's *The Architect's Dream* and Childe Hassam's *Rainy Day—Boston—*almost too reminiscent of *Place de L'Europe on a Rainy Day* by Gustave Caillebotte (see Chicago), but a fine Hassam nevertheless.

The last seven years have been years of astounding growth, as the museum's catalogue, *Treasures for Toledo,* will attest. An Egyptian relief and a Palmyrene funerary relief, *Portrait of a Lady,* have moved in. The decorative arts have been desegregated and now team up with painting and sculpture in a series of galleries that give the total feeling of place and period.

As a delightful special feature, a concert hall, or peristyle with a ceiling that turns blue to emulate the sky when the lights dim, seats 1,700. This Hellenistic amphitheater is one of the most beautiful auditoriums in the country. And it's acoustically perfect.

BUTLER INSTITUTE OF AMERICAN ART

524 Wick Avenue, Youngstown, Ohio
Hours: Tues.–Sat., 10–4:30; Sun., 1–5;
closed Mondays.
Free.

J. G. Butler, Jr., was on a train headed for New York when he received word that his house, with his collection of paintings, had burned down. Twenty-four hours later the redoubtable Mr. Butler was making plans with architects McKim, Mead and White for a fireproof museum. Two years later, in 1919, the Butler Art Institute opened. The present director, Joseph G. Butler, the grandson of the founder, is the only hereditary museum director in the country.

In Youngstown, a town of one industry (steel) and many nationalities, where the Poles did not speak to the Italians or the Italians to the Germans, Grandfather Butler's decision to buy nothing but American art for his museum, a startler at the time, worked as a bridge between nationalities.

The oldest paintings usually hang in the entrance gallery: Copley, Stuart, a delightful Earl of *The Strycker Sisters*. The big

Junius Brutus Stearns (1810–1885): *The Marriage of Washington* (1849) (The Butler Institute of American Art, Youngstown, Ohio)

three of the nineteenth century are well represented: Homer by *Snap the Whip* and a drawing and wood engraving of same, Eakins by *The Coral Necklace* and *Portrait of General Cadwalader*, and Ryder by a small *Roadside Meeting*. Another beauty is Whistler's *The Thames from Battersea Bridge*. One downstairs gallery shows sculpture and ceramics of the region, no mean collection, as some of the top ceramists we have work around Cleveland. On the stair landing is a complete set of miniatures of the Presidents of the United States. All those predating Woodrow Wilson were once owned by Diamond Jim Brady, who is said to have lost them in a poker game . . . but not to Mr. Butler. A gallery upstairs has a sea theme, the second-generation Mr. Butler's hobby. Primitive paintings, engravings, ship models, and Henry Mattson, and Reginald Marsh's lusty *Belles of the Battery* enjoy each other's company.

Sole survivor of the fire that inspired the museum is a unique Indian group (it was on loan to the library at the time). Much of the work is by E. A. Burbank (cousin of the naturalist, Luther) and J. H. Sharp. Burbank worked among the Sioux, Apaches, Crows, and Zunis, while Sharp went north to the Blackfoot tribes. In small oil paintings of chiefs—Charging Skunk, Kicking Bear, and Little Wound—each man had an intimate approach and fresh, vital style. No monotony here.

Though the watercolor gallery is large, it can display at one time only a third of what the Butler owns. Generally on view are Burchfield's *September Wind and Rain*, Wyeth's *Sunset*, and Shahn's *Inside Looking Out*. Among contemporary painters there is the romantic realism of Colleen Browning and the starker realism of Carroll Cloar. The action painters, the pop, op, and minimal painters, the experimenters and pacesetters are missing. This is a museum whose director can afford the Renaissance gesture of purchasing and exhibiting only what he believes in. And he does.

BROOKS MEMORIAL ART GALLERY

Overton Park, Memphis, Tennessee
Hours: Tues.–Sat., & holidays, 10–5; Sun., 2–5;
closed Thanksgiving, Dec. 25, Jan. 1.
Free.

In 1966 the Brooks Memorial Art Gallery celebrated its fiftieth birthday. Set in the green of Overton Park, the building's marble façade is a copy of New York's Morgan Library. Another wing

Ralph E. W. Earl: *Portrait of General Andrew Jackson* (Brooks Memorial Art Gallery, Memphis, Tennessee)

was added when the Kress Foundation, whose founder Samuel Kress began his career as a storekeeper in Memphis, gave thirty works of art to the gallery. Two of these to which the museum points with particular pride are the Canaletto, *View of the Grand Canal at San Vito,* and the Romanino, *Mystic Marriage of St. Catherine.*

The gallery boasts one of the finest collections of English portraiture and landscape in the South: Gainsborough, Reynolds, Raeburn, Hoppner, Hogarth, Lawrence, Lely, and Romney, among others. The Richard Wilson painting, *Temple of the Sibyl at Trivoli,* is one of the best examples of this artist's work in the country. Van Dyck's splendid portrait of *Queen Henrietta-Maria of England* was in Charles I's collection. American paintings range from Copley to contemporary. Ralph E. W. Earl, son of the well-known eighteenth-century painter Ralph Earl, did the *Portrait of General Andrew Jackson, President of the United States.* So successful was he that he spent the last twelve years of his life painting Jackson and is buried beside Jackson's own tomb at the Hermitage, Jackson's mansion in Nashville. Some contemporary Americans at the Brooks Gallery: Kenzo Okada, Theodoros Stamos, Andrew Wyeth, Josef Albers, Carroll Cloar, William Congdon, and Edward Giobbi.

A new feature: a "Deep South" collection depicts the unique life of the Delta region in paintings, drawings, and sculpture.

UNIVERSITY OF WISCONSIN: ELVEHJAM ART CENTER

Madison, Wisconsin
Hours: Mon.–Sat., 9–5; Sun., 1–5; closed major holidays. Free.

When the Elvehjam Art Center opens late in 1968 the play will be on a dramatic blend of new concepts and functional design.

It is named for President Elvehjam, who in 1958 instigated a study of campus needs which resulted in the handsome four-storied building which has an auditorium and library on the two lower floors; on the mezzanine and two upper floors, galleries circle a skylighted open court. Paintings range from sixteenth-century Italians and Dutch to the present. The *pièce de résistance* of the Kress group is a marble *tondo, Madonna and Child,* by the Florentine sculptor Benedetto da Maiano. The print collection, large and varied, stretches from Dürer and Rembrandt to four original engravings of William Hogarth, *The Election Series,* plus works by his two rowdy compatriots Rowlandson and Cruikshank, to such current workers as Hayter, Peterdi, Lasansky, and Ben Shahn. Wisconsin may seem an unlikely place for a collection of Russian paintings and icons, including an outstanding fifteenth-century triptych. But there they are, a gift of His Excellency Joseph E. Davies, Ambassador to Russia during the troubled years of World War II. The triptych is from the monastery of Klevo–Pecherskaya–Larva.

With the art center's conservation laboratory, conference and seminar rooms, exhibition construction and planning space, and its generous gallery facility, a new day is dawning for the students and citizens of Madison, who will share the university's good fortune.

MILWAUKEE ART CENTER

750 North Lincoln Memorial Drive,
Milwaukee, Wisconsin
Hours: Mon.–Sat., 10–5; Sun. & holidays, 1–5; Thurs., 10–10;
closed Jan. 1, Dec. 25.
Free.

Though Milwaukee has had a museum since 1888, when civic-minded Fredrick Layton gave his collection and a building to house it to the city, the dynamic force that operates today came with the opening in 1957 of the War Memorial Building and Art Center designed by Eero Saarinen. The effect from three sides is compactness, but from the Lake Drive monumental proportions emerge. Lake Michigan is the picture framed by the fourth side. In 1963 space was opened for ten new galleries and a whopping number of important gifts poured in. The museum's forte is its paintings, especially twentieth-century. Americans begin with

Wassily Kandinsky: *Composition VII, Fragment I* (Courtesy of Milwaukee Art Center)

Benjamin West and come almost full circle to Roy Lichtenstein. Most major movements, such as German Expressionism, French Cubism, and Fauvism, are well represented. Some outstanding canvases are Zurbarán's *St. Francis,* a brooding brown-robed figure contemplating death through the skull he holds in his hands; Picasso's large oil, *The Cock of the Liberation,* immortalizing France's freedom from German occupation; Bonnard's *Vue de l'Atelier Midi.* Nolde, Klee, Appel, Kokoschka, Okada, Giacometti, and Marini bring an international flavor.

A recent gift of a sumptuous private house, Villa Terrace, gives the Art Center a separate decorative arts museum. Built on a cliff not far from the center, with terraces cascading down the cliff to the lake, the museum will emphasize American and English period rooms, especially the strong eighteenth-century Palladian influence in both countries. David Adler, one of the "last great revival architects," designed the villa.

WESTERN CENTRAL ART MUSEUMS

COLORADO SPRINGS FINE ARTS CENTER AND TAYLOR MUSEUM

30 West Dale Street, Colorado Springs, Colorado
Hours: Mon.–Sat., 9–5; Sun., 1:30–5;
closed Mon. from Sept. to June. Library. Free.

A remarkable woman, Mrs. Alice Bemis Taylor, infused the Arts Center with her own remarkable taste. Mrs. Taylor was interested in American Indians and got permission to visit the storage rooms of the Grand Canyon Hopi House belonging to Fred Harvey, whose restaurants and souvenir shops punctuated the Santa Fe Railroad lines. Harvey—in spite of his souvenir counters —was an astute collector. Mrs. Taylor was so impressed by what she saw that she bought many of his finest things and shipped them home to Colorado, without a thought of what she was letting herself in for. Today her artifacts of the Navaho, Hopi, and Northwest Indians, and the Spanish colonial art with which

Christ (Spanish-American, probably nineteenth-century) (Collection of the Taylor Museum of the Colorado Springs Fine Arts Center)

Walt Kuhn: *Trio* (1937) (Collection of the
Colorado Springs Fine Arts Center; gift of
El Pomar Foundation)

she later became enamored, form an important part of the
museum.

The exact date when the Spanish Franciscan friars left Mexico
to work among the Indians is not known, but the Palace of the
Governors in Santa Fe was begun about 1610. The missionaries
were versatile, making pulpits, altar rails, and tabernacles, and
carving religious statues, some crude, some marked by considerable skill. The first paintings were on animal hides. Later ones on
wooden panels show a definite Spanish or Mexican baroque style.
During all of this time the friars were teaching the Spaniards and
the Indians to carve statues for their homes and more ambitious
figures for their churches. As was the tradition in Spain, many
of the *bultos* (figures carved in the round) were dressed in actual
clothing made of anything from calico to damask, though occasionally garments were painted on the carvings.

Most *retablos* (paintings) and *bultos* were undated and un-
signed; the earliest examples, done under the tutelage of the
friars, are delicately carved, the expressions on the faces benign.
The ones executed by the Penitentes, a semireligious sect, reflect
their belief in a God of blood and vengeance and are stark,
macabre, and chilling. Colorado Springs examples are tops in the
country.

In building the permanent collection the criterion has been to
obtain canvases from significant artists who have been associated
with the center either as students or as teachers. Walt Kuhn is an
example. He is represented by his handsome *Trio* and twenty-
nine oils comprising his slightly ribald *Imaginary History of the
West*. Recent acquisitions include Lawson, Bierstadt, Callahan,
Broderson, Cremonini, Kamihira, and Sage.

The Fine Arts Center, designed by John G. Meem and opened
in 1936, is an elegant, clean-lined, functional structure. Conceived

to serve all the arts, it was the first museum to have a complete professional theater with a deep stage, elaborate lighting board, dressing rooms, and a high loft for building and painting scenery. The painting galleries are large and flexible and there are apartments for visiting artists. Practically the only thing not built in is the staggering view of Pike's Peak.

DENVER ART MUSEUM

West 14th Avenue at Acoma, Denver, Colorado
Hours: Mon., 1–5; Tues.–Sat., 9–5; holidays, 2–5;
closed major holidays.
Library.
Free.

Architects Gio Ponti of Milan and James Sudler of Denver are masterminding a six-story museum in Denver's Civic Center, site of the former museum. Its present south wing—air-conditioned, grid-lighted, and with flexible walls—will remain in continuous operation during the building phase. Eventually it will connect with the new tower building, which includes an elevated space for sculpture, a video-auditorium, seminar rooms, and ten loft-type galleries arranged in a construction of twenty-eight sections of ribbon walls.

The museum, starting in 1893 as the "Artists' Club of Denver" when the town was not much more than an overgrown mining center, has progressed to the leading museum of the Rocky Mountain region. Its overall aim is to show the most influential periods in the history of art. Antiquities begin with a head of *Queen Nefertiti* (1365 B.C.). The Oriental galleries are rich in objects from all the Asian countries: the goddess of love, *Lakshmi,* from the great temple complex of Khajuraho; *Kuan Yin,* goddess of mercy from the T'ang Dynasty, is here—not in her usual heroic size, but delicately carved in small, worldly grace.

The Italian Renaissance is portrayed by Pesellino, Carpaccio, Ghirlandaio, and works from the ateliers of Da Vinci, Botticelli, and Mantegna; the Italian baroque by Veronese and Tintoretto. Spain and Northern Europe are represented by paintings of Murillo, Cranach, Terborch, Rembrandt, and many others. Lucas

Defendente Ferrari: *Christ in the House of Martha and Mary Magdalen* (Denver Art Museum; Samuel H. Kress Collection)

van Leyden's tapestries from the series representing *The Months*, done for Rome's Barberini Palace, were presented by William Averell Harriman to museums at terminal points along his Union Pacific Railroad; Denver's is titled *December*. The museum's extraordinary period rooms include a Spanish baroque, an English Tudor, and one of the most complete Gothic rooms outside France.

Monet, Pissarro, Sisley, and Renoir headline the French Impressionists. The Marion Hendrie bequest has given the museum a group of star-studded gems. Miss Hendrie, a birdlike little woman who played a key role in the museum's early development, made important purchases in the 1930s, including Paul Klee's *Palast Teiliveise Zerstört;* a Picasso Cubist-period canvas *Nature Morte;* and a great Rouault, *Portrait de Femme.* There are also outstanding examples of Braque, Modigliani, De Staël, Gris, and Dubuffet.

The primitive art, including Denver's celebrated North American Indian collection formerly in Chappel House, will be incorporated into the new museum. Colonial America ranges from Copley and Benjamin West to the anonymous Spanish-American *santeros* (see Santa Fe). The nineteenth century offers Peale, Ryder, Homer, and Bierstadt. Rico Lebrun's *Figures on the Cross with Lantern* and the Italian Mirko's strange and vital bronze *Chimera* highlight the contemporary section.

DAVENPORT MUNICIPAL ART GALLERY

1737 West 12th Street, Davenport, Iowa
Hours: Tues.–Fri., 12–4:30; Sat., 10–4:30; Sun., 1–4:30.
Library.
Free.

The lively exhibitions at the new Davenport Art Gallery challenge one's interest; an added delight is the view from the tall windows that frame the treetops and the broad Mississippi beyond. The serene, open-style architecture throughout the building and the hanging stairway in the entrance hall allow for maximum arrangements.

Iowa's General Assembly enacted legislation establishing the gallery in 1925, when the C. A. Ficke collection was given to the city. An old armory, effectively remodeled, housed an active program until the opening of the present building in 1963.

The permanent collection is modest, with a few outstanding Flemish works, German fifteenth to nineteenth century, Dutch, Hudson River School. Of the fine print and drawing section in the making, the Rembrandt prints are the most important; but there is also a good Japanese print group, old and contemporary. Two exceptions make the Davenport unique: distinguished Mexican and Spanish colonial painting and a gathering of Grant Wood's art and personal effects that would be the envy of any archivist. Recently purchased from Wood's sister are paintings, graphics, ink sketches, bas-reliefs, and mementoes spanning Wood's lifetime, from his silver baby cup to the flag that draped his coffin. Many objects used in his paintings, the sketch box and palette he designed when he was a young man and used until his death, are set in a special area. A short dividing wall holds a

Baltasar de Echave (Mexican, 1580–1660): *Adoration of the Magi* (Davenport Municipal Art Gallery, Davenport, Iowa)

lucite exhibit case of Wood's sculpture and three-dimensional objects. And here he belongs. For Grant Wood is as much a part of Iowa as the tall corn. Though the avant-garde discount him and he fell into a trap of stylization in his landscapes, his gently satirical *Daughters of the Revolution* (see Cincinnati) and the sturdy *American Gothic* may some day stand with the best of our historical painting.

DES MOINES ART CENTER

Greenwood Park, Des Moines, Iowa
Hours: Tues.–Sat., 11–5; Thurs., 11–9; Sun., 1–6;
closed Mon.
Library.
Free.

For years energetic Des Moiners held exhibitions wherever they could find enough wall space and were allowed to drive nails. In 1948 a local businessman, James D. Edmundson, financed the building of a museum in Greenwood Park, and their wandering ceased. Designed by architect Eliel Saarinen, the center was one of the most advanced of its time. The museum's new, well-defined policy is to concentrate on contemporary art highlighted by historic examples aesthetically related to the contemporary.

Non-American works are: Courbet's splendid *La Vallée de la Loue*, Joan Miró's *Woman, Bird and Stars*, Paul Klee's *Remember the Kaiser*, and one of Rodin's great sculptures from the *Burghers of Calais* series, *Pierre de Voissant*. In 1884 Rodin did a heroic monument to these burghers, a group of six men who, in the fourteenth century, offered their lives as forfeit to the king of England in order to save their besieged city. The figure in the finished monument is clothed, but so particular was Rodin about the structure of the body that he always made his life-sized studies, like this one, in the nude. Goya's *Don Manual Garcia de la Prada*, in yellow satin breeches and blue waistcoat, is an imposing figure, all 9 feet of him.

For so young a museum (most of its purchases were made since 1948), the sculpture is impressive. A huge Calder mobile swings from the ceiling of the entrance gallery.

Two paintings brought from the old art center that have stood time's test are George Bellows' *Aunt Fanny* and Robert Henri's *Ballet Girl in White*. Henri, an inspiring teacher in the early part

LEFT: Interior, Des Moines Art Center, Des Moines, Iowa (Edmundson Art Foundation, Inc.); Jose de Rivera sculpture in foreground. ABOVE: Henry Moore: *Seated Woman* (Permanent Collection of the Des Moines Art Center, Edmundson Art Foundation, Inc.; Nathan Emory Coffin Memorial)

of the century, whose ideas embodied a whole philosophy of art, infuriated academicians and paved the way for the acceptance of modern art. The present generation, as shown here, includes Shahn, among whose four examples are *Integration—Supreme Court* and a drawing called *National Pastime*—yes, baseball—so popular that the center has to nail it down to keep it at home. Every drawing exhibition in the country wants to borrow it. Feininger, Bouche, Kuniyoshi, Knaths, and lately, moving into a more abstract field, Rothko, Stamos, and Kepes are represented; also sculptors Arp, Laurens, Noguchi, and Moore.

To double the space, a new wing which makes a happy marriage with the Saarinen building has been designed by I. M. Pei. A large, enclosed, two-level sculpture court opens to a view of the gardens in Greenwood Park. Connecting galleries on either side join the wing to the present building and enclose the large reflecting pool. The material is similar in tone and texture to the parent structure.

UNIVERSITY OF IOWA: MUSEUM OF ART

Iowa City, Iowa
Hours: Tues.–Fri., 10–5; Sat., 10–1; Sun., 2–5;
closed Mon. and holidays. Library. Free.

The art department of the University of Iowa is acquiring simultaneously an important collection and an important building. Designed by Harrison & Abramowitz, the new museum, opening late in 1969, will have 14,000 feet of exhibition space, an auditorium, lounges, lending gallery, and a large laboratory for conservation and restoration. The style of the building, with its horizontal reach and long panels, is suggestive of a Japanese influence. A center sculpture court has a floor level lower than the main galleries and a clerestory at the top.

The base of the collection is a gift of Mr. and Mrs. Owen Elliott and comprises a large group of prints, eighteenth-century silver, approximately sixty French paintings from the period after 1904, and a few important Expressionist paintings. Among the latter are landscapes by Munch and Kokoschka, an unusual nude by Franz Marc, a large Lyonel Feininger, early major portraits by Jawlensky and Soutine, Fauve Paintings by Vlaminck, and a portrait by Delaunay when he was under Pointillist influence. There are additionally, Braque, Juan Gris, Kandinsky, Picasso, Utrillo, De Chirico's *Disquieting Muses,* still lifes by Morandi and Jacques Villon, a Matisse interior with figures and a Breton landscape by Paul Gauguin.

The university's own permanent collection complements that given by the Elliott's, being mainly in the twentieth-century American field. There are two Jackson Pollocks, including a huge mural painted in 1943, an early Paris landscape by Stuart Davis, a Marsden Hartley of 1915, the preliminary oil sketch for Jack Levine's *Gangster Funeral,* and other works of the period. The collection also includes an important triptych by Max Beckman.

There will be two drawing and print galleries as print making has long been a high point in the art school's tradition. The collection, aside from the moderns, has a substantial old master print group including Dürer, Schongauer, twenty-five Rembrandts, and a first and third edition of Goya's *Disasters of War.*

Marsden Hartley: *E* (1915) (The University of Iowa Museum of Art, Iowa City)

UNIVERSITY OF KANSAS: MUSEUM OF ART

Lawrence, Kansas
Hours: Mon.–Sat., 9–4:45; Sun., 1:30–4:45;
closed Thanksgiving, Dec. 25, Jan. 1, July 4.
Library.
Free.

When the university library moved out of its Romantic Revival building in 1924, the museum rounded up its treasures scattered about campus and moved in. Gradual reorganization and modernization turned the library nave and narthex (it was based on a basilica design) into a good working museum. The institution publishes *The Register*, a scholarly journal of its collections, twice a year and has a photographic reference collection for the study of art and architecture. The collections start with the ancient and early Christian world and with some good examples of fourth- and fifth-century Coptic weaving. Capitals from Languedoc and the Auvergne introduce the Middle Ages; a highlight is a *Madonna and Child* by Tilman Riemenschneider from the collection of the Prince of Lichtenstein. Carved with delicacy and grace, the Madonna is erect and vital in spite of the Gothic curve of her posture. The Kress study collection holds interesting Renaissance canvases and a striking seventeenth-century pair of portraits by the Netherlander Nicolaes Maes. There is a good

Tilman Riemenschneider: *Virgin with the Christ Child* (ca. 1499) (The University of Kansas Museum of Art, Lawrence)

small decorative arts section. Modern Europeans include Maillol, Kolbe, Epstein, Dix, Monet, Manet. In the American section is an especially appealing Rembrandt Peale, *Mrs. John Brice and Child*, and a fine Winslow Homer genre painting, *Cloud Shadow*.

WICHITA ART MUSEUM

619 Stackman Drive, Wichita, Kansas
Hours: Daily, 1–5;
closed Mon., Easter, Thanksgiving, Dec. 25.
Library.
Free.

Though Mrs. Roland P. Murdock was the first professional interior decorator in Kansas and traveled about the state lecturing on the importance of aesthetically pleasing homes, she never stressed works of art. However, when she died in 1915, Mrs. Murdock asked her city to build and maintain a museum so that her estate could be used to purchase acquisitions for it. She drew no boundary lines but did indicate a strong preference for American art. Plans for a handsome building were drawn. The style, for lack of a better designation, might be called "modified Mayan." The central portion, opened in 1935, has just been enlarged to provide a gallery for temporary exhibitions, a library, a sales-rental gallery and a children's museum. Under the skillful and final authority of Mrs. Murdock's executor, Mrs. Rafael Navas, the collection continued to grow. Works by Mark Tobey and John Heliker are two noteworthy additions.

There is no heterogeneous gathering of big names, but an astutely chosen sampling of every important period of American art, slowly and carefully put together. Although the emphasis is on the contemporaries, two excellent Copleys, *James Otis* and *Mrs. James Otis*, and a Feke testify to our colonial blossoming. And how many small Midwestern museums can boast of a fine Ryder, a Homer (*In the Mowing*), and three Eakinses?

Seven of The Eight, or "Ashcan School," as they were derisively labeled, are represented in Wichita. This group of artists, young at the beginning of the twentieth century, rebelled against the slick academic painting of the time. They preferred painting life around them as they saw it: the back alleys, the city tenements, the clotheslines of reality. Beauty lay for them in form and color, and in the ability to catch and hold the mood and meaning of ordinary scenes.

The museum and Mrs. Navas refused to be stampeded by the popularity of "American Scene" collecting in the thirties, although one of its masters, John Steuart Curry, was a Kansan. There is, quite properly, an important Curry—*Kansas Cornfield,* with giant, shooting stalks of corn whipping in the breeze, surely as close to abstraction as that realist ever came.

Space limits the sculpture, but John Flannagan, Zorach, Umlauf, Wayne Williams, Oliver Andrews, De Creeft, and Lachaise are shown in notable examples. Indeed, it is impossible to emphasize too strongly the quality of each and every piece in the Murdock collection, the result of a determination to acquire not just the available, but only the fine representation of any artist's work.

To offer the public an understanding of growth and the diversity of style, some major artists are represented by several examples each. There are five Marins and three Walt Kuhns, one of them a strong, typical *Clown in White and Silver* by that master of the sawdust arena. The four Hoppers are enviable; two large canvases by Kuniyoshi complement each other across a gallery.

Edward Hopper: *Sunlight on Brownstones* (Wichita Art Museum, Wichita, Kansas; Roland P. Murdock Collection)

His *Bouquet and Stove* is from his middle period, when Kuniyoshi left his early world of sly dreams and painted, with such extraordinary quality, realistic subjects like this good old American pot-bellied stove. His *Revelation,* done twenty years later, shows him reaching back, taking from his ancient heritage the symbolic masks and the bright, subtle colors of his people.

All labels give short sketches of the artist's career, plus discriminating comments on the particular painting or the artist's philosophical approach to his work.

The lively Wichita Art Museum Members, Inc., was founded in 1960 for the purpose of extending the services of the museum to the community. The Wichita Art Museum Members Foundation, Inc., composed of young business executives, was organized in 1964.

This treasure trove is not only well worth a stop for lovers and students of American art, it's worth a pilgrimage.

UNIVERSITY OF MINNESOTA: TWEED GALLERY

Duluth, Minnesota
Hours: Daily, 7:45–4:30 P.M.; Sat.–Sun., 2–5;
closed university holidays.
Free.

George P. Tweed was a financier and public-spirited son of Duluth. The gallery named for him forms a spirited link between two wings of the new humanities building. Light and contemporary in feeling, its brick walls and wide glass façade provide an excellent backdrop for the assertive canvases of some of its changing exhibitions. Students passing through receive, perhaps in spite of themselves, a broad visual education.

The Alice Tweed Tuohy gallery, opened in 1965, doubles the space. Paneled in walnut, it is congenial with the nineteenth-century French and American art which dominates the permanent collection. Some Frenchmen here are Corot, Rousseau, Millet, Daubigny, Cazin, Jules Dupré, and Boudin; some Americans, Martin, Twachtman, Luks, Glackens, Maurer, Homer's *Watching the Sea,* Inness' *Aproaching Storm,* and an unusually direct Sargent, *Portrait of a Young Man in Khaki.* In addition to its university chores, Tweed is the only gallery serving northern Minnesota, upper Wisconsin, and a certain part of Canada. For these far reaches, it is the community museum.

Lipchitz: *Sieur du Luth* (University of Minnesota, Duluth)

Outside the gallery entrance in the Ordean Court is Jacques Lipchitz' 9-foot statue of Daniel Greysolon, Sieur du Luth. Lipchitz has presented Du Luth in a costume mixture of American trapper and French dandy. He wears the long wig popular at the courts of the Louis' (two were found in Du Luth's Montreal apartment). Having no likeness to guide him, Lipchitz said, "He will look like a builder, a man who looks at a place and says, 'This is where I want a city.'" He stands on a 13-foot column, jaunty, arrogant—commanding the city of Duluth to be brought into being.

MINNEAPOLIS INSTITUTE OF ARTS

201 East 24th Street, Minneapolis, Minnesota
Hours: Tues., 10–10 P.M.; Wed.–Sat., 10–5; Sun. & holidays, 1–5; closed Mon.
Library.
Restaurant.
Free.

Half a dozen northwest empire builders ran Minneapolis, lock, stock, and culture, around the turn of the century. Though the Minneapolis Society of Fine Arts had been founded in 1883, nothing much happened until 1911, when the bankers and bakers, restive at the philistine state of affairs, gave a dinner and, between the sherry and the champagne, pledged $350,000 to build the biggest art museum west of Fifth Avenue.

The rotunda, two stories high, presented a problem handsomely solved in 1959 by Ernst Barlach's monumental 18-foot statue, *The Fighter of the Spirit*, originally commissioned as a World

War I monument for Kiel, Germany. It was denounced by the Nazis as degenerate and was dismantled, but fortunately the pieces were later reassembled.

The institute is rich in Oriental bronzes and European paintings of the seventeenth, eighteenth, and nineteenth centuries. The Alfred F. Pillsbury bronzes are notable for their quality and their scope. A wine vessel, shaped like an owl with a Picasso face, is a sheer delight—ascribed to the Shang-Yin period or early Chou Dynasty.

Among the antiquities is the wonderfully fluid Greek *Figure of a Muse*, known as the "Tiber Statue." Hellenistic and first century B.C., it was found in modern times in an excavation for a Roman apartment house.

In the fine decorative arts section is a tea service made by the Revolutionary silversmith Paul Revere. Over the mantel in the Queen Anne Room drowses Hogarth's *Sleeping Congregation*, dated 1728, one of his finest excursions into high satire. Everyone but the droning preacher is fast asleep—a point Hogarth underlines with the inscription on the side of the pulpit: "Come unto me all ye that labour and are heavy laden and I will give you rest." Downstairs in the print room, two engravings of the same subject show slight variations in treatment.

The second-floor rotunda gallery is filled with important French nineteenth-century painters: Degas, Cézanne, Matisse's *White Plumes*, Bonnard with his hot and glowing *Dining Room in the Country*, Pissarro, Monet, Gauguin, Renoir, all in top form. In Degas' *Portrait of Mlle. Hortense Valpinçon* the canvas's unremitting pattern would be impossibly busy in less skillful hands. As it is, the bright colors are tied down by the tablecloth's black background, the calculating little face under the pert hat, the white of the apron and shawl.

Long neglected by everybody except art historians, Poussin is today being regarded in a new light. Minneapolis has *The Death of Germanicus*, of which that self-appointed art critic Napoleon Bonaparte said, "One can never forget compositions like the Germanicus—once having seen them. The French school of painting must return to the ideas of Poussin." El Greco's *Christ Driving the Money Changers from the Temple* was a work of his early thirties. A later version is in the Frick in New York. El Greco has painted in the lower-right-hand corner four portraits of people to whom he felt indebted, Titian, Michelangelo, Giulio Clovio, and Raphael. Strangely, in all the years that El Greco worked in Toledo, a few miles from

BELOW: Balthus: *The Living Room* (1941–1943) (The Minneapolis Institute of Arts; the John R. Van Darlip Fund and the William Hood Dunwoody Fund) TOP: G. B. Castiglione: *Immaculate Conception* (1650) (The Minneapolis Institute of Arts)

Philip II's court, he got only one commission, *St. Maurice and His Legion,* from Philip; and though it remains in the Escorial, it was never placed over the altar for which it was designed. Philip preferred the opulent paintings of the Italians, especially Titian, whose pupil El Greco was. Recent purchases have been the Fra Angelico *St. Benedict,* and the large Prud'hon *The Unity of Love and Friendship.*

For many years Rembrandt's *The Suicide of Lucretia* was thought to have been painted before she "sheathed in her harmless breast a harmful knife," for her gown was spotless, her dagger poised. Following the cleaning of the painting in 1965, her fate was seen to be accomplished in the bloody stain on her dress.

Giovanni Benedetto Castiglione's *The Immaculate Conception,* considered the most important Castiglione outside Italy, has just come to the museum. A number of drawings connected with it are in the Windsor Castle collection.

Important twentieth-century canvases are *La Vie Conjugale* by Roger de La Fresnaye, *Still Life* by Juan Gris, and Léger's cubist *Table and Fruit.* Beckman's enormous triptych *Blindman's Buff,* Marca-Relli's *Trial,* and Larry Rivers's vast *Studio* dominate the contemporary room and bring the collection to the present.

UNIVERSITY OF MINNESOTA: UNIVERSITY GALLERY

316 Northrop Memorial Auditorium, Minneapolis, Minnesota
Hours: Mon.–Fri., 8:30–4; Sun., 2–5;
closed Sat., holidays.
Free.

Rich as the museum fare goes in the Twin Cities, the visitor should not forego a trip to the University Gallery. The permanent collection is mainly twentieth century, but you might encounter an exhibition that spans centuries. Marsden Hartley and Alfred Maurer are well-ensconced. So is notable contemporary sculpture. A study collection is in the making. By the time you get there, the gallery will have settled into its new home on the West Bank campus.

WALKER ART CENTER

1710 Lyndale Avenue South, Minneapolis, Minnesota
Hours: Tues.–Thurs., 10–10; Fri., Sat., 10–5; Sun., 12–6;
closed Mon., holidays.
Library.
Free.

Add the Walker's name to the list of museums and cultural centers being built by distinguished architects around the country. Edward Larabee Barnes created this one, which will open in 1970. The address will be the same, and the museum will share a common entrance with an enlarged Tyrone Guthrie Theater.

The building is set on a broad base with a series of rectangular cubes spiraling upward to form a helix. The progress inside winds one up broad stairs that alternate with ramps and put some galleries at half-floor levels. The top opens onto sculpture roof gardens and a terrace restaurant. For those long Minnesota winters, indoor dining space adjoins. All levels can be reached by elevator as well. Monumental sculpture by Manzu, Marini, Moore, Somaini, Richter, Noguchi, David Smith, Tony Smith, and others will silhouette against the sky line.

T. B. Walker, a lumber magnate, was one of the omnivorous turn-of-the-century collectors who amassed Chinese ceramics, armor, Renaissance paintings, snuffboxes—you name it, he collected it. By 1879 he had enlarged his house and opened it to the public. Eventually he had fourteen rooms full of art, and Mrs. Walker had to hire a maid to do nothing but answer the doorbell.

In 1926, when Walker was eighty-seven, he built the present art center and set up a foundation to maintain it and permit further purchases. Thereafter, late Depression doldrums hit lumbering and consequently the museum. The W.P.A. arts project moved in and saved the day by establishing a lively community arts program. This changed the traditional direction the museum was following. They plunged into an ambitious design program, building in 1941 a model "Idea House" on the museum's grounds and incorporating within a given budget new design in furniture and materials. *Design Quarterly,* museum-spawned, became an important publication in the field. Today the handsome, experimental Tyrone Guthrie Theater occupies the site of "Idea House." The World War II boom revived the lumber business, and the center was once more self-propelled. Top-flight experts reassessed Grandfather Walker's collection and only choice pieces remain on view. The first floor holds an auditorium and information gallery where various visual and audio aids prepare one for the collections above.

One lower floor gallery houses jade, ceramics, bronzes, and wood and stone sculptures. Paintings from the T. B. Walker collection are periodically on display. Barent Fabritius' *Women Taken in Adultery,* ascribed to Rembrandt till the dark and murky varnish was cleaned away, is one of these. When *The Holy Family* by Rubens and Panneels was cleaned, smug little Victorian faces were wiped off the Christ child and St. John, revealing underneath the true childish countenances of the original painting.

The contemporary section has its roots in such paintings as Franz Marc's *Blue Horses* and Joseph Stella's *American Landscape.* Marc, with Klee, Kandinsky, and others founded the Blue Rider group in Germany before World War I. Through rhythmic movement and color, rather than by using natural forms, they sought to convey the artist's mood. *The Blue Horses* typifies this idea. Animals were Marc's forte before his promising career ended in death in the trenches.

No one in America has better realized Abstractionism than Stuart Davis. Unlike Joseph Stella, who worked back to realism, Davis started with it, then undertook the semiabstractions of gas stations and egg beaters. (It is said that he disciplined himself by nailing an egg beater to a table and painting it over and over for a year.) These canvases are collectors' items. Other im-

George Segal: *The Diner* (Courtesy of the Walker Art Center, Minneapolis, Minnesota)

portant artists in the collection include: Gottlieb, Baziotes, Morris Louis, Brooks, Marca-Relli, Indiana, Trova, Wesselman, Paolozzi, Segal, Held, Judd, Ortman, and sculptors Lipchitz, Stankiewicz, Agostini, and Chryssa, to name but a few from this lively group.

While every U.S. museum has had a rise in attendance, the center's has been huge. Part of this is due to its involvement with the Tyrone Guthrie Theater, a site for programs in jazz, chamber music, dance, theater, and opera, whose audience the Walker shares.

Occasionally historical shows that feed into the background of modern art are mounted, but the orientation now is toward new forms, whether on canvas, scrap iron, plastic, or neon; whether regional, national, or international. Minnesotans, and indeed the whole country, through the museum's excellent circulation program, see some of its important exhibits.

ST. PAUL ART CENTER

30 East 10th Street, St. Paul, Minnesota
Hours: Mon.–Sat., 10–10; Sun., 1–5.
Free.

The art center recently moved from a mansion on Summit Avenue, a period-piece street that still retains its turn-of-the-century character and conjures up memories of F. Scott Fitzgerald, now inhabits a smart, streamlined, limestone and polished granite building and shares space with the science museum. In the adroit interior design, the only common science–art space is the entrance and auditorium. Exhibitions are held in one large gallery that breaks successfully into smaller units, some more or less in permanent installation. "Windows" along a wide corridor display the center's applied arts material.

Two important activities are: the National Bi-annual Craft

Klaus Ihlenfeld: *Cluster of Butterflies* (1962) (St. Paul Art Center, St. Paul, Minnesota; gift of Mr. and Mrs. Robert W. Sarnoff)

Show (confined to fiber, clay, metal) and the National Bi-annual Drawing Exhibition. Leading craftsmen such as Peter Voulkos, Christian Schmidt, Jo Roper, the Natzlers, Warren Mackenzie, Toshiko Takaezu, and Trude Guermonprez are importantly represented, as are, in the drawing field, Lebrun, Weber, Shahn, Peterdi, Cuevas, Graves, and Rattner.

The small Oriental collection contains some great fabrics, screens, Sung and Ming pots. The Chester Harding collection of religious art from the twelfth through seventeenth centuries is on indefinite loan. A twelfth-century Breton Madonna and a crudely carved, polychromed, stone Virgin are highlights. Important contemporary sculptures are Masayaki Nagare's *Progression—1967*, Klaus Ihlenfeld's *Cluster of Butterflies*, and George Rickey's *Square #1*. Abbot Patterson, Bernard Reder, Guitou Knoop, Fritz Koenig, and Ludvik Durchanek appear with distinction.

The center has just received one-half the estate of native-son sculptor Paul Manship. The other half goes to the Smithsonian's National Collection of Fine Arts. While known chiefly for his monumental pieces, *Prometheus Fountain* in Rockefeller Center, his *Lincoln as a Youth, Fort Wayne*, etc., it is Manship's small works in St. Paul that stand out. These are not models for his many commissions, but vital little pieces free of the academic "setness" of his large productions.

WILLIAM ROCKHILL NELSON GALLERY OF ART AND ATKINS MUSEUM OF FINE ARTS

4525 Oak Street, Kansas City, Missouri
Hours: Tues.–Sat., 10–5; Sun., 2–6.
Library, restaurant.
Admission 25¢, children 10¢; free Sat., Sun.

Kansas City was a town of mud streets and unadorned one-story frame buildings when William Rockhill Nelson arrived there in

1880. As a crusading young journalist, he campaigned for sidewalks and parks. As its editor, he built up the great tradition of the *Kansas City Star* and spent his life fighting to make the city the best possible place to live.

The idea for the museum was probably conceived when Nelson stood before Rembrandt's *Night Watch* at the Rijksmuseum in Amsterdam. Nelson promptly hired a Dutch artist to do a full-sized copy of the *Night Watch*, approximately 12 by 14 feet. When he met the Pisani family in Florence, he persuaded them to part with their gallery of copies of masterpieces. One hundred paintings were shipped home to hang in the basement of the Kansas City Public Library, which became known as the Gallery of Western Art.

Nelson's heirs, in accordance with his wishes, willed his entire estate for the purchase of works of art. Mary M. Atkins left funds to build a museum. Experts, heady with the knowledge that millions were accruing, scoured the art markets of the world. From Europe and the Orient to the heart of our wheat and beef belt flowed great treasures. Few museums have arrived on the scene so well accoutred. A forest of colossal black marble was imported from the Pyrenees to the Missouri prairies, where it was carved into twelve gigantic columns for the great central hall. When the building opened in 1933 it was the last word in classical opulence.

The painting galleries were deliberately kept small, to each room its own period. Gallery III, for instance, holds the Flemish painters, Brueghel, Memling, Gossaert, Patinier, and the beautiful *Madonna and Child in a Gothic Room* by Petrus Christus, who helped to initiate the Renaissance in Northern Europe. In one of the French rooms is that imaginative beauty of Boucher's, *Landscape in the Environs of Beauvais*. This is not Boucher the decorator, nor Boucher of the slick and silken ladies, but Boucher the painter.

With range and distinction, Kansas City presents France in sculpture, painting, and drawing. There is Poussin's *Triumph of Bacchus*, one of the finest Poussins in America, from a series of bacchanals commissioned, oddly enough even for so worldly a churchman, by Cardinal Richelieu. Another of the series hangs in the Louvre, while *Triumph of Neptune* was purchased from the Hermitage for the Philadelphia Museum. Kansas City has one of the drawings for *Triumph of Bacchus*. It also has the original small wax study for Rodin's *The Thinker*, of which many U.S. museums, including Kansas City, have large bronze casts.

In Gallery XI, are the great Spanish painters—Goya, Velázquez,

Petrus Christus (Flemish, ca. 1410–1472): *Madonna and Child* (William Rockhill Nelson Gallery of Art, Atkins Museum of Fine Arts, Kansas City, Missouri)

and El Greco with a glowingly subdued *Penitent Magdalene* and his worldly *Portrait of a Trinitarian Monk*. In the portrait, El Greco's elongated exaggeration is replaced by solid forms. The friar's great weight rests on a simple chair. He is alert, spectacle case in hand, ready to mete out mercy or punishment with equanimity. It seems probable that this was a commissioned portrait and that El Greco lacked sympathy for his sitter, for the face is in sharp contrast with most of El Greco's conceptualized men of God.

To the right of the museum's entrance, the ancient Near East is dramatically represented by *The Kneeling Bull*. This capital from the Hall of One Hundred Columns at Persepolis, each column 65 feet high, is in a black marble gallery where the bituminous limestone of the bull luminously plays black against the dark-veined marble. He shares this elegant background with the stern, finely chiseled *Head of Hammurabi*, first lawgiver of Babylon. Examples from the Etruscan, Egyptian, Greek, and Roman civilizations lead on to medieval and Renaissance sculpture. In a tranquil cloister from a monastery near Beauvais, a splendid French Romanesque capital is used as a wellhead. Near it stands a late Gothic alabaster carving of *St. Thomas Aquinas*, a reminder of the days when a universal Church husbanded the arts, built the cathedrals, and founded the universities. The Medieval sculpture gallery adjoining holds examples of ivories, enamels, and Gothic sculpture.

Of the period rooms, the Louis XIII Gold Room is the grand climax.

Upstairs, except for a few galleries of American art, the famed Oriental and Asiatic collections take over. The Indian bronze group is the largest in this country. The Indian temple room, a composite of several temples, with its lacy, intricate ceiling and complex paneling somehow manages a unity that enhances the bronze and wood sculptures it holds.

There are five galleries of Chinese art. One room is a reconstruction of a Chinese temple, one holds porcelains, another Shang-Yin and Chou bronzes. A highlight in Chinese painting is *Views from a Thatched Cottage,* Hsia Kuei, Chinese Southern Sung Dynasty (1127–1279). Ink on silk, the scroll is 7 feet long. Important in the Japanese section is a pair of luminous sixfold screens, Momoyama period (1568–1615).

The American wing starts with Benjamin West and includes Raphaelle Peale's teasing *trompe-l'oeil, After the Bath.* In the George Caleb Bingham gallery are the genre paintings for which he was famous, such as *Canvassing for a Vote.* Bingham, an ardent Whig, painted it in 1852 and sent it to Paris to have engravings made. It was lost and turned up again in 1954, when a Florida physician, knowing the museum owned several Binghams, wrote to their conservation department concerning the care of his *Canvassing for a Vote.* In time the museum was able to purchase the painting. Bingham is little known outside the Middle West for his portraits, but most of Missouri's prominent families commissioned him to "do a likeness." Kansas City's ancestral citizens are shown in a range from Bingham's first brittle trials through the softer, Sullyesque style found in *Portrait of Elizabeth Dillingham Keller.*

A rich decorative arts section includes the Burnap collection of English pottery, with unique precious examples from every period, beginning with primitive medieval wares. The *Codrington Punch Bowl,* largest known covered bowl, has joined the distinguished Atha collection of English silver.

Nelson stipulated that no work of art should be purchased with his bequest until thirty years after the artist's death. However, "The Friends of Art" purchase the latest in art trends for the museum and the museum in turn stages in-depth exhibitions of some of the most advanced art forms prevailing.

The Nelson has recently added a gallery of primitive art. If past performance is a criterion the department will soon achieve important proportions.

CITY ART MUSEUM OF ST. LOUIS

Forest Park, St. Louis, Missouri
Hours: Wed.–Sun., 10–5; Tues., 2:30–9:30;
closed Mon., Dec. 25, Jan. 1.
Library, restaurant. Free.

In the heart of the city, on a hill in Forest Park, the museum dominates and invites. The building is the central portion of the Palace of Art constructed for the Louisiana Purchase Exposition in 1904. Its architecture is unabashed Roman classical.

Dividing the museum into symmetrical wings, the barrel-vaulted sculpture court runs from the entrance to the gardens. Few museums are so well adapted to the display of monumental masterpieces. The St. Louis museum provides a stunning showcase for major twentieth-century works by such sculptors as Moore, Lipchitz, Wotruba, Somaini, Pomodoro, Nagare, Maillol.

Practically all the important cultural facets of civilization are represented, some with stunning examples, such as the *Bearded Bull's Head* (Sumerian, 2800–2600 B.C.) and the notorious *Egyptian Cat* (Saite, *circa* 500 B.C.). When it was purchased in 1937 for $14,000 with city funds during a year of unemployment (the city museum is supported by a mill tax levy), the jobless picketed with such signs as "Cash for cats but not for humans." The same summer the public made no protest when the municipal zoo paid $10,000 for a sea elephant which sickened and died in a month. Museum personnel understandably gloated over the fine state of health of their cat. Since Egypt no longer allows its ancient art to leave the country, it would be nearly impossible today to obtain such a treasure.

Another great piece of sculpture is *Satyr*, considered one of the finest High Renaissance carvings in America. It is now identified as the work of Giovanni Angelo Montorsoli, a Florentine. Long attributed to Michelangelo, it stood for generations in the Barberini Palace in Rome before it was brought to St. Louis. In 1937 Prince Urban Barberini wanted to sell the piece in New York, but the Pacca Law of 1905 forbids exportation of important works of art. The Prince finally made a deal with Mussolini, who drove a hard bargain. Barberini had to give a Raphael to the government before *Satyr* could leave Italy.

In a strong medieval section are Romanesque columns and capitals, a tempera panel by Ugolino da Siena, and a rare French, twelfth-century, polychromed wood Madonna. The Etruscans, the Greeks, Near Eastern art, Chinese jades and bronzes—each is given its importance. A gallery of pre-Columbian art includes a wide range of Peruvian pottery and textiles. Western Mexico and the Gulf Coast are well represented. Two pieces of Cholula polychrome are notable. The group also samples the pre-classic, Tomec, Teotihuacan, and Aztec cultures. Panama, Costa Rica, and Colombia are represented by both ceramics and gold work.

In a small gallery off the main hall, the life of ancient China teems in miniature. Scratching hens and playful children, temples, houses, and model figures all made of clay are arranged to recreate a village street during the Han Dynasty (206 B.C.–221 A.D.). The whole effect of everyday life in the hamlets along the great Chinese trade routes is charmingly and vividly displayed.

But it is in its painting collections that St. Louis scores most vividly, showing in every field distinguished examples and astuteness of judgment. Certainly, purchasing Manet and Sisley in 1915 and 1916 was farsighted.

A few treasures of North European art: *A Portrait of Lady Guildford* by Hans Holbein the Younger; Cranach's *Judgment of Paris,* one of several known versions, is of unusual quality; a small, round *Crucifixion* by Gerard David reminds, with its precise, glowing colors, that the artist was also an illuminator of books. There are stunning examples in the Dutch school of Rembrandt, Frans Hals, Terborch, and De Hooch.

The High Renaissance group is crowned with paintings by Titian, Veronese, and Tintoretto. In medieval times, craftsmen

Frans Hals: *Portrait of a Woman* (1648–1650) (City Art Museum of St. Louis)

and painters worked more-or-less anonymously under the patronage of the Church, but as kings and rich men, such as the Medicis, began to rival the Church as patrons of art, artists emerged as individuals. In Florence, Rome, and Venice, masters like Titian wielded considerable influence on their times and places. The *Ecce Homo* by Titian was painted in his high, or late, phase. A skeptical Pilate, bejeweled and dressed as a contemporary prince, is accompanied by the inevitable page boy of Renaissance courts. Only the resigned and suffering figure of Christ is timeless. Our own Jack Levine, in his bitter commentaries on social justice, owes much to this kind of painting.

Another beauty is Zurbarán's *Still Life* of fruit and flowers. An important recent gift is Henri Matisse's *Bathers with Turtle.* Painted in 1908, the intensity of the color and the powerfully delineated figures showing the female form in three attitudes give the canvas a richness and solidity that mark it one of Matisse's masterworks. Acquired by a German, Karl Osthaus, the painting was taken from the Folkwang Museum in Essen by the Nazi government and ordered sold at auction in 1939 in Switzerland, where it was purchased by Mr. and Mrs. Joseph Pulitzer, Jr.

The entire collection of Western painting has recently been regrouped—culminating in a stunning gallery of twentieth-century art—adjacent to the sculpture court. The American section, beginning with colonial, goes through the different sagas of our painting history and keeps up with today. A late acquisition is one of Ellsworth Kelly's outsized paintings. One early picture by John Greenwood, the satirical *Sea Captains Carousing in Surinam,* is one of few pieces of eighteenth-century genre painting by an American artist. St. Louis does well by George Caleb Bingham; though born in Virginia, he was known as "the Missouri artist" and in 1875 became the state's adjutant-general. His *Raftsmen Playing Cards* is probably the best-known Bingham in the collection, but the small, atypical, quieter, *The Old Friend Horse* delights too.

Henri Matisse: *Bathers with Turtle* (1908) (City Art Museum of St. Louis)

Few museums show the art and artifacts of their regions as effectively as St. Louis. A downstairs wing, informally referred to as the "Cowboy and Indian Department," presents a picture of culture in the Mississippi Valley from the days when St. Louis was a fur-trading post through the glamorous years when side-wheelers plied the broad river. The conquering of the redskin, whether by treaty or treachery, is depicted in painting, sculpture, and prints. Included is one of the quieter pictures by the Swiss artist Charles Bodmer, who accompanied Prince Maximilian of Prussia when that naturalist explored the West; he seems to have been artist-in-residence at more than one Indian massacre. Sagas of buffalo hunts, of trappers and traders and wagon trains, are by artists from Catlin to Remington.

Though the mill tax levy for museum support has aroused occasional resentment, as in the case of the Egyptian sculpture, most of the time it gives the citizens of St. Louis a proprietary feeling toward their museum.

WASHINGTON UNIVERSITY GALLERY OF ART

Steinberg Hall, Forsyth Boulevard, St. Louis, Missouri
Hours: Mon.–Fri., 9–5; Sat., 10–4; Sun., 1–5.
Free.

Though the Washington University Gallery of Fine Arts in Steinberg Hall was built in 1960, the history of the university collections began almost a hundred years earlier, when through the enthusiasm of one man, Halsey C. Ives, free evening art classes for eighteen people were established at the university. The horse-and-buggy-days project seems to have been jet propelled, for within a year 288 were receiving art instruction. In 1879 a department of fine arts was established.

In 1881 Wayman Crow, a St. Louis merchant, gave a building to the university which was to be known as the St. Louis Museum of Fine Arts. Situated at 19th and Locust Streets, it consisted of five large galleries, classroom, studios, and an auditorium. From then until the turn of the century, St. Louisans did a great deal of collecting and gave generously to the university. The William Bixby Fund was established to purchase works of American art.

With the closing of the Museum of Fine Arts in 1905–1906, the collections came on hard times. Housed in the new City Art Mu-

Interior sculpture court of the Washington University Art Gallery, St. Louis, Missouri.

seum of St. Louis, which was established after the St. Louis World's Fair of 1904, the paintings, as the new museum grew, were relegated to storage and strewn about corridors and classrooms on campus. With the coming of Horst W. Jansen to the university in 1941, the department sprang back into life.

The collections were reassessed and drastic measures taken to bring them up to date, since practically *no* twentieth-century work was represented. A purchasing plan to encompass the past forty years of European and American modern art developed. Within a year, about thirty significant pieces had been bought, including Braque, Beckmann, Baziotes, Stuart Davis, Max Ernst, Juan Gris, Guston, Tamayo, Zerbe, Miró, Moore, Degas, and Calder. Nothing but a top example of a painter's work was eligible. The dollar went further in 1945's art market.

Steinberg Hall is a handsome building set on the edge of the campus, accessible to one of St. Louis's main traffic arteries. A center section of glass shows off a large, arresting Lassaw and other pieces of sculpture, as well as changing exhibitions and the now-rich permanent collection. Of the three galleries on the lower floor, one houses the Morton D. May collection of New Guinea and Oceanic art. This material is on indefinite loan, as are many canvases of May's famous German Expressionist group.

A small group of early European paintings—Murillo, El Greco, Albert Cuyp, Daumier's beautiful *L'Ecrivan*—form a background for the ever-increasing contemporary group. The sculpture includes Lipchitz, Hepworth, Chillida, Consagra, among others.

The tradition of displaying works of art throughout the university carries on. Professors have been known to stoop to various forms of chicanery in order to hang behind their desks a favorite painting.

UNIVERSITY OF NEBRASKA ART GALLERIES:
SHELDON MEMORIAL ART GALLERY

Lincoln, Nebraska
Hours: Tues., 10–10; Wed.–Sat., 10–5; Sun., 2–5;
closed Mon., holidays.
Free.

Not the least of the works of art at the University of Nebraska art gallery is the building itself. Designed by Philip Johnson, the Sheldon is modest in size, monumental in conception. Its simple travertine exterior is bisected by a large sculpture hall composed of glass arches that rise to the building's height. Large golden discs set into the ceiling provide light patterns at night that make the gallery a glowing showcase from a block away. A sculpture garden will grow at the rear façade. To de-parch the Nebraska summer, the sculpture will stand among trees on watered islands. The key to the serenity of the entrance hall is its restraint. Instead of the frequent jungle of sculpture, only four noble pieces stand here: Lipchitz's *Bather*, Noguchi's *Song of the Bird*, Brancusi's *Head of a Girl*, and a nineteenth-century American wooden horse that looks as though he's pranced out of the T'ang Dynasty.

An art collection came to this prairie campus long before many an Eastern university could claim one. The first painting exhibition was shown in 1888 under the auspices of what is now the Nebraska Art Association. Progress was steady, if slow; but since 1930 the purchasing of works of art of discrimination has been

Interior court of the Sheldon Memorial Museum, Lincoln, Nebraska; photograph by Ezra Stoller Associates, Rye, N.Y.

Marsden Hartley: *Mount Katahdin, Autumn No. 1* (ca. 1942) (University of Nebraska Art Galleries, Lincoln; F. M. Hall Collection)

accelerated. Though primarily an American collection, a few foreign contemporaries such as Kirchner, Barlach, and Brancusi are seen at their best.

Some twentieth-century "old masters" are well represented: Walt Kuhn, Max Weber, Stuart Davis, Edward Hopper, Mark Rothko, Morris Louis, James Brooks, Helen Frankenthaler, Conrad Marca-Relli, Robert Motherwell, and Robert Indiana are seen at their best. Marsden Hartley, with four works, ranges from the poetic *Autumn, Lake and Hills,* 1907, to his much stronger, much later *Mt. Katahdin.* Cole, Blakelock, Eakins, Moran, and Ryder speak for the nineteenth century. The art gallery has recently acquired eighteen paintings and drawings from Blakelock's family (he died in 1919). Importance must be attached to this fact, as Blakelock is one of the most forged American masters. The quality is high, and some of the oils show a style which is unexpected and unique in the artist's work.

A print gallery whose walls are effectively covered with biscuit-colored carpeting also has a print cabinet for scholars' use.

Sold in Nebraska's museum shop are only original works of art, small sculpture, prints, ceramics.

JOSLYN ART MUSEUM

2218 Dodge, Omaha, Nebraska
Hours: Tues.–Sat., 10–5; Thurs., 10–9; Sun., 1–5;
closed Mon., holidays. Library. Admission 25¢; Thursday free.

A stone's throw from Main Street, a city-block-sized, pink marble, Egyptian-style temple houses the museum. Even the reliefs that ornament the façade, dedicated to Indians, buffaloes, and Mr. Joslyn's business activities, are in the two-dimensional profile style of the early dynasties. The illusion is disturbed only by four classical columns at the portico. On a first visit, use the main entrance into the floral court. Here the architecture of the Spanish Moors takes over, its arches borne on thin columns, its fountains green tile. Off the court an interesting area, "The Ancient World," features Egyptian, Greek, and Roman works.

Not a rich institution, the museum uses its masterpieces in conjunction with minor works to evoke specific periods in the history of art. The Middle Ages begin left of the Moorish court. A model of the twelfth-century church St. Trophime at Arles, France, shows the low, massive strength of Romanesque construction, the grandeur of the sculpture in the center-door tympanum. A photographic blowup of Carcassonne Citadel sets the stage for a medieval suit of armor. Illuminated manuscripts, silver, carved ivory, round out the period. Lorenzo di Credi's *Madonna and Child with Angels,* a handsome Spanish-Romanesque fresco, dominates the early Renaissance gallery. Everything from coins of the realm to small bronzes illustrate the period.

Joslyn rightly boasts of one of the fine Titian portraits in America, *Man with Falcon.* Here the statesman General Giorgio Carnaro gazes intently at the falcon, as if trying to define the power of so small a bird; the burnished red and gold of the falcon's jacket and the gleam of the general's sword accent the monumentality of the figure in its slate-gray and brown garb. Titian has built into this portrait, with its noble head and powerful body, all the dignity and richness of Venetian sixteenth-century life.

Copley's *Lord Cornwallis* typifies eighteenth-century America. The general stands in his red coat, his hand resting on what was to Colonials the real symbol of his power, a cannon.

A smaller but succinct version of Renoir's *Two Girls at Piano*

Titian: *Man with Falcon* (Joslyn Art Museum, Omaha, Nebraska)

keys the French Impressionist gallery. Several large galleries to the right of the courtyard are used for changing exhibitions and contemporaries, among them Pollock, Lipchitz, and Grant Wood's *Stone City, Iowa*. Downstairs galleries record life on the American prairies. Because there is no natural history museum in the region, the physical environs of Nebraska, and especially their effect on artists, are carefully studied. One case shows comparisons between Indian tools and modern tools—there is a surprising similarity. Push buttons reveal slides of the Plains Indians and their con-quests. In artifacts, engravings, painting, and sculpture the story unfolds: the French in the Northwest Territory, the Lewis and Clark expedition, the Indians and the army of the frontier, the evolution from sod house to log cabin, the record in paint by Alfred Jacob Miller, Seth Eastman, and George Catlin of buffalo hunts and tribal rites. Catlin was the first artist of stature to go West for the express purpose of documenting the tribes pictorially. Important indefinite loans are Charles Bodmer watercolors from the Prince Maximilian expedition, 1832–1834, to the interior of North America; and Alfred Jacob Miller's field paintings when he accompanied Captain Stewart's expedition. Finally, there is the territorial expansion that followed the building of the railroads. A large section is devoted to Indian crafts, and the work of the Aleutian Islanders and Eskimos should not be missed. The paint-ings on elk hide have the charm of much of the early cave painting.

Period rooms show the evolution of Omaha parlors, from Pony Express to Late Antimacassar style. A handsome auditorium seats 1,200.

BUFFALO BILL HISTORICAL CENTER,
THE WHITNEY GALLERY OF WESTERN ART

720 Sheridan Avenue, Cody, Wyoming
Hours: May–Sept. daily, 8–5; June–Aug., 7 A.M.–10 P.M.
Admission 50¢, children 25¢.

It's a long time between museums out on the Western plains, so don't miss this one. The simple building's entrance lounge frames a sandy mesa reaching to a spectacular mountain range and a heroic-sized bronze equestrian sculpture of Buffalo Bill—*The Scout,* done by Gertrude Vanderbilt Whitney. Mrs. Whitney was instrumental in acquiring this large tract of land for the historical

Gertrude Vanderbilt Whitney: *Buffalo Bill the Scout* (Buffalo Bill Historical Center, Cody, Wyoming; photograph by Jack Richard Studio, Cody)

center, of which the gallery is a part. All the aspects that made up frontier life, the grandeur of the untouched landscape, the Indian, the buffalo, the frontiersmen are recorded on canvas and in bronze —"As the story of the Old West fades into legend the testimony our artists left us becomes increasingly important."

Some of the best paintings here were collected by William F. "Buffalo Bill" Cody and displayed at the Irma Hotel which he built in Cody in 1902. The equestrian portrait of *Buffalo Bill* by the French artist Rosa Bonheur was done in 1889 in Paris, where Cody had taken his "Wild West Show." A few years later, when Cody was notified that his home was burning, he telegraphed back, "Save Bonheur picture, let home burn."

Among the Albert Bierstadts is *Last of the Buffalo* and *Wind River, Wyoming*, eloquent portrayals of our Western saga. Seventy-two George Catlin paintings of his journey up the Mississippi, from the Paul Mellon collection, are on indefinite loan from the National Gallery. The Alfred Jacob Miller paintings show the territory that is now Wyoming. Frederic Remington, Charles M. Russell, and other artists who documented our Western saga are shown. One gallery displays the entire contents of Remington's studio at the time of his death in 1909, memorabilia from every facet of pioneer Western life.

The museum is happily situated on routes 14 and 20—the eastern gateway to Yellowstone National Park.

SOUTHWESTERN ART MUSEUMS

PHOENIX ART MUSEUM

1625 North Central Avenue, Phoenix, Arizona
Hours: Tues.–Sat., 10–5; Sun., 1–5;
closed Mon., major holidays, August.
Free.

Until 1959 Phoenix was said to be the largest city in the United States without an art museum. A handsome new complex—a triumvirate of library, theater, and museum—silenced the accusers that year. The mortar was scarcely dry before the architect was at work again. Six years later a new museum wing of 50,000 square feet was added.

As John Mason Brown so neatly phrased it: "Women are the Typhoid Marys of American culture." In 1915 a determined handful of Phoenix Woman's Club members decided the "calendar" art exhibited at the state fair needed upgrading, and encouraged regional artists to show their work. Mrs. Dwight Heard, one of the members, formed the Phoenix Art Association in 1925 and instigated the conveyance to the city of the land where the fine arts project finally materialized.

The original museum presents medieval, Renaissance, baroque, eighteenth- and nineteenth-century art. The new wing contains

Tartar Guard (T'ang dynasty, 618–907 A.D.) (Phoenix Art Museum, Phoenix, Arizona; gift of Mrs. Elsie Sackler)

Mexican, Far Western, American, and Far Eastern art, full-scale period rooms, and a sculpture garden and court containing six Jacob Epstein bronzes, including a portrait of Somerset Maugham.

Not to be caught napping, generous donors have enhanced the collections a hundredfold. To date, these range from a pert T'ang figure of a *Tartar Guard* to a portrait of jazzman *Count Basie* by the contemporary Dutch artist Karel Appel. Other handsome acquisitions are a strong Courbet, *The Wave; Paysage à Varengeville,* a sunlit landscape by Camille Pissarro; Archipenko's economical yet lyrical *Torso;* Germaine Richier's *The Horse;* Marini's *The Equestrian,* to name but a few in this leaping complex.

UNIVERSITY OF ARIZONA ART GALLERY

Olive Road and Speedway, Tucson, Arizona
Hours: Mon.–Sat., 10–5; Sun., 2–6;
closed Jan. 1, Dec. 25. Free.

Edged by one of Tucson's main thoroughfares, this campus museum is accessible to students and visitors alike. The heart of the institution is the Kress collection and the heart of the Kress collection is the fifteenth-century *retablo* of the Cathedral of Ciudad Rodrigo, consisting of twenty-six large panels attributed to Fernando Gallego, an important painter of the Hispanic-Flemish fifteenth-century style. It represents an all-encompassing narrative of Creation to the Last Judgment. The painter of another Kress work, *Madonna and Child,* is called the Master of Ovile, because of his most important work in St. Pietro a Ovile, Siena. A few others represented are Taddeo di Bartolo, Lorenzo Lotto, Lucas Cranach the Elder, and Jusepe da Ribera.

The museum is strong in twentieth-century holdings. Edward Hopper is shown in an important canvas, *The City,* as is Charles

Jean Dubuffet: *Paysage avec Quatre Personnages* (The University of Arizona Art Gallery, Tucson; Edward Joseph Gallagher III Memorial Collection)

Joan Miro: *La Naissance du Jour* (The University of Arizona Art Gallery, Tucson; Edward Joseph Gallagher III Memorial Collection)

Burchfield with *The Quiet Pond*. With the gift of the Edward Joseph Gallagher III memorial collection, the gallery has come into "the big time" in modern art. The collection's size and range is extensive, the examples creditable to tops; included are Arp, Hebald, Calder, Kline, Hultberg, Baziotes, Stamos, Pollock, and De Kooning's smashing *Woman Ochre*. The European range: Tanguy, Miró, Appel, Nolde, Léger, Matisse, Dubuffet, Mathieu. In-depth exhibitions of such masters as Henry Moore, Walt Kuhn, John Marin, and Winslow Homer make the university galleries a popular place to visit.

ROSWELL MUSEUM AND ART CENTER

11th and Main Street, Roswell, New Mexico
Hours: Daily, 10–5; Sun., holidays, 1–5.
Free.

The modest adobe building on Route 70, built as a Federal Arts Project in 1937, is the only museum within a large radius. Through its museum, Roswell honors prominent New Mexican residents, the artist Peter Hurd, the poet Witter Bynner, and Paul Horgan, writer, whose *The Great River* won the Pulitzer Prize.

Most of the paintings in the permanent collection are Southwestern, either in origin or in subject matter. There are an important Georgia O'Keeffe, *Ram's Skull with Brown Leaves*, an early Marin of a *Scene in Taos*, and several examples of Marsden Hartley's painting done in New Mexico. In the Peter Hurd gallery is the main body of this native son's work, devoted to the people of the countryside and landscapes of its dramatic panoramas.

In a new section, the cream of Witter Bynner's collection of

Georgia O'Keeffe: *Ram's Skull with Brown Leaves* (Roswell Museum and Art Center, Roswell, New Mexico)

Chinese painting and jade has been installed. Although modest, it is well chosen. During his years in China translating Chinese poetry, Bynner made friends with many scholars and in his selection was, he said, "prevented from indulging or enjoying my own ignorance."

The museum has added science to art with another new gallery, in honor of Dr. Robert H. Goddard, who, between 1930 and 1941, conducted his world-renowned research in the development of high-altitude rockets just northwest of Roswell. The outdoor exhibit includes his first launching towers and his models of various stages in rocket progression. Indoors are his original drawings and some pieces of experimental apparatus.

MUSEUM OF NEW MEXICO: FINE ARTS MUSEUM

124 East Palace Ave., Santa Fe, New Mexico
Hours: Mon.–Sat., 9–5; Sun. & holidays, 2–5; winter, 2–4;
closed Jan. 1, Thanksgiving, Christmas.
Free.

Though international work is shown, the main emphasis in sculpture and painting here is on New Mexican artists and those who, since the opening of the West, have been drawn to record her history or the awesome beauty of her landscape. George Catlin, Ralph Blakelock, and Albert Bierstadt, and later Robert Henri, Randall Davey, and John Sloan painted here. The latter two settled close to Santa Fe for long periods. Sloan encouraged contemporary Indian artists and helped in the preservation of their older art forms. The Indian Arts Fund collection of jewelry, blankets, pottery, and clothing is housed in the museum.

MUSEUM OF NEW MEXICO:
MUSEUM OF INTERNATIONAL FOLK ART

Old Pecos Trail, Santa Fe, New Mexico
Hours, May 15–Sept. 15: Mon.–Sat., 9–5;
Sept. 15–May 15: Tues.–Sat., 9–5; Sun., holidays all year, 2–5;
closed Jan. 1, Thanksgiving, Dec. 25. Library. Free.

The museum of New Mexico is a complex of complexes, of which
the Folk Art museum is one of five. Exhibitions in the charming,
indigenous-style building run the gamut from Tibetan, Nor-
wegian, Mexican, and Japanese to New Mexican and Spanish
colonial folk art. A fine catalogue vividly documents the religious
and secular art of the Spanish colonial period. The furniture,
whether crudely or skillfully done, is elegant in line; the religious
paintings and carvings evidence a sturdy faith that survived
massacre and isolation. The rarest paintings are those done on
buffalo hide by the Franciscan friars after the reconquest of the
territory by the Spaniards in 1692. The colonials, isolated and
lacking tools, had to do everything in the simplest manner. Under
the missionaries' guidance they, along with the half-castes and
the Indians, learned to paint and carve in the round. By 1800
native image-makers created everything from altar screens to
small *bultos* for homes. Properly, a *bulto* is a religious object
carved in the round, while a *retablo* is a painting. We are inclined
to use the misnomer *santos* for both forms. The *santero*, or "saint
maker," could do either, moving from settlement to settlement,
executing commissions for church or home. Handed down from
father to son, the art flourished in remote villages well into this
century. The handsomest example of colonial baroque in the
Southwest is an altar executed by order of the governor of Santa

Señor Santiago, or *Saint James the
Greater* (New Mexican artist, ca. 1920–
1925) (Museum of International Folk
Art, Santa Fe, New Mexico)

Fe in 1760. It is now in the Church of Cristo Rey, a beautiful adobe church not far from the center of Santa Fe.

OKLAHOMA ART CENTER

3113 Pershing Blvd., Oklahoma City, Oklahoma
Hours: Tues. and Thurs., 10–9; Wed., Fri., Sat., 10–5; Sun., 2–5.
Closed major holidays. Library. Free.

Since the art center was established in 1936 as a W.P.A. arts project, it has been lively with lectures, concerts, and traveling exhibitions. National and international shows have kept Oklahomans in touch with world art movements, while at the same time there has been concentration on the Southwest. The center is host to an Eight-Side Exhibition of Painting and Sculpture, Young Talent, Oklahoma Annual, and the All-Oklahoma Biennial and is now working toward the establishment of a more general art museum. The collection now consists of American contemporary painting and sculpture, some old master paintings and prints, good contemporary prints recently enriched by a gift of German Expressionist graphics, American glass, and some Chinese porcelain. Some of the American holdings are Louis Eilshemius, Cameron Booth, Morris Kantor, Emil Carlson, Julian Levi, Nicolai Cikovsky, Cleve Gray, and George Bellows.

Ground was broken for the present building in 1957. A round structure, its hub is an open circular court, ideal for sculpture.

PHILBROOK ART CENTER

2727 South Rockford Road, Tulsa, Oklahoma
Hours: Tues.–Sat., 10–5; Tues. eves., 7:30–9:30; Sun., 1–5;
closed Mon., holidays.
Library.
Admission 25¢, children under 15 free.

When oil magnate Wait Phillips retired, he left his ornate villa and his gardens to the museum. The change of pace from columned Italianate decor on the ground floor to adobe-style galleries below is interestingly abrupt. In the adobe galleries, pottery is grouped according to pueblos and tribes. Clark Field, who assembled the pottery, chose only the best specimens from those made for the Indians' own use. The American Indian wove into his baskets the history of his culture. Those found in caves of Colorado, Utah, and New Mexico tell of our early civilization. More importantly, the museum is actively helping the modern Indian to express himself creatively. Using new techniques and idioms, they draw on their own rich past for inspiration. It is, after all, not such a big step from the design of a Navaho blanket to Abstractionism.

The museum owns about three hundred American Indian paintings, which are constantly rotated, and holds an annual juried exhibition of Indian painters. The Taos Room shows the Spanish colonial influence as well as native Indian styles, while the Santa Fe Room combines Remington and Russell with Indian objects.

The upper galleries are used for changing exhibitions and to display the Kress and Clubb collections. Kress representation is in Italian art from the fourteenth to the eighteenth centuries. When her husband struck oil, Laura Clubb was teaching school in Kaw City, Oklahoma. Mr. Clubb asked his wife what they should do with "all that money," and Laura was ready with her own answer. She headed for Northwestern University and a course in the history of art. The next step was Europe. Her best buys, however, were the Americans Blakelock, Wyant, and Thomas Moran.

In 1871 Moran made his first of three trips with the Geological Survey of the Territories into the almost unexplored Yellowstone region. The artist's canvases, with their sense of grandeur and extravagant beauty of Yosemite and Yellowstone, showed Americans the wonder of this enchanted, unknown land and led to the preservation of much of the area in national parks. Moran's quick watercolor sketches gave Easterners their first idea of the magnitude and glory of the West. In 1872 and 1874 the government,

Thomas Moran: *Grand Canyon* (Philbrook Art Center, Tulsa, Oklahoma)

through an Act of Congress, purchased two large Moran oils, *Grand Canyon at Yellowstone* and *Chasm in the Colorado.*

Another innovation at the Philbrook, which is doing so much to preserve the visual record of the West, is a gallery of Southwestern architecture, commencing with today's skyscrapers and going back to Indian pueblos and cave dwellings.

THOMAS GILCREASE INSTITUTE OF AMERICAN HISTORY AND ART

2401 W. Newton Street, Tulsa, Oklahoma
Hours: Mon.–Fri., 10–5; Sat., Sun., holidays, 1–5;
closed Christmas.
Library.
Free.

The only portrait made from life of President James Madison (by Charles Willson Peale) is but one of many surprises to be found at this museum. When Thomas Gilcrease, part Cree Indian, discovered oil at the age of twenty-one and became an instant millionaire, the first thing he did was buy a painting. That was in 1912. In 1963 a new museum was erected to house the prodigious collection of Remingtons (21 oils, 18 bronzes), Russells (29 oils, 25 watercolors, 28 bronzes), Catlins (74 oils, 137 watercolors), and a cache of works by Alfred Jacob Miller, the first painter of the Rocky Mountain territory. This collection is second only to the one in the Smithsonian. But Gilcrease's interest went far beyond the saga of the West. There are remarkable portraits of great Americans painted by artists of the caliber of Robert Feke, Ralph Earl, John Smibert, Benjamin West. Albert Bierstadt, Ralph Blakelock, and Charles Wimar are shown in important examples, while Thomas Moran fills a handsome gallery with his romantic scenes.

When in 1955 Gilcrease found himself financially embarrassed and offered his collection to Tulsa for $2,500,000, grateful citizens voted four to one for a bond issue for purchase. When he became solvent again he continued to add to the collection. When he died, one and a half years before the present building opened, Gilcrease had given years of his life to furthering America's historical art heritage.

A wealth of other material is still being catalogued: Mound Indian and Eskimo artifacts, Central American jades, Olmec terra cottas, Incan and Mayan treasures.

The library collection is staggering: Cortez' papers, including his proclamation of the conquest of Mexico; Columbus' first known letter to his son from the New World; the original of Penn's Treaty; and the letter written by General Warren in 1775 telling Paul Revere to "proceed on a ride with all dispatch."

UNIVERSITY OF TEXAS: ART GALLERY

San Jacinto and 23rd Street, Austin, Texas
Hours: Mon.–Fri., 10–6; Sat., 9–5; Sun., 1–5;
closed Thanksgiving, Dec. 25.

The university art department and gallery could not be more felicitously situated than it is, on the broad avenue that is the heart of the campus and at the foot of the hill leading to the Lyndon B. Johnson Memorial Library. The football stadium lies directly across the street, and the museum's director claims that before the game on Saturday at least 5,000 of the audience visit his museum.

The building's first floor contains an auditorium, exhibition galleries, library, and research department. Art is looked at, talked about, and studied all on one floor. The library and print cabinet are open to the public. Trained docents give lectures at stated times during the week.

In its collecting, the museum emphasizes mainly prints, drawing, and sculpture. Its chief interest is the North American continent, European baroque as it influences American art, and primitive and prehistoric material.

In its exhibitions program, the museum shows the arts of major areas concerned with the community. Provincial? Not when one remembers that the pipeline that runs through Saudi Arabia originated in Texas. Not without reason have many of King Faisal's sons been enrolled on the campus. The high-level studies in geology and petrography, as they relate to the Near East, make exhibitions of the arts of Iran and Iraq logical.

So diverse and lively, yet scholarly, is the program that as Austin becomes more and more a convention city, hotel managers have begun calling the museum to check on their exhibitions and lecture activities. The more important catalogues are issued in hard cover by the excellent University of Texas Press.

The museum is a major repository of book arts and literary iconography, including important unpublished material on colonial Mexico, much of it visual in nature. The fine James A. Michener collection of 260 contemporary paintings has just been given to Austin. It will form the visual art basis of their new (still in the planning stage) $7 million Humanities Research Center.

DALLAS MUSEUM OF FINE ARTS

Fair Park, Dallas, Texas
Hours: Tues.–Sat., 10–5; Wed., 10–9; Sun., 2–6;
closed Mon., Dec. 25.
Library. Free.

The Dallas Art Association was formed in 1903 by a group of women to stage art exhibits in the public library. In the twenties, after a good deal of soul-searching, they finally decided to allow men to serve on their board. The present museum opened in 1936 in the Fair Park, just a short walk from the Midway.

Nowhere is the spirit of expansion and change that pervades the whole museum world more evident than in Dallas. The main entrance has been moved to lead into a new wing around a sculpture court dominated by a large Barbara Hepworth. Intimate galleries for drawing and craft exhibits are here also. Upstairs a series of galleries designed for temporary exhibitions lead into the permanent installations beyond.

Recently the museum has changed its orientation. Though the collections formerly included some art of the past, the emphasis was on Texas and regional art. The aim now is to build a group of prime-quality objects of all periods, with the strength in twentieth-century work and the art of the Americas. Already fine Etruscan pots and gold ornaments, a unique pre-Archimedian piece, and a large fourth-century Greek figure found near Athens have arrived. The French school's best example is the happy *Apple Pickers*, a product of Camille Pissarro's Pointillist period. Excellent American examples are Gilbert Stuart's *John Ashley, Esquire* and *Mrs. Ashley,* George Bellows' *Emma in Blue,* Edward Hopper's *Lighthouse Hill,* and Andrew Wyeth's *Becky King.*

A huge two-storied court that used to be the entrance, and could logically revert to it again, is dominated by Henry Moore's

Figure of a young man (Greece, ca. 330 B.C.)
(Dallas Museum of Fine Arts; gift of Mr. and Mrs.
Cecil H. Green, 1967)

Woman. Its vast scale is matched around the white brick walls
by canvases of Motherwell, Adolph Gottlieb, and Jimmy Ernst.
Other distinguished works are by Lee Bontecou, Louise Nevelson,
James Dine, George Rickey, Alicia Penalba, Hans Arp, Dimitri
Hadzi, and Jackson Pollock.

The Mexican Tamayo's *El Hombre* stands 18 feet high in
smokey blue and red earth colors, showing man wrestling with
the universe. It was commissioned especially for this court.

The Dallas museum remains unique in its care and treatment
of native artists. Their work and their lives are documented with
biographies, photographs, and slides. A gallery of Texas painters
is always on view and there are yearly exhibits of their work.

MEADOWS MUSEUM

Southern Methodist University, Dallas, Texas
Hours: Daily 12–5: Sun. 1–5;
closed major holidays.
Free.

This newest of University museums endowed by the Meadows
Foundation in 1965 occupies a large corner of the university's
handsome Fine Arts Center. Its dedication is to Spanish culture.
Among masterpieces in the leaping collection are: Zurbarán's
Mystical Marriage of St. Catherine; Murillo's *Jacob Laying the
Peeled Rods before the Flocks of Laban.* This canvas is one of a
series of five paintings on the life of Jacob. William B. Jordan,
director of the museum, has followed in scholarly fashion the
peregrinations of the paintings (*Art Journal*, Spring 1968). The
Cleveland Museum acquired one in 1966. Two were purchased

Diego Rivera: *Portrait of Ilya Ehrenburg* (1915) (Meadows Museum, Southern Methodist University, Dallas; photograph by O. E. Nelson, New York)

by the Czar of Russia in 1811 and remain in the Hermitage in Leningrad. The fifth canvas was sold in London in 1870 and has not been heard of since. Another star in the collection is Velázquez's portrait of *Philip IV*, one of a series of ten the artist did of his patron. It is Velázquez's earliest portrait of the King to have survived in visible pigment. There are canvases by Juan de Sevilla and Valdes Leal and five Goyas plus early first editions or trial proofs of all four sets of Goya etchings. These editions were until 1953 in the library of the Dukes of Lerma. The group of Spanish nineteenth-century paintings is the largest in America. The museum is also beginning to collect Latin American and Spanish twentieth-century works. Fine examples of Juan Gris and Joan Miró make a good starting point.

AMON CARTER MUSEUM OF WESTERN ART

3501 Camp Bowie Blvd., Fort Worth, Texas
Hours (Sept. 1–June): Tues.–Sat., 10–5; Sun., holidays, 1–5:30; closed Mon. Library. Free.

In 1961, this small, handsome museum opened its doors. It was established under the will of the late Amon Carter for the study and documentation of western North America, a program expressed in scholarly publications, exhibitions, and permanent collections related to the many aspects of American culture, historic and contemporary, which find their identification as "Western."

The color of baked honey, the building is made of a shell stone quarried near inland Austin, on which some errant sea urchin has left nostalgic patterns that speak of the sea as clearly as a

Interior view of court, Amon Carter Museum, Fort Worth, Texas.

conch shell held to the ear. The architect, Philip Johnson, has given the museum a two-storied glass façade segmented by tapering columns. All the galleries in the teakwood and bronze interior face out into the entrance court. The museum becomes a platform for viewing the city, with Fort Worth's skyline sweeping the distance. Set in alien grandeur, skimming the top of the flowering trees on a lower terrace, is Henry Moore's *Upright Motives No. 1–2–7.* The similarity of these forms and the totem poles of the North American Indians is striking. (Moore and a charming small portrait of Buffalo Bill done by Degas when the "Wild West Show" was in Paris are among the few non-American works in the museum.)

This is a personal collection brought together by a man who through tradition and predilection was involved with our Western frontier in its romantic cowboy-and-Indian phase. Built primarily on outstanding Remingtons and Russells, the collection has been expanded by extensive works depicting nineteenth-century Indian and hunting scenes on the Western plains, early views of Western towns, and a growing group of important twentieth-century American artists involved with the West. Georgia O'Keeffe and other artists such as Marsden Hartley foraged and recounted their impressions of the desert country on canvas.

A few museum books: *Standing Up Country* by C. Gregory Crampton, *Taos and Santa Fe* by Van Deren Coke, *Santos* by George Kubler. Much of the West's great heritage is succinctly bound in this elegant Philip Johnson building.

FORT WORTH ART CENTER

1309 Montgomery Street, Forth Worth, Texas
Hours: Tues.–Sat., 10–5:30; Sun., 1–5:30;
closed Mon., Dec. 25.
Free.

When in 1909 Mrs. Jennie Scheuber, librarian, hung on her library walls the first exhibition that the American Federation of Arts sent across the country, the first step toward a museum was taken. After that showing, "Miss Jennie" began begging, cajoling, driving to build a collection. She wheedled $10 out of each of seventy women to buy Eakins' *The Old Swimming Hole,* and even so, payments had to be sent along on the installment plan, since it took a long time to convince all those women that one painting was worth all that money. Today it is appraised at well over $50,000. An art association was established after this venture and was housed in the library until 1954, when Herbert Bayer designed the present art center on a rise of green in Carter Square, which, together with the recently opened William Edrington Scott Theatre, makes this a focus for all the performing arts: theater, opera, ballet and music, as well as visual arts.

The theater's entire plan was conceived by Donald Oenslager, one of America's foremost scenic designers. Aesthetically and functionally satisfying, it makes the average Broadway theater seem like an antique. Mr. Oenslager also executed the mural in the lobby, depicting the theater through the ages; th scenes run the gamut from the Greeks through the Restoration to today.

The art center's collection, mainly American, includes Gilbert Stuart's *Miss Clementina Beach* and George Inness' *Approaching Storm.* Among the latter-day canvases are Feininger's *Manhattan, New York #2,* Rattner's *Still Life with Chair,* and Josef Albers' *Intaglio Due E.* Renoir's *Jean with a Hoop* is the center's first excursion into Impressionism. Picasso's important *Femme Couchée Lisant,* the first picture acquired by an American museum through Tel-Star auction, has recently come into the collection. The William Edrington Scott contemporary painting collection, catholic in range, includes examples of the Texas sculptor Charles Umlauf and painters Sheeler, O'Keeffe, Tamayo, Andrew Wyeth, and Morris Graves. An excellent group of about seven hundred prints begins with Dürer and carries through to the present.

One cannot leave this spot without saying a word about the

Pablo Picasso: *Femme Couchée Lisant* (1960) (Collection of the Fort Worth Art Center; The Benjamin J. Tillar Memorial Trust)

concentration of art and architecture on Amon Carter Square. Within sight and walking distance are the Amon Carter Museum of Western Art, Fort Worth Art Center, The Children's Museum (parents, don't park your children here—stay with them, it's well worth it). The Kimbell Museum, designed by Louis Kahn, is in the building stages and promises to bring to the area a world range of art treasures.

KIMBELL ART MUSEUM

Carter Square, Fort Worth, Texas

The Kimbell art museum, so new that it is not quite off the drawing board, is nonetheless an established fact made possible by the late Kay Kimbell. Kimbell made a fortune in such disparate enterprises as oil, grain, insurance, and supermarkets. He collected art avidly, if not always with notable discernment. However, the museum's director, Dr. Richard F. Brown, is free to weed as he pleases. A good man with a hoe, he will surely transplant only choice specimens. Meanwhile, his ear to the ground, his hand frequently leaving his pocket, Brown zooms between continents acquiring topnotch art definitive of its period and medium. There will be no attempt to create a milieu of the original ambiance of an art object. Rather, the impression will be that of a private collection of catholic taste—and considerable means. Minoan may face Mondrian.

On a 9½ acre park, the building will take up 100,000 square feet. The architect, Louis Kahn, proposes to execute the structure on low, broad, deceptively simple lines to fit the terrain, weaving into the building, gardens and sculpture courts. Parking will be solved underground. A conservation center will offer its services to institutions of the region. The collection will burst into full bloom on the night the building opens on Carter Square, which is fast becoming the acropolis of the Southwest. But, at writing, the art works in hand so far are known only to the director and the trustees.

BAYOU BEND COLLECTION OF THE MUSEUM OF FINE ARTS

1 Westcott Street, Houston, Texas
Hours: Tues. and Thurs., 1:15–4:30; Wed. and Fri., 10–4:30;
Sat., 10–1:15;
closed major holidays and San Jacinto Day.
Admission by reservation. Minimum age, 16.

The home and beautiful gardens of Miss Ima Hogg were opened to the public in 1966. This collection of eighteen rooms of furniture, decorative arts, and paintings (1650–1825) was selected over a period of years for the express purpose of bringing to Houston fine examples of our American cultural heritage. The Newport Room, faithfully reproduced from the Nichols–Wanton–Hunter house, shows fine examples of Rhode Island craftsmanship. The music room is a perfect Federal-period assemblage, including a Duncan Phyfe piano. The Philadelphia Hall contains Chippendale furniture made in Philadelphia when that city was the leader of the Colonies.

CONTEMPORARY ARTS ASSOCIATION

6949 Fannin Street, Houston, Texas
Hours: Tues.–Fri., 10–5; Sat.–Sun., 1–5;
closed Mon., major holidays. Free.

Since its founding in 1948, the association has undergone a series of changes. Always lively with film series, lectures, and art classes, it has sponsored some distinguished one-man exhibitions: Van Gogh, Max Ernst, Tamayo, and Calder. For several years, activities such as poetry readings, musicals, experimental TV programs prevailed, but lately the trend has been to return to the showing of works of art, with emphasis on the arts of the Americas.

Exhibitions span six weeks. A larger home is being sought, and there is every indication that the museum plans to resume its role as a vital center for the presentation of contemporary art and its related activities. Permanent holdings will be expanded. They now include Matta, Calder, Max Ernst, Joseph Cornell, and Jacques Lipchitz.

MUSEUM OF FINE ARTS OF HOUSTON

1001 Bissonnet Street, Houston, Texas
Hours: Tues.–Sat., 9:30–5; Wed. 9:30 to 10 P.M. (Oct.–June);
Sun., 12–6; closed Mon., major holidays, San Jacinto Day.
Library.
Free.

There is a tranquility about the Houston Museum that is difficult to reconcile with the high-voltage charge of some of its art. The simple white walls, the economy of hanging contribute, but it is essentially the feeling of order, the balance of objects of uniformly high quality that pervades and sets the stage.

The Houston Public School of Art League was founded in 1905 to purchase reproductions of old masters for school use. Motivated by the same movers, the present Museum of Fine Arts became an impressive reality, situated on a triangular park in the center of the city. Later, the starkly beautiful Cullinan Hall, designed by Mies van der Rohe, was added. Fitting neatly between two wings, it will serve as an inner court when ultimate expansion plans are completed. Its noble space is admirable for large sculpture such as Chillida's or Calder's 20-foot mobile or paintings from the collection by Soulages, Kline, Motherwell or others who employ the heroic-size canvas. By hanging the paint-

Interior, Cullinan Hall, the Museum of Fine Arts of Houston, Texas.

ings on wires suspended out in the gallery from the ceiling, an extra and arresting dimension is created.

One usually enters the museum through the south gallery, where the contemporary permanent collection is often rotated. A sampling might be: Alberto Burri, Antonio Tapies, James Brooks, Enrico Donati, Luis Feito. A junior gallery to the right adjoins young people's classrooms and supplements a practical program of art education for youth. The galleries on the second floor are more static, since many of the collections must be shown intact. The Robert Lee Blaffer memorial wing holds a top Cézanne, *Portrait of Madame Cézanne;* important panels by Giovanni di Paolo; a retable, school of Avignon, fifteenth-century, from the chapel of Notre Dame des Sceaux. Here also is one of the museum's most popular paintings, Renoir's *Still Life with Bouquet,* an allegory of the arts within which Renoir copied a sketch of Manet's which Manet did after a painting by Goya.

Three arresting portraits by Corneille de Lyon hang in an area outside the Blaffer galleries. In the Kress collection of old masters are works by Tintoretto, Magnasco, Sebastiano del Piombo, and *Market Place in Pirna, Saxony* by Bernardo Bellotto. Bellotto did for Pirna on the Elbe what his uncle, Canaletto, did for Venice on the Adriatic—and with less to work with. The Edith A. and Percy S. Straus collection of Italian Renaissance paintings and sculpture encompasses bronzes by Cellini, Giovanni da Bologna, and Verrocchio; paintings by Hans Memling and Rogier van der Weyden. Fra Angelico is here at his endearing best in the predella *Temptation of St. Anthony, Abbot.* The gold of the coins that tempt the saint play against the gold of his halo. The soft blue-violet tones of the panel are sharpened by a pungent pink church perched on a hilltop.

Frederic Remington, that recorder of the Plains and the Plains Indians, has a gallery to himself. The museum's Bayou Bend collection of Indian art of the Southwest is one of the finest and includes pottery of the Hopi and Zuni. The museum has lately been strengthening its native art galleries with North and Meso-American, Mayan, Oceanic, African, and Australasian pieces. One of the most arresting sculptures in volcanic stone is *Standing Female Figure* from Costa Rica.

All roads seem to bring one logically back to Cullinan Hall. From either upstairs wing staircase, on whose mezzanine nine monumental sculptures rest, one descends into the great hall conversely, for the sculpture beckons one up . . . especially *Ephebus,* a 91-inch bronze sculpture and one of the great Greek figures in existence. Prints and drawings are shown in space below the Cullinan wing. Drawings for Robinson Crusoe by Thomas Sully are unique. A lively art school offers a Bachelor of Fine Arts degree here.

MARION KOOGLER McNAY ART INSTITUTE

6000 N. New Braunfels Street, San Antonio, Texas
Hours: Tues.–Sat., 9–5; Thurs., 9–9; Sun., 2–5;
closed Mon., Jan. 1, July 4, Thanksgiving, Dec. 25.
Library.
Free.

Marion Koogler McNay contributed her name, her house, and her works of art to form the San Antonio Art Institute. Even as the large Hispano-Moorish building went up in 1929, Mrs. McNay was thinking of it in terms of a public trust. Hence, the spacious rooms and outside loggias ribboning a fountained patio are ideal for this eclectic collection. Mrs. McNay, stirred by the Armory Show of 1913, began to buy the work of those artists who deeply influenced twentieth-century painting. Perhaps because she was herself a watercolorist, she concentrated on that difficult and rewarding medium, and today the museum has a distinguished roster of such names as Cassatt, Boudin, Bonnard, De La Fresnaye, and Klee. Pascin is splendidly represented by 218 drawings and watercolors, from the erotic to the witty. Redon, in *Profile with Flowers,* displays his trademark—brilliant, wet-eyed anemones. Demuth's *From a Kitchen Garden* and Homer's *Scotch Mist* are two American beauties.

During the last fifteen years of her life, Mrs. McNay focused on acquiring a few important oils of the first-generation Post-Impressionists: *Portrait of the Artist with the Idol* by Gauguin, Van Gogh's *Women Crossing the Fields,* Pissarro's *Haymakers Resting,* and Cézanne's *Portrait of Henri Gasquet.*

The second collection here is the Frederic Oppenheimer, primarily Gothic and medieval material, unique in the Southwest. A new and charming Gallery of Folk Art of the Southwest illustrates the art of the *santero*—both *retablo* paintings and *bultos.*

A small print cabinet has been established; its aim is to purchase editions of the highest quality. A proof impression of

Redon's *Centaur Visant les Nues* is the only known example in sepia. Print aficionados will be happy here.

Contemporary changing exhibitions are shown on the second floor, and a purchase fund allows for constant surprises, such as fine examples of Barbara Hepworth's and Germaine Richier's sculpture and the five bronze studies for Rodin's *The Burghers of Calais.*

WITTE MEMORIAL MUSEUM

3801 Broadway, San Antonio, Texas
Hours: Mon.–Fri., 9–5; Sat., Sun., holidays, 10–6.
Admission 25¢; under 17, 10¢.

The Witte museum is a natural science, history, and art showcase devoted mainly to the Southwest and the antecedent cultures that

Paul Gauguin: *Portrait of the Artist with the Idol* (Marion Koogler McNay Art Museum, San Antonio, Texas)

went into its making. Spacious upstairs galleries hold the permanent art and decorative arts collections and changing exhibitions. Behind the main building are four reconstructed early Texas homes.

WEST COAST ART MUSEUMS

UNIVERSITY OF CALIFORNIA AT BERKELEY:
THE UNIVERSITY ART MUSEUM

Berkeley, California
Hours: Daily, 12–6;
closed Christmas, New Year, July 4.
Free

In building its new art center the University of California at Berkeley is bringing to the museum world one of the most exciting realizations of the century. By holding a national competition, it has put some of the most creative minds in architecture to work on the problems of museum building. Of the seven finalists out of 400 entries, Mario Ciampi Associates of San Francisco were chosen. The center is scheduled to open in 1969.

The university's collections, accumulated over nearly a century and now scattered about the campus, will be brought together in a building that in the words of the museum's director, Dr. Peter Selz, must express "utility, firmness, and grace." The architectural

Peter Paul Rubens: *Road to Calvary* (University Art Museum, University of California, Berkeley)

historian Spiro Kostof describes the boldly cantilevered galleries as a series of five trays that fan out in a 90-degree angle, stepping down as they do so. Ramps will lead from the lobby to these and to galleries stacked farther up, which will be circumscribed on one side by a pleated glass wall.

Though the collections cover most periods in the history of art, much emphasis is placed on the contemporary. Hans Hofmann's splendid gift, shortly before he died, of forty-five of his important canvases plus a princely sum to house them makes a fine rallying point. A few others on today's scene are: Zoltan Kemeny, Jason Seley, Wilfred Zogbaum, Sam Francis, Pierre Alechinsky, Roy de Forest, Glenn Wessels, Cleve Gray, and James Gill. Other distinguished acquisitions: a High Renaissance gem, a *Pietà* by the Venetian painter Savoldo; and one of Rubens' great oil sketches, *Road to Calvary.*

One wing will be devoted to primitive art, which will be on extended loan from the university's Lowie Museum of Anthropology. One of the great primitive collections in the world, it is especially strong in Peruvian, Northwest Coast Indian, African, and Oceanic art. With the gathering together and enriching of its treasures, the university brings a new dimension to Berkeley the campus and Berkeley the town.

LA JOLLA MUSEUM OF ART

700 Prospect Street, La Jolla, California
Hours: Tues.–Sun., 12:30–4:30; Wed. also 7–10 P.M;
closed Mon., Jan. 1, Dec. 25. Free.

Very little, if anything, is left of the Ellen Browning Scripps house that in 1941 became the home of La Jolla's first art center. A series of additions has more than doubled its space, including a luxurious auditorium, joined to the original building by a sculpture garden and a large open gallery. Abbott Pattison's *Family Group,* George Baker's *Watcher VII,* and Peter Voulkos' large and complex *Big Remington III* usually inhabit the garden. A wing plunges down the hill at the rear for studios, an art school, and the most distracting view along the Southern California coastline.

The permanent collection roams from prehistoric to Larry Bell but, of over two hundred paintings and sculptures, the major portion is in the twentieth century. German Expressionist Ernst

Nicholas Krnshenick: Untitled (La Jolla Museum of Art, La Jolla; gift of Mr. and Mrs. Martin Gleich)

Ludwig Kirchner's vivid *Portrait of Max Lieberman,* father of the Secession movement, companions his splendid 1905 *Portrait of the Artist with Nude Model.* A recent gift brought seventy oils and watercolors by John Marin and Marsden Hartley to La Jolla. Considerable gallery space is devoted to Oceanic, African, and pre-Columbian sculpture and to the twentieth century.

The print collection begins with seventeenth-century European etchings and engravings and ranges to a group of over four hundred lithographs from the Tamarind Workshop in Los Angeles. Tamarind was founded to provide facilities for artists, similar to those of the print shops in Paris, where the great print-makers such as Toulouse-Lautrec and Picasso worked. Many of America's well-known artists experimented at Tamarind.

LOS ANGELES COUNTY MUSEUM OF ART

5905 Wilshire Boulevard, Los Angeles, California
Hours: Tues.–Sun., 10–5; Fri.,1–10;
closed Thanksgiving, Dec. 25.
Restaurant.
Ahmanson Gallery, free;
Lytton Gallery, 50¢; children 25¢.

The best thing to report about an art museum, aside from the lure of its collections, is its functionalism. The Los Angeles County Museum definitely has both. A person wishing to see a current exhibition goes directly to the Lytton Pavilion. For the permanent collection, he proceeds to the Ahmanson. (In the bookshop on the main floor, buy the *Handbook of the Collections;* its where-to-find-it section is most useful.) For a concert or

Krishna as the Dancing Butter Thief
(South India, Vijzyanagar period)
(Los Angeles County Art Museum,
Exposition Park)

lecture, he steps from the plaza to the Leo S. Bing Center.

While many gifts have enriched the Los Angeles County Museum of Art since it opened in 1913 as a section of the Science and Natural History Museum, it was William Randolph Hearst who, with his gargantuan appetite for collecting, raised it in the 1940s to a first-class power. At the height of his buying, Hearst's acquisitions represented a quarter of the sales of art objects in the world; warehouses bulged; his agents ranged from Tucumcari to Tibet. That he was an indiscriminate buyer of art (a misconception fostered by the story of his ordering his agents to get him a rare piece which he already possessed but had forgotten) is disproved here. Outstanding Hearstian treasures in residence are in the field of Hispano-Moresque pottery, silver, Gothic tapestries, and English furniture. But Greek, Etruscan, Hellenistic, and Roman sculptures, and a large group of Greek pottery are not to be ignored. Among the paintings is one of the country's best Sir Thomas Lawrences: *Portrait of Arthur Atherly as an Etonian.*

The museum has a major new East Indian collection, the Herramaneck Group, which puts its Indian holdings on a par with those of the Boston, Cleveland and Kansas City museums.

Set on broad and busy Wilshire Boulevard, the museum, designed by William L. Pereira & Associates, consists of three pavilions arranged on a central raised plaza in a reflecting pool. Faced with hand-set marble tiles and surrounded by colonnades of slender columns, the buildings seem to grow out of the reflecting pool, much as a Venetian *palazzo* appears to grow from the canal. Promenades topped with clear plastic domes provide covered walks between the buildings. At the rear in two large pools segmented by a slab walk leading into Hancock Park's green lawns are three large Calder mobiles, the tallest entitled *Hello Girls.* With jets of water pinging merrily away at their witty surfaces, they are in perpetual motion, like three irresponsible young women out for a lark.

The ambiance in the painting galleries is luxurious. The carpeted floors and velvet walls satisfy some, produce aesthetic trauma in others. The first-level galleries contain the antiquities. Some highlighs are the five Assyrian Assur-Nasir-pol reliefs, the Camer sculpture, and an especially fine example of Haniwa art, *Figure of a Sitting Man.* (Haniwa was funerary genre sculpture of the third to seventh centuries A.D.) That these delicate Japanese terra cottas have survived earthquakes, wars, and the plain passing of time is a miracle.

On the second floor, an astonishingly moving religious carving, a German Swabian *Descent from the Cross,* rises 6 feet high. Two remarkable early canvases are Hans Holbein the Younger's *Portrait of a Woman* and Petrus Christus' *Portrait of a Man.* Holbein, a German, spent many years in England, his last six in the pay of the court of Henry VIII. The portrait is a glowing, vital likeness of a petulant young woman. In Christus' portrait the sitter wears a grave, enigmatic dignity, his face molded as though it were sculptured.

The third floor is the address of the nineteenth-century French and contemporaries. Among the French are a great Cézanne, *Still Life with Cherries and Peaches,* and Degas' *Two Sisters.* Another portrait of them hangs in the Wadsworth Atheneum in Hartford. Other French pleasures are provided by Gauguin and Matisse; Modigliani's *Portrait of Jean Cocteau;* six Picassos, with *Courtesan with Jewelled Collar,* painted when he was only twenty-three; Rouault's *Samson Turning the Millstone.* The galleries are arranged to facilitate a survey of developments in

Pablo Picasso: *Courtesan with Jeweled Collar* (Los Angeles County Museum, Exposition Park; gift of Mr. and Mrs. George Gard De Sylva)

European and American art since 1800. The German Expressionists are especially articulate. Among the contemporaries are California's Rico Lebrun, William Brice, John McLaughlin and John Paul Jones, along with Rothko, Pollock, MacIver, Motherwell, Stuart Davis, Guston, and Nakian. Many young painters are being added to the collection. An extensive outdoor sculpture plaza on this level changes the pace from the painting galleries. In fact, one of the features seems to be an ever-at-hand pleasant plaza in which to contemplate sculpture, pools, park, and sky.

The print and drawing galleries rove exploratively from a rare print, *St. Jerome in Penitence* (*circa* 1470) by an unknown German, to the latest from Los Angeles' Tamarind Lithography Workshop. The print and drawing study room is open to the public Tuesday through Friday, 10 to 5. The textiles and costume section also contains a research center used by appointment by hundreds every year. Decorative arts, aside from ancient and classical, begin with the Gothic. One spectacular room holds Louis XV furniture and Rose Gobelin tapestries.

Elaborate supervisory data centers have been installed which electronically control temperature and humidity and bring monitored television to the galleries. An interior loading dock, sealed from the outside, accommodates three outsize vans, so that a large exhibition can be moved at minimum risk.

UNIVERSITY OF CALIFORNIA AT LOS ANGELES: ART GALLERIES

405 Hilgard Avenue, Los Angeles, California
Hours: Mon.–Fri., 12–5; Sun., 1:30–5;
closed Jan. 1, May 30, month of August, Thanksgiving, Dec. 25.
Free.

As with many university art galleries, the emphasis here is on the fine, scholarly, in-depth exhibition program rather than on building a permanent collection, although in contemporary sculpture the museum seems to be leading the way in Southern California. Set among eucalyptus, jacaranda and pine trees or bedded down on a pink brick terrace are twenty-seven monumental pieces by David Smith, Calder, Lipchitz, Laurens, Hepworth, Chadwick, Consagra, Rosenthal, Archipenko, Matisse, and Henry Moore, among others.

On the first floor: architecture, design, painting, sculpture exhibitions. On the second floor: permanent collection and print cabinet. A thirteenth-century bodhisattva figure welcomes one upstairs to nineteenth-century and twentieth-century paintings, prints, and drawings: Lebrun, Rouault, Oliveira, and the German Expressionist Kirchner's last painting, found on his easel after his suicide.

The print collection, built primarily from the Grunwald Graphic Arts Foundation, is second largest on the coast: old masters; the Japanese group, largely Hiroshige; all of Renoir's output but one; Matisse, second only to the Museum of Modern Art; German Expressionists. An annual set of Tamarind prints were purchased so the cabinet has the whole history of this fine workshop. For specialists in design, there's the ornament collection, including rare pattern and design sketch books by such masters as Chippendale and Sheraton.

OAKLAND ART MUSEUM

970 Fallon Street, Oakland, California
Hours: Daily, holidays, 10–5;
closed Jan. 1, Dec. 25.
Free.

Occupying a 7-acre site in downtown Oakland overlooking Lake Merritt, this museum designed by Kevin, Roche and John Dinkaloo Associates (who also did the stunning new Ford Foundation building in New York) is one of the most beautiful and satisfying new art complexes in the United States. The three major galleries, for art, history, and science, are linked in one brilliant concept of connecting gardens, sometimes depressed below ground level, all enclosed by galleries and arcades. The roof of one gallery becomes the garden terrace leading into another. The interests of the three units flow into each other ideologically as well as physically, for the overall aim is to present the comprehensive story of the arts, the cultural history, and natural sciences of California and to show their interrelation. No less than six sculpture courts, both large and intimate, encircle the art museum. There the work of such artists as Peter Voulkos, Robert Howard, Roger Bolomey, and the Rodin of California, Arthur Putnam, are shown. The large central gallery is devoted to California art; its core is the Kahn collection of nineteenth-century art, which consists of works either by California artists or on Californian sub-

David Park: *Solitaire* (Oakland Art Museum, Oakland, California; gift of the members of the Museum Guild)

jects. Two Bierstadts, Martin Heade, George D. Brewerton, who rode with Kit Carson on the great crossing of 1848, are among the displays which manifest California's rich heritage. Adjoining galleries house prints, photographs, changing exhibitions, and the work of such California contemporaries as John Mason, David Parks, and Richard Diebenkorn.

PASADENA ART MUSEUM

46 North Los Robles Avenue, Pasadena, California
Hours: Tues., 10–9; Wed.–Sat., 10–5; Sun., 2–5;
closed holidays.
Free. Special exhibits $1.

Digging has started in Carmelita Park on Pasadena's new art museum. The H-shaped building will quadruple former space as galleries of different height, shape, color, and size flow into each other. One feature will be an Oriental garden and a wing for Oriental sculpture and ceramics and for such Japanese masters as Hiroshige, Hokusai, and Haronobu.

Hopefully, the doors will open early in 1969. Then the museum will show to advantage its remarkable "Blue Four" collection, an integrated and distinguished group of works by Feininger, Kandinsky, Jawlensky, and Klee, artists who worked together in Germany before the world wars, gift of Madame Galka E. Scheyer, the artists' American agent. The Klee and Jawlensky holdings are among the nation's finest. Interesting are Klee's comments on the problem of naming the group for an American

Paul Klee: *Refuge* (Pasadena Art Museum, Pasadena, California; photograph by I. Serisawa, Los Angeles)

showing. They were, he insisted, bound together only in friendship but if they were to send work to a new country they should have a catch name; but in no case was it to end in "isms" or "ists." Because of the association with an earlier group in Munich who founded the Blue Riders, Madame Scheyer called Klee and his three friends the Blue Four. Pasadena has an enviable cache of Klee's work—forty-one in all.

Although a general museum with pre-Columbian art, Oriental art, and prints from all periods, Pasadena's new policy is to emphasize twentieth-century art, including the most contemporary. It led the field in giving Pop art prominence and claims to have instigated the first shows in the West of Kandinsky, Klee, Diebenkorn, and Duchamp. A good start has been made in the permanent collection with Miró, Marcel Duchamp, Picasso, Archipenko, Nolde, Schwitters, and such current painters as De Kooning, Diebenkorn, and Sam Francis.

Long a leader in the field of design, especially involving California craftsmen, the museum after its move will use the present building to establish a design center.

E. B. CROCKER ART GALLERY

216 O Street, Sacramento, California
Hours: Daily, 10–5; closed Mon.
Free.

E. B. Crocker was one to put the cart before the horse. Before he moved to Europe in 1870 to build a "collection" of European

Rufino Tamayo: *Laughing Woman* (1950) (E. B. Crocker Art Gallery, Sacramento, California)

masters, he had started erecting a gallery in Sacramento in which to house them. Because his trip coincided with the Franco-Prussian War, Crocker settled in Germany; but art dealers were soon bringing him paintings from all over Europe. Five years later, when he died, the museum was filled with over seven hundred works of art, many of them naturally by German artists. In 1885 the museum was given to the city by Crocker's widow.

Directors through the years have succeeded in weeding much of the inevitable dross that comes with such impulsive gathering. Some fine Dutch and Flemish masters remain: Jan de Heem, Jan van Goyen, David Teniers, Philips Wouwermans are shown in good examples, and there is a beautiful fifteenth-century panel painting of *St. Bernard of Clairvaux Receiving the Stigmata from the Virgin.* However, the strength of the collection lies in the remarkable print and drawing section: Dürer, Rembrandt, Fragonard, David are a few of the artists represented by important drawings.

The Oriental collection's *pièce de résistance* is its large and distinguished assemblage of Korean pottery.

The long-neglected contemporary section received new impetus with the formation, in 1959, of the Crocker Art Gallery Association. The Mexican Rufino Tamayo's brilliant painting *Laughing Woman* proclaims the museum's intention to collect twentieth-century masters on an international scale.

FINE ARTS GALLERY OF SAN DIEGO

Balboa Park, San Diego, California
Hours: Tues.–Sat., 10–5; Sun., 12:30–5;
closed Jan. 1, July 4, Thanksgiving, Dec. 25.
Library.
Free.

For San Diego's International Exposition in honor of the opening of the Panama Canal in 1915, architect Bertram G. Goodhue designed a Spanish town of cloisters, towers, and palaces around a great plaza. When the fair ended, the public demanded that the whole complex, including the Fine Arts Gallery done in the ornate plateresque style of the seventeenth century, remain in the park.

Spanish art is the high point here, with the Venetian, Renaissance, and baroque schools next in importance—all based on gifts of three post-Victorian maidens, the Misses Putnam, recluses who lived in an Italian villa surrounded by 10 feet of wrought-iron fence. Lately a wing has been added to the museum, and an adjacent, small, elegant structure, the Timken Gallery, has been built exclusively for Putnam Foundation paintings. Some of the fine canvases in the Timken are Hieronymus Bosch's *Christ Taken in Captivity;* Rogier van der Weyden's *Pietà,* Petrus Cristus' largest canvas, *Death of the Virgin;* Titian's *Portrait of Cardinal Bembo,* a truly great portrait full of elegance and energy; Goya's brilliant *Portrait of Marquis de Sofraga,* painted in 1798 at the peak of the artist's career; Francisco de Zurbarán's *St. Jerome* and delightful atypical little *Agnus Dei;* El Greco's *The Penitent St. Peter.* Juan Sanchez Cotan's *Quince, Cabbage, Melon and Cu-*

Fray Juan Sanchez Cotan (Spanish, 1561–1637): *Quince, Cabbage, Melon and Cucumber* (The Fine Arts Gallery of San Diego, California)

Goya: *Portrait of Marquis de Sofraga* (ca. 1795) (The Fine Arts Gallery of San Diego, California)

cumber makes brilliant mathematical use of objects to create light and shadow. One gallery houses icons collected early in the century when the Putnam girls visited Russia with their father.

The main museum has its own Spanish gallery to the left of the entrance. Most of the permanent collection of European painting and sculpture and also the American section is in the new wing. An atrium open to the California sky is enhanced by greenery and by two sturdy stone-carved Korean sheep of the Koryu Dynasty (918–1392). From here one looks beyond to a wall of Chinese sculpture. The museum's graphic section has excellent holdings, especially in early master prints. The Timken Gallery has added an extra dimension of quality to art in California.

CALIFORNIA PALACE OF THE LEGION OF HONOR

Lincoln Park, San Francisco, California
Hours: Daily, 10–5; holidays, 1–5.
Restaurant.
Free.

San Francisco is that rare phenomenon among American cities—a three-art-museum town. Each of these has its distinctive character, yet they are alike in that each started under the aegis of a great San Francisco name. The Spreckels' built the Legion of Honor; M. H. de Young sired the museum that bears his name; the Crocker family has always given its support to the San Francisco Museum of Art. There was feuding and fighting and even gunplay between the three tycoons who helped shape the dappled-gray city. Today, the stories amuse—their monuments endure.

The "Palace" occupies a spectacular site. Its broad front lawn, sweeping downhill, looks north across the harbor to the Golden Gate Bridge, east to the beauty of the city, while below it is a cool forest of plane trees.

When Mr. and Mrs. Adolph Spreckels gave the building to the city, they asked permission from the French government to copy the Paris Palace of the Legion of Honor, formerly the Palais de Salm, where Mme. de Staël held her famous *salon*. It is in the French classical style which developed in the period of Louis XVI.

The Spreckels' generosity and Mrs. Spreckels' Francophile taste gave the museum its stamp, personified in rare treasures of French culture. Other citizens helped build the collection, but essentially it takes the Spreckels direction.

Auguste Rodin aided Mrs. Spreckels in selecting many of his works which are now in the central sculpture court. *The Burghers of Calais* is an original bronze. An early marble piece was done when Rodin was only twenty-one. The powerful *St. John the Baptist* is an example of his mature style.

On either side of the sculpture gallery is an octagonal garden court, filled with that virile foliage only California can produce. Great sculptural masses of plants provide a green haven and tease the skylights.

Among the Dutch and Italian paintings are many fine works, including Rembrandt's *Portrait of a Rabbi,* but the French art and *objets d'art* made the museum famous. It would be difficult

François Boucher: *Vertumnus and Pomona* (California Palace of the Legion of Honor, San Francisco; Mildred Anna Williams Collection)

Jean Honoré Fragonard: *Self-portrait* (California Palace of the Legion of Honor, San Francisco; gift of Mr. and Mrs. Louis Benoist)

to find a comparable collection of eighteenth-century French furniture in all America. Much of it came from Collis Huntington's house at 57th Street and Fifth Avenue, New York City, where Tiffany's now is. Collis' son Archer inherited the house on condition he live in it, but, preferring California, he let it go to Yale and gave the furniture to the museum.

Fragonard's *Self-Portrait* shows him, benign and small, painting at a desk—an intense and intimate little canvas, free of the frivolity of the court of his patron, Mme. du Barry. Carle Van Loo's four paintings of the muses—music, painting, sculpture, and architecture—were commissioned by Mme. de Pompadour for her charming Château de Bellevue. La Pompadour, who collected châteaux and pavilions the way other royal mistresses collected jewelry, lavished her not-inconsiderable talents on Bellevue. The paintings in time passed into the Rothschild collection in Vienna and were confiscated by the Nazis during World War II. Thomas Howe, director of the museum, first saw them in the salt mines in Alt-Aussee, Austria, where the Nazis had secreted them, when he was Deputy Chief, Monuments, Fine Arts Section, for the U.S. Forces. Returned to the Rothschilds, they were later consigned to New York dealers, where Mr. Howe saw his official sticker still on them. He decided then and there that the Fates meant them for his museum.

Largillière's *Portrait of the Marquis de Montespan* is as much a portrait of an epoch as of a man. All the luxury, elegance, and pomp of the Sun King's court are exemplified in Louis XIV's bedizened, peruked courtier. Nattier, Oudry, Le Nain, Corot, Manet, and Renoir are all seen in top form. More rare French treasures have lately arrived. One is a superb Louis XVI *salon* from the Hôtel d'Humières, Paris. For some years it graced the town house of the late Otto Kahn and then, as often happened to such treasures, became the property of Lord Duveen. The museum's brochure on the subject makes fascinating reading. The *salon* has been reconstructed at one end of the gallery of eighteenth-century French painting and furniture.

Several galleries are devoted to contemporary paintings and changing exhibitions, and much of the decorative arts collection (again mostly French) is beautifully installed on the lower floor. The Achenbach Foundation for Graphic Arts has assembled the most complete print and drawing section west of Chicago's Art Institute. Open to qualified students is work of all periods and nationalities. Spacious galleries hold changing exhibitions in graphic art, and the department generously sends exhibitions through the West and Southwest.

In the Legion of Honor you see a good general cross section of art imbued with a lusty "*Vive la France!*" A restaurant, the museum's latest addition, no doubt features French cuisine.

M. H. DE YOUNG MEMORIAL MUSEUM

Golden Gate Park, San Francisco, California
Hours: Daily, 10–5.
Library.
Free.

When the California Midwinter Exposition closed in 1895, all its appurtenances were junked, except the Japanese tea garden, the Fine and Decorative Arts Building, and the heavily ornamented "Royal Pavilion." Through the efforts of a group of San Franciscans, led by M. H. De Young, owner and editor of the *Chronicle*, a museum was established in the latter two buildings. De Young had flair and a gift for showmanship (he and his brother bought 80,000 lots in Los Angeles for $10,000 and gave one away to anyone who bought a ticket to their theater, the Alcatraz). His first purchases for the new museum were from what was nearest at hand—the material that foreign governments had displayed at the fair. This ran to Sèvres and Royal Worcester porcelains, Greek vases, and some fine primitive carvings, the best from the South Sea Islands.

In a grove of cypress and linden trees, its grounds heavy with flowers that form Matisse patterns, the museum has undergone many changes. Today it is a thoroughly pleasant and up-to-date building with spacious galleries and two verdant garden courts.

The entrance opens into the William Randolph Hearst Memorial Court, its walls covered with what must be the biggest Flemish Gothic tapestries in existence. The Hearst collection leads directly into the Kress collection, exhibited in three especially designed galleries. Here are Spanish, Dutch, French, and Italian masters, such as Fra Angelico, Titian, Pieter de Hooch, and an El Greco of the city's own patron, St. Francis. In the portrait of *Vittoria Colonna*, Bronzino has caught this remarkable woman in the dignity and disillusionment of old age, noble but weary. A youthful Vittoria, by Del Piombo, hangs in the Columbus, Ohio, museum.

Two acknowledged masterpieces in the De Young are Rubens' *Tribute Money* and El Greco's *St. John the Baptist*. Rubens, that supreme portrayer of men's motives, paints the sea of faces pressing around Judas, contorted with avarice, cunning, and skepticism, while the traitor shows simple astonishment at the enormity of his crime. Even the figure of Christ is subordinated to the sudden articulation of grief on Judas' face. In the *St. John*, El Greco has set the saint, looming and majestic, in the foreground while, characteristically, despite historical demands of period and place, the Baptist finds himself against the mauve-drenched background of the painter's beloved Toledo, with the saint's constant symbol, the white and woolly lamb, adding appeal to the composition. For the small *Christ Appears to Mary Magdalen after His Resurrection*, Rubens executed the figures, while Jan Brueghel the

El Greco: *St. John the Baptist* (ca. 1600) (M. H. DeYoung Memorial Museum, San Francisco)

Elder painted the encompassing, frosty, blue-green landscape. Georges de La Tour leaves his usual candlelighted shadow world to capture solidly both craftiness and humor in his French *Peasant Woman*. One of the pleasures of wandering through the De Young is the constant discovery of compelling works by unknown masters, and painters few laymen are familiar with.

The European sculpture is exciting, in particular Verrocchio's *Reclining Boy*, an enchanting frolic in marble; and what may be one of El Greco's rare sculptures, a terra cotta of St. Jerome. The figure has the elongated asceticism, the rapt mystical expression of El Greco's painted saints. One of the most celebrated art patrons of history, *Cosimo de Medici*, is commemorated in marble by the equally celebrated sculptor and goldsmith Cellini.

The *Wespien Room*, one of a series of important interiors, came from the palatial residence of the Lord Mayor of Aachen. Built in 1735, most of the palace was destroyed by bombs in the last war. A Spanish room has a fifteenth-century Mudejar ceiling; there's an original oak and paneled Elizabethan room. An elaborately carved French rococo room from a château near Rouen leads into a Louis XVI Parisian room. These delightful French rooms look out into a formal garden.

The new Avery Brundage wing adds another dimension to the museum and to the West Coast, for with the exception of the Stanford University collection little Asian art was to be seen along this gateway to the Orient. Avery Brundage, amateur sportsman and president of the International Olympics Committee, encountered the arts of the Orient at the first major Chinese art exhibition held outside Asia (Royal Academy, London, 1935). It was first-sight love and led to a passion to possess. The setting for the treasures is austere in its simplicity; a large window at the end of one of the galleries looks off into the trees and the old Japanese tea garden. The Chinese section makes up about one-half of the group; the ceramics alone range from neolithic times to the present day. The 700 pieces of jade span 3,000 years of history. History again picks up the thread as Buddhism is traced in stone and gilt bronze. The principal paintings are mainly Japanese, screens of the Muromachi, Momoyama, and Edo periods and Kamakura scrolls. Japanese sculptures, including five of the sixth-century Haniwa period, are of wood, terra cotta, bronze, and dry lacquer. Temple sculpture, steles, bronzes from India, Thailand, and Korea fill out this rich pattern. Mr. Brundage continues to collect.

SAN FRANCISCO MUSEUM OF ART

Van Ness Avenue and McAlister Street, San Francisco, California
Hours: Tues.–Fri., 10–10; Sat., 10–5; Sun., 1–5;
closed Mon., holidays.
Library.
Free.

Do not be put off by the tomblike entrance; take the elevator to the fourth floor and step into a lively world of modern art. The museum channels a continuous flow of important exhibitions of contemporary art. Print, watercolor, and drawing shows line the wide hallways. In addition, one gallery is set aside for a permanent collection. Notable are Picasso's portraits of *Sara* and *Michael Stein*, Georges Braque's *Table*, Paul Klee's *Nearly Hit*, Matisse's *The Girl with the Green Eyes*, an early Jackson Pollock, a Clyfford Still (his first canvas to be acquired by a museum), and other modern masters, Arp and Calder. Recent acquisitions include an impressive Philip Pavia marble sculpture and canvases by Esteban Vicente and Gene Davis.

Files recording the collections of Bay Area art lovers, biographical dossiers on local artists, and a comprehensive study of the private gallery system are a part of the museum's archives. The traditional Bay Area Annual Exhibition has been suspended for a time, making way for a National Invitational to be held on the even-numbered years. The SFMA remains the heart of experiment and leadership in the West Coast avant-garde.

Henri Matisse: *The Girl with the Green Eyes* (San Francisco Museum of Art; Levy bequest)

HENRY E. HUNTINGTON LIBRARY
AND ART GALLERY

1151 Oxford Road, San Marino, California
Hours: Tues.–Sun., 1–4:30;
closed Mon., Oct., national holidays.
Free.

Here hang—in the unreproducible original—Lawrence's *Pinkie* and Gainsborough's *Blue Boy.*

Before he set about amassing his truly staggering collection of eighteenth-century art, Henry E. Huntington built his library, which contains one of America's great collections of British books. His fabulous gardens were originally designed to woo his bride away from the East Coast—with 5 acres of camellias, with rare Oriental plants, and the largest selection of desert greenery outside the desert. From all over the world, Huntington brought strange and wonderful trees to shade and decorate the grounds of his San Marino ranch, on which he had built in 1910 an English manor house. (This was a period when U.S. millionaires tended to erect Renaissance *palazzi* on the Wabash and French châteaux on the prairies.)

In 1913, by marrying his Uncle Collis' widow, Arabella, Henry Huntington consolidated the vast real estate and railroad fortune which Collis had established and Henry, as his West Coast manager, had rapaciously expanded. That avid and astute dealer Sir Joseph Duveen had already guided Mrs. Collis Huntington into the rarefied world of Rembrandt, Velázquez, Hals, and Bellini. When Arabella married her nephew-in-law, budding collector Henry, the eighteenth-century interiors were soon filled with paintings, sculpture, furniture, and *objets d'art,* some French, but most of them English. Henry Huntington's penchant for English portraiture coincided, happily, with a time when taxes and death duties were forcing the British aristocracy to dispose of their more valuable ancestors. Duveen provided Huntington with one of the best collections of Gainsborough now under one roof.

S. N. Behrman, in his hilarious book about Sir Joseph, later Lord Duveen of Milbank, tells the story, probably apocryphal, of how one picture, which has been so often reproduced that it is nearly as familiar to Americans as the *Mona Lisa,* came to California. Duveen and Huntington were making a trip to Europe

Gainsborough: *The Blue Boy* (Henry E. Huntington Library and Art Gallery, San Marino, California)

together and were dining in the "Gainsborough Suite" on the *Aquitania,* where one of its ubiquitous reproductions hung. Henry asked about the "boy in the blue suit." The canny Duveen knew, as he made it his business to know, that the owner, the Duke of Westminster, might, if the price was right, be persuaded to part with the painting. He made a calculated guess that he could lay hands on it for maybe $600,000. Huntington saw his way clear to parting with such a sum, and Duveen was off like a shot for the Duke the minute the *Aquitania* docked. Apocryphal or no, several months later *The Blue Boy* was delivered to Huntington. Later, Gainsborough's *The Cottage Door* and Reynolds' masterpiece, *Sarah Siddons as the Tragic Muse,* came from Westminster through Duveen to Huntington. In 1926, Duveen got *Pinkie,* Sir Thomas Lawrence's charming painting of Elizabeth Barrett Browning's aunt, at auction for $377,000. He offered it first to Andrew Mellon, on the principle that he must keep all his millionaires equally happy, but Mellon balked at the price. The next day he telephoned Huntington, and *Pinkie* went to California. Another stunning acquisition was Gainsborough's portrait of his friend *Karl Friederich Abel,* court musician to Queen Charlotte.

The living rooms of the mansion remain much as they were. Huntington's first purchases from Duveen were the incomparable Boucher tapestries *The Noble Pastoral,* woven in Beauvais. The Savonnerie carpets were part of a series woven for the Palais du Louvre.

When Arabella died in 1924, Huntington added a memorial wing to the library. It is fitting that the fifteenth- and sixteenth-century paintings, the Renaissance bronzes, and most of the

French sculpture and *objets d'art* are here. Mrs. Huntington's taste was the more catholic and her interests deeper. The Houdons fascinate. *Portrait of a Lady* is a tour de force in marble. In *Sabine*, Houdon makes unbelievably whimsical use of marble to portray his piquant daughter. The sculpture collection concentrates on Giovanni da Bologna, the Frenchmen Falconet, Clodion, Houdon, and the work of sculptors from the ateliers of these masters. Both connoisseurs and students can play sleuth among them.

The Rogier van der Weyden *Madonna and Child* stands out in the Renaissance room, among twelve other Madonnas of the same luxuriant period.

Except for Mrs. Huntington's contributions, the collection is primarily English, with such masters as Blake, Turner, and Constable. An outstanding small Constable of *Salisbury Cathedral* (there are four other versions in U.S. museums) was given by the Bishop of Salisbury to his daughter as a wedding present. At the Bishop's special request, the flexible Constable obligingly inserted a small piece of blue sky into his usual cloudy one to make it more suitable to the occasion.

John Russell Pope, architect of the National Gallery, was commissioned by Henry Huntington to create a mausoleum for his wife and himself. Deep in an orange grove, there they lie now, like a Medici couple, not far from the main house in which they amassed their treasures. They left behind them an endowment of $8 million to protect their monuments from everything short of an atomic bomb.

Houdon: *Portrait of a Lady* (Henry E. Huntington Library and Art Gallery, San Marino, California)

SANTA BARBARA MUSEUM OF ART

1130 State Street, Santa Barbara, California
Hours: Tues.–Sat., 11–5; Sun., 12–5;
closed Mon., national holidays.
Free.

A United States post office in the Spanish colonial style was remodeled by Chicago's famous architect David Adler, in 1939, to
house Santa Barbara's burgeoning art collection. In a cool white
court, one step from the busy street, are antiquities which include
a fountain made from an interchangeable bridal-funeral urn
(Greek, second century B.C.) and other treasures ranging from
the sixth century B.C. to the second century A.D., many from the
Wright Ludington collection.

A splendid drawing collection starts with the Renaissance and
is continuously being enlarged: a primitive arts gallery includes
Oriental musical instruments. The museum has been a pioneer in
the development of American art on the West Coast. The Preston
Morton wing built in 1961 houses this rich lode, which begins with
Benjamin West and includes Copley's portrait of *General Joshua
Winslow* and goes through the Hudson River School, with an
important new Frederick Church, to a full complement of "The
Eight." Mrs. Sterling Morton's gift in 1960 doubled in distinguished representation eighteenth- and nineteenth-century painting. It has fine examples of such twentieth-century masters as
Weber, Hopper, Albers, Kuniyoshi, and Kuhn, and also attunes
its exhibitions and purchases to the young activists on the art
scene.

The most popular painting is *The Buffalo Hunter* (*circa* 1830)
by an unknown American who had the ability to combine the

Buffalo Hunter (American
artist, ca. 1830–1840)
(Santa Barbara Museum of
Art; Buell Hammett Me-
morial Fund)

drama of his subject matter with rhythmic lines and an architectural sense of space. A strong document from our colorful past, the *Hunter* still roams the Plains from one Western exhibition to another.

Watercolors and drawings by Marin, Demuth, Miró, Picasso, Matisse, and Degas have come from the fine Wright Ludington collection. Old masters' paintings include *A Franciscan Monk* by the seventeenth-century painter Francisco de Zurbarán and *The Holy Family* by Pieter de Witte. There is also a sizable collection of Oriental art and an ever-growing modern European section.

The active exhibition program, which includes over twenty varied exhibitions a year, keeps the Santa Barbara Museum one of the most interesting on the Coast.

STANFORD UNIVERSITY: STANFORD MUSEUM

Stanford, California
Hours: Tues.–Sat., 10–5; Sun., 1–5.
Free.

"The Stanford Museum is the only museum to the writer's knowledge which can lay claim to the distinction of having given birth to a university," wrote John La Plante, Stanford's long-time curator of Asian art. It is quite a claim, for Stanford has become one of the world's leading universities. Senator and Mrs. Stanford conceived the museum as a memorial to their only son, a brilliant boy who, though barely sixteen when he died, had a predilection for collecting works of art. While developing the museum, plans for a university took shape. The oldest art museum in the West (1891), the handsome building was badly damaged and much of its collection destroyed during the 1906 earthquake.

Today the collections are housed in the Leland Stanford, Jr., Museum and the Frances Wetten Stanford Art Gallery built in 1917. The latter is used throughout the school year for changing exhibitions as well as for housing part of the permanent collection. The range is ancient and classical, Asian, European, and American art. The Egyptian material runs pre-dynastic to Saitic and is choice partly because the Stanfords were members of the Egyptian Exploration Fund, a society formed to finance excavations in Egypt, the material to be distributed to subscribers.

Impatient to stock their museum, the Stanfords purchased out-

Wang Kai: *Landscape in the Manner of Chu-jan* (Stanford Museum, Stanford, California; gift of the Committee for Art)

right some distinguished collections. In 1896 the Metropolitan Museum obligingly sold them about half of its Cesnola group of Cypriot antiquities. The Baron Ikeda collection endowed them with Chinese and Japanese ceramics, paintings, and Japanese lacquers. The McAdams group of American Mound relics was also acquired.

Since those early days many gifts have made the Asian collection into one of the finest in the West. Eleven rare Chinese paintings, from the collection of Dr. Victoria Contag, have just been purchased. They include hangings, hand scrolls, and albums, and range through the Ming (1368–1644) and Ch'ing (1644–1912) Dynasties. They were brought together in Shanghai before the Communist takeover in 1944.

European painting starts with fourteenth-century Italy and is rather rich in seventeenth- and eighteenth-century Italian furniture and paintings. Two Longhis present a charming and vivid view of Venice. Guardi's *Landscape with Ruins*, the Magnasco, and Zuccarelli should also be noted, as well as the genre of seventeenth-century Flanders. American and English painting runs to portraiture. There are over forty works by nineteenth-century California artists; the twentieth century is getting under way, with Karl Knaths, Morris Broderson, and Carl Morris as a hopeful triumvirate.

The California Room, a mixture of art and memento, is dominated—even overwhelmed—by the "Governor Stanford," California's first locomotive, brought around the Horn and assembled in San Francisco. Used as a work engine on the building of the Central Pacific Railroad, from which most of the Leland Stanford wealth derived, it is but fitting that it should be honored by the university its labors helped to create.

HONOLULU ACADEMY OF ARTS

900 South Beretania Street, Honolulu, Hawaii
Hours: Tues.–Sat., 10–4:30; Thurs., 10–9:30; Sun., 3–6.
Library.
Free.

Founded in 1927, the Honolulu Academy is the only museum of a general nature in the broad Pacific. Around an Oriental court, galleries present European material, and around the Spanish court, Western. Most galleries open onto garden courts so rich with tropical plants that one is torn between staying outside with nature or inside with works of art. The second floor is given over to the contemporaries and to changing exhibits. But for all the museum's sensible emphasis on balance, it is best known for its Oriental holdings, both qualitatively and quantitatively. Asiatic art covers early China through all its periods in painting, sculpture, and decorative arts; the Buddhist arts of Japan, Momoyama and Edo periods, and a famous group of folding screens from the height of the classical period. Celebrated is the Chinese ink and brush drawing on paper of geese and rushes referred to as the *One Hundred Geese* scroll. It is usually attributed to the master Ma Fên. The academy also houses one of the world's important groups of Korean ceramics. The Western section embraces the ancient Mediterranean world, medieval and Renaissance art, and the Kress collection of Italian painting. Decorative arts emphasize eighteenth-century England and France.

Late paintings include Pissarro, Cézanne, a splendid Monet, *Water Lilies*, Gauguin's *Two Nudes on a Tahitian Beach*, Van Gogh's blazing *Wheatfields*, Chirico, Braque, and Picasso. The

Paul Gauguin: *Two Nudes on a Tahitian Beach* (ca. 1890) (Honolulu Academy of Arts; gift of Mrs. Charles M. Cooke)

modern section grows with such artists as Karl Knaths, Helen Frankenthaler, Karel Appel, Kenzo Okada. In its changing exhibition program the academy brings to the island a varied fare of art movements around the world.

UNIVERSITY OF OREGON MUSEUM OF ART

Eugene, Oregon
Hours: Tues., Thurs., 11–5; Wed., Fri.–Sun., 1–5;
closed national holidays.
Free.

The Murray Warner collection of Oriental art given to the museum in 1921 inspired the building of what was then the largest state university art museum in the country. Since then the arts of the Pacific Northwest have joined the Oriental, which consists mainly of Japanese and Chinese, with some Korean works. Four Japanese Buddhist sculptures, from late Jōgan (794–897 A.D.) to late Fujiwara (1086–1185 A.D.) are most impressive. A unique piece presented by New Yorker Winston Guest in 1957 is the Imperial Jade Pagoda from the palace of the Emperor K'ang near Peking. All jade and 9 feet tall, the pagoda was rescued when the British and French fired the palace in the middle of the nineteenth century. Finally sold to a Shanghai jeweler, it eventually came into the hands of our own famous Oriental firm of C. T. Loo. India and Nepal are also represented, and one gallery is given to Persian miniature painting and manuscripts.

The contemporary section centers mainly on a talented group of Northwestern artists: Morris Graves, Tom Hardy, Mark Tobey, James McGarrell, Carl and Hilda Morris, Kenneth Callahan, Louis Bunce, and, of course, C. S. Price (see Portland). While each has developed his personal idiom and unique physical character, the drama of the Puget Sound area, ringed by mountains and tall pines, seems subconsciously to permeate much of the work.

The museum is less campus-oriented than most university museums for the simple reason that funds for the building were raised not only by the state but by private individuals who felt the need for a museum in the community. The recently organized Friends of Art, not a feature on other college campuses, do much to promote the museum to Oregonians.

PORTLAND ART MUSEUM

South West Park at Madison Street, Portland, Oregon
Hours: Tues.–Fri., 12–10 P.M.; Sun., 12–5;
closed national holidays.
Library.
Free.

In 1914, the venturesome spirit of the Portland Art Association manifested itself defiantly when the rest of the art world was still rocking from the punches New York's Armory Show had delivered the year before. Portland borrowed the most controversial painting of them all—Marcel Duchamp's *Nude Descending a Staircase.* Around it, lithographs and photographs recreated the Armory Show.

Portland's history established a climate for art. Her early settlers, sea captains and professional men, sailed round the Horn in comparative luxury, their libraries and *objets d'art* stowed in the ships' holds. As early as 1892, with a population close to fifty thousand, the city organized an art association, which authorized one of its members to select a hundred casts of Greek and Roman sculptures in Europe. In 1926, Miss Sally Lewis presented the museum with a distinguished collection of original classical antiquities. She has also given contemporary works including Brancusi's *Muse.*

The collection is well rounded but best known for the artifacts which Axel Rasmussen, superintendent of schools at Skagway, Alaska, gathered throughout his lifetime. The culture of Indians, northern California to Alaska and east to the Cascades, is shown in heraldic columns and grave posts, as well as minute carvings. Huge trees were turned into totemic monuments, while five or six tiny animals, each individually expressive, may be seen carved with exquisite delicacy on the end of a spoon. For the

Mask, *Spirit of Dead Man* (Tlingit; from Wrangel, Alaska) (Portland Art Museum, Portland, Oregon)

Northwestern Indians art was a part of life—"art for art's sake" unknown.

The Chinese collection is small but fine, one of its top treasures a wild little horse carved in wood around the fourth century B.C. Portland also has probably the most impressive assembly of Japanese prints on the West Coast. The pre-Columbian group, too, is small but strong.

The increasingly important English silver collection, with some seven hundred fifty items, has concentrated on the Huguenot silversmiths working in London.

Latter-day paintings include canvases by Corot, Courbet, Renoir, and Soutine's fine *Pastry Cook*, with his sad eyes looking like yesterday's oysters. The contemporary roster embraces Beckman, Feininger, Rouault, Albers, Hofer, Maurer's portrait of *George Washington,* and northwest artists Tobey, Graves, Carl Morris, and Darrel Austin.

One of the vitally individual painters of twentieth-century America, C. S. Price, spent the last twenty years of his life in Portland, where he died in 1950. Price, never east of the Mississippi, left his imprint up and down the Coast. Certainly, painters like Diebenkorn and Carl Morris responded to his power. The tigers and swamp ladies in the eerie world of his next-door neighbor, Darrel Austin, bear their creator's unmistakable stamp, yet seem related to the lonely animals that haunt Price's paintings. Originally an illustrator, Price moved into Impressionism and gradually into "Abstract Expressionism," around 1919, before *that phrase* was coined. Portland is fortunate in having drawings, models, and paintings by this significant artist.

The building, designed by Pietro Belluschi, now dean of the School of Architecture and Planning at M.I.T., is as contemporary in design today as it was in the thirties when its handsome brick and travertine walls went up.

SEATTLE ART MUSEUM

Volunteer Park, Seattle, Washington
Hours: Tues.–Sat., 10–5; Thurs. eve., 7–10; Sun., holidays, 12–5.
Free.

The Seattle Arts Society came into being in 1904, and in 1933 Mrs. Eugene Fuller and her son, Richard E. Fuller, founded the present museum by giving the building to the city. Like Youngstown's, it is a family museum, and Dr. Fuller has been its president and director from the start.

Mrs. Fuller began collecting *bibelots*. A trip to the Orient changed that. In fact, the spine of the body of art is Far Eastern, with the Chinese and Japanese galleries showing practically every facet of those cultures in historic sequence. Initially the emphasis was on Chinese jade, for which the museum is famous and which is always on exhibit. The collection was expanded beyond the Oriental to embrace works from almost every age and culture. Two great pieces that have lately come to the museum are: a marble tenth-century Indian carving from the cupola of a Jain temple, a *Dancing Girl* about 40 inches high; and a stunning Sassanian silver plate from Reshi, Iran, third century A.D. The building's expansion now gives the visitor a fascinating survey of ancient Mediterranean art. In the "classic corner" fine pieces are always on exhibition.

The opening in 1965 of the Seattle Art Museum Pavilion in the remodeled United Kingdom Pavilion of the Seattle World's Fair has solved certain space perplexities. It offers hospitality to the annuals and traveling exhibitions that previously took up gallery space.

Dr. Fuller, always on the prowl for opportunities, made a find in Gump's warehouse in San Francisco. For decades, huge marble animal and human figures, former guardians of princely Chinese tombs, had lain wrapped in rope; today these simple, monolithic sculptures of the twelfth to the seventeenth centuries make up a unique collection. Two ancient Chinese camels flank the museum's entrance, their massive backs accessible to children playing "nomads."

Dancing Girl (Indian; tenth century A.D.) (Seattle Art Museum, Seattle, Washington)

Two galleries house the Kress collection, which includes Veronese, Tintoretto, and Canaletto. Rubens' sketch for *The Last Supper* (the finished painting, done for an Antwerp church, was destroyed by fire) is especially fine.

Little-known forerunners of Impressionist painters, like Paul Camille Guigou, teacher of Courbet and friend of Corot, are shown in top examples. Latter-day painters include Léger, Marcel Duchamp, Picabia, Moholy-Nagy, Pollock, and Sam Francis. The museum takes pride in its works by local artists. Citizens Mark Tobey, Kenneth Callahan, and Morris Graves hung here long before they achieved international fame.

ACKNOWLEDGMENTS

The acknowledgments listed in the brief bibliography represent but a fraction of my obligations, most of which are to the directors, curators and staff of every institution noted in this book. My gratitude goes out to them all for their unfailing patience, friendliness and helpfulness in allowing me to roam through their museums at will, often after closing hours and at times inconvenient to them, thus making an arduous cross and crisscross country schedule tolerable for me. I am grateful to them for making available to me catalogues and other material on the history of their institutions and collections.

BIBLIOGRAPHY

Brown, Milton. *American Painting from the Armory Show to the Depression.* Princeton, Princeton University, 1955.

Cahill, Holger. *American Painting and Sculpture.* Newark, Newark Museum.

Carter, Morris. *Isabella Stewart Gardner Museum and Fenway Court.* Boston, Houghton Mifflin, 1940.

Cartwright, W. Aubrey. *Guide to Art Museums in the U.S.* (Southeast Coast section). New York, Duell, Sloane & Pearce, 1957.

Coke, Van Deren. *Taos and Santa Fe.* Amon Carter Museum of Western Art publication.

Dana, John Cotton. *American Art.* Woodstock, Vt., privately printed.

Eliot, Alexander, and Editors of *Time. Three Hundred Years of American Painting.* New York, Random House, 1957.

Faison, S. Lane Jr. *A Guide to the Art Museums of New England.* Harcourt, Brace and Co., 1958.

———. *Art Tours and Detours in New York State.*

Flexner, James T. *Short History of American Painting*. Boston, Houghton Mifflin, 1950.

Fryxell, Fritiof. *Thomas Moran*. East Hampton, New York, East Hampton Free Library, 1958.

Gilbert, Dorothy. *American Art Directory*. New York, Bowker, 1957.

Hendy, Philip. Isabella Stewart Gardner Museum, Catalogue of the Collections, Boston, Gardner Museum.

Howe, Winifred. *History of the Metropolitan Museum of Art* (2 volumes). New York, Columbia University Press, 1946.

Iglaurer, Edith. "Housekeeping at the Big Museum," *Harper's*, February, 1960.

Kubler, George. *Santos*. Amon Carter Museum of Western Art publication.

Lansdale, Nelson. "Mrs. Jack Gardner's Palace," *Horizon*, July, 1959.

Larkin, Oliver. *Art and Life in America*. New York, Rinehart, 1949.

Lewis, Oscar. *Big Four*. New York, Knopf, 1946.

Lyon, Peter. "Adventurous Angels," *Horizon*, May, 1959.

Overmeyer, Grace. *Government in the Arts*. London, Norton & McLeod, 1939.

Pach, Walter. *The American Art Museum*. Pantheon Books Inc., 1948.

Pach, Walter (translator). *Journal of Eugene Delacroix*. New York, Crown, 1948.

Phillips, Duncan. *The Enchantment of Art*. New York, J. Lane, 1914.

———. *The Leadership of Giorgione*. Washington, American Federation of Arts, Inc., 1937.

Rewald, John. "Degas," *Gazette des Beaux Arts*, August, 1946.

Richardson, E. P. *Painting in America*. New York, Crowell, 1956.

Roberts, George and Mary. *Triumph on Fairmount:* Fiske Kimball and the Philadelphia Art Museum. Philadelphia, Lippincott, 1959.

Saarinen, Aline B. *The Proud Possessors*. New York, Random House, 1958.

Sandberg, W. and H. L. C. Jaffe. *Pioneers of Modern Art*. McGraw-Hill, 1961.

Taylor, Francis Henry. *Fifty Centuries of Art*. New York, Harper, 1954, 1960.

Tebbel, John. *The Life and Good Times of William Randolph Hearst.* New York, Dutton, 1952.

Watson, Forbes. *Art in Federal Buildings.* Washington, U.S. Treasury Dept., 1936.

Wunder, Richard P. *The Smithsonian Institution's National Collection of Fine Arts.* Connoisseur, May, 1968.

INDEX OF PERSONS
AND WORKS OF ART

[Dates are given only for artists who are no longer living. Asterisk denotes illustration.]

This lively and informative guide is for the traveler who, unfamiliar with a local gallery or museum and with little time to visit, still wants to feel he has seen the institution's most distinguished works of art. *American Art Museums* puts you directly in touch with the most important museums and art galleries all over the country.

New, revised and up-dated to include the latest acquisitions made during the past five years, the book now includes college and university collections as well. Addressed to the layman, this unique "introduction to looking" is illustrated throughout. The present edition covers every aspect of the art world in America, from the history of collecting to the actual directions on how to get to a given museum, whether or not it charges admission, and the hours that it is open to the public. Ideal for planning an itinerary, it is also a fund of information about the treasures you might not have realized were buried in your own bailiwick.